ON STAFF

On Staff

A PRACTICAL GUIDE TO STARTING YOUR CAREER
IN A UNIVERSITY MUSIC DEPARTMENT

Donald L. Hamann

OXFORD
UNIVERSITY PRESS

OXFORD
UNIVERSITY PRESS

Oxford University Press is a department of the University of Oxford.
It furthers the University's objective of excellence in research, scholarship,
and education by publishing worldwide.

Oxford   New York
Auckland   Cape Town   Dar es Salaam   Hong Kong   Karachi
Kuala Lumpur   Madrid   Melbourne   Mexico City   Nairobi
New Delhi   Shanghai   Taipei   Toronto

With offices in
Argentina   Austria   Brazil   Chile   Czech Republic   France   Greece
Guatemala   Hungary   Italy   Japan   Poland   Portugal   Singapore
South Korea   Switzerland   Thailand   Turkey   Ukraine   Vietnam

Oxford is a registered trademark of Oxford University Press in the UK and certain other
countries.

Published in the United States of America by
Oxford University Press
198 Madison Avenue, New York, NY 10016

Library of Congress Cataloging-in-Publication Data
Hamann, Donald L.
On staff : a practical guide to starting your career in a university music department /
Donald L. Hamann.
pages cm
Includes bibliographical references and index.
ISBN 978-0-19-994704-1 (alk. paper)—ISBN 978-0-19-994702-7 (alk. paper)
1. Music in universities and colleges—Vocational guidance.   2. College teaching—
Vocational guidance.   I. Title.
ML3795.H26 2013
780.23—dc23
2012043306

Contents

About the Companion Website

www.oup.com/us/onstaff

The materials contained in the OUP companion website are offered as additional resources to assist you in the preparation of your documents. While you will find individual variation among the documents, you will also find commonality through the use of accepted, recognizable organizational ideas and models. It is my hope that these ideas and models will stimulate your creative process, help clarify and focus your thoughts, and enable you to produce original, meaningful, and distinct documents that exemplify your strengths and attributes. If you are preparing for a job search, you may find the examples of academic and performance-oriented curricula vitae, cover letters, and philosophy statements useful as you prepare your documents. For those institutions preparing to fill a music position, a step-by-step job preparation checklist is available that should assist both search committee members and administrative personnel in this task.

The examples presented on the website are actual materials from individuals in the profession. Many of the names and most of the contact information have been changed to maintain anonymity, but the documents have not been altered. Some of these documents may resonate with you, others may not, but the process of finding that ideal forum in which you choose to present yourself is the goal of this book and subsequently this website. May this website and book enable you to be as successful as the individuals represented through these examples.

You may access the website using the following:

Username: Music3

Password: Book3234

Preface

YOUR HIGHER EDUCATIOn music career begins with your first post. In order to qualify for a higher education music post, you need years of educational training. To secure that post, you must convince a search committee that you are the most appropriate choice for that position through the application and interviewing processes. To that end, the contents of this book will prepare you for those processes. Additionally, they will prepare you for what lies beyond the application and interview—tenure, promotion, and career advice. Whether you are just beginning or an established music professor, you will find that *On Staff: A Practical Guide to Starting Your Career in a University Music Department* provides detailed, step-by-step information that will assist you or your graduate advisees in securing that first higher education music post.

What's In This Book?

On Staff: A Practical Guide to Starting Your Career in a University Music Department will guide you through the steps to applying for, acquiring, and holding a position in higher education. Each chapter is designed to assist you in one or more of the following:

- locating and understanding position announcements,
- preparing dynamic and clearly articulated application materials,

- understanding the process of the job search committee in relation to your application,
- planning and preparing for your interview,
- learning what questions you could be asked in an interview,
- discovering what search committee members and administrators are looking for in candidates,
- completing a successful interview,
- negotiating a contract,
- getting started and succeeding in your position,
- becoming tenured and being promoted, and
- developing your career.

How Is This Book Organized?

The book is organized in a sequential manner. You will first discover how university music jobs are created, advertised, and listed. *On Staff* will show you how to:

- prepare and construct a successful curriculum vitae (CV),
- create appealing letters of application,
- develop a teaching philosophy statement,
- write innovative research statements, and
- select your reference providers.

You will be apprised of the steps needed to apply for a university position, including the time lines associated with that process. Have you ever wondered:

- what's important to search committee members and administrators,
- how you prepare for a telephone or Skype interview or an on-site interview,
- what you would do and whom you would meet in an interview,
- what questions you might be asked during your interview, or
- what you should wear and what you can eat at your interview?

On Staff will provide that information. After a successful on-campus interview and a job offer, discover what one might typically ask for in the negotiation process. And finally, *On Staff* will discuss your first days in your new position and present the blueprint for the development of a successful higher education music career.

Why Should I Read This Book?

If you are just now planning to enter the university job market, have recently become a university music professor, are a university music faculty advisor, or are serving on a search committee, either as a chair or member, you will want to read this book. *On Staff* will enhance or supplement your knowledge of the university application and interview process. For those who are entering or have recently entered higher education, *On Staff* provides information to help you succeed in the field. If you are an established professor and graduate student adviser, this book will supplement information you provide to your students. As the chair or member of a search committee, *On Staff* will refresh or provide you with information relevant to successfully conducting a higher education music position search.

Where Do the Musician Examples Come from?

Music educators, theorists, composers, performers, and others have contributed to these examples. While names, addresses, and other such information may have been altered to protect the anonymity of the individuals, the basic information provided in those examples remains unchanged.

The illustrations in the text and Oxford companion website provide you with various examples of CVs, cover letters, and so forth. While these illustrations conform to a structured and accepted or common framework, you will also see how each author has creatively and effectively individualized his or her materials. From these examples, you will develop your own unique approach to "selling" yourself through your originally created documents.

Academia and You

Your higher education career journey begins with your first university music position. For some, the academic journey also concludes with the first position, but for others, the first university music position becomes a stepping-stone to other posts. One of the most challenging tasks you will face in your career, as a university music professor, is staying current, motivated, and interested. Your continued professional and musical growth through teaching, research, and/or service will help insure your lifelong interest in the profession. I wish you success in your higher education music career and hope you find this book to be of continued service and enlightenment. Welcome to the world of higher education!

Acknowledgments

I would like to thank all of those individuals, too numerous to list, who have contributed to this book. I would especially like to thank Oxford University Press for their support of *On Staff: A Practical Guide to Starting Your Career in a University Music Department*, with very special thanks to Todd Waldman, OUP Editor, Music Books, Professional and Applied. I would also like to thank Laura Mahoney and Michael Durnin for providing editorial support and Norman Hirschy and Jeff Iorio, who worked on the production of this of this book.

POSITION ANNOUNCEMENT DESCRIPTIONS

Introduction

Congratulations! You've decided to secure a position in higher education. Securing a position in higher education is a multistep procedure. Beginning with the identification of appropriate positions, one must next apply for those posts. After applying, and while patiently waiting as a job search committee considers your application materials, you must next begin your preparations for a telephone or Skype interview, followed, one hopes, by an on-campus visit. Assuming you've had a successful interview, your next step is to negotiate an amenable contract. After all of this you can finally begin the process of becoming a faculty member in your newly acquired position. You will be launching your higher education music career, and as a new faculty member there will be much to consider, such as securing tenure and promotion. Your first post will become your first foray into the development of your unique and successful career in higher education.

On Staff: A Practical Guide to Starting Your Career in a University Music Department will help guide you through the steps to acquiring and holding a position in higher education. Each chapter is designed to assist you in one or more of the following:

- locating and understanding position announcements,
- preparing your application materials,
- understanding the process of the job search committee in relation to your application,
- planning and preparing for your interview,

- completing an interview,
- negotiating a contract, and
- getting started and succeeding in your position and developing your career.

Welcome to the world of higher education!

Position Announcements

To begin the journey of your higher education job search, you must first locate appropriate positions to which you would like to apply. There are several vehicles you may choose to use in your search for higher education openings. Some of the more common sources are the *Chronicle of Higher Education* (www.chronicle.com/jobs or www.chronicle.com/jobcategory/arts/2/); national accreditation or professional association exchange listings (such as the National Association of Schools of Music [NASM] and American Educational Research Association); and higher education position professional listing services provided through organizations such as the College Music Society, state websites, and university websites (many university postings are noted on *Jobs in Higher Education* at www.academic360.com, *Diverse Issues in Higher Education* www.diverseeducation.com, and *Higher Education Jobs* http://www.HigherEdJobs.com/). Other sources are listed in "Additional Job Listing Resources" at the end of this chapter.

Once you have identified positions of interest, you will want to know what qualifications are being sought and what the requirements are for these positions. The components of job descriptions can vary from position to position. The majority of job descriptions have standard information pertaining to the position. National position advertisements may contain only limited information due to cost factors associated with publication or advertising costs, but lengthier position descriptions can often be found on an institution's website, in distributed, printed announcements provided by the hiring department, and/or through such sources as the NASM position announcements. Information concerning the following is generally provided in job announcements:

- the type of position, music education, theory, performance/studio, and so forth,
- the rank at which the position is being supported and whether it is an adjunct, tenure track, non-tenure track, special hire, and so forth,
- the position's duties and responsibilities,
- the minimum and maximum qualifications for hiring consideration

- the minimum and maximum qualifications for hiring consideration, additional preferred qualifications,
- a closing or review timeframe.

Additionally, job announcements may have the following:

- salary range, benefits, and so forth,
- the date the position begins,
- brief descriptions of the hiring institution,
- information on the department, school, or college,
- a depiction of the institution's locale.

As you view the job description, it would also be prudent to research the mission of the school to which you are considering application. While this topic will be discussed in further detail later in this chapter, it is very important to point out that your skills and interests must match those of the school you are considering. If there is not a good match between your goals, objectives, interests, and skills and those of the school's mission, neither you nor the school will be content with the "fit." Hence it is critical that you research the mission of the school to determine whether it is analogous with your skills and interests—that there is a good fit.

Type of Position

The three most common categories of positions are tenure-track, non-tenure-track, and a group of individualized positions that shall be referred to as "special hire" positions, all of which will be discussed in this chapter. While other types of positions may be advertised, tenure-track, non-tenure-track, and "special hire" positions cover the majority of offerings. It would behoove the reader to understand what is commonly offered at institutions so that exceptions can more clearly be recognized and understood.

TENURE-TRACK POSITIONS

Tenure-track positions are the most common position offering. There has been considerable discussion concerning the system of tenure and creating/offering tenure-track positions. Some universities have attempted to implement programs in which tenure-track positions are not offered, due to budget constraints or legislative or public pressures. Subsequently, part-time positions have become more prominent in the higher education teaching force (Wilson 2010). However, even though the tenure-track system has come under scrutiny in the academic world, many universities still offer a majority of their full-time positions as tenure-track appointments.

What then is a tenure-track position? According to the 1940 *Statement of Principles on Academic Freedom and Tenure* from the American Association of University Professors (AAUP) and the Association of American Colleges, "Tenure is a means to certain ends; specifically: (1) freedom of teaching and research and of extramural activities, and (2) a sufficient degree of economic security to make the profession attractive to me and women of ability" (American Association of University Professors 2012: 1). Tenure-track positions offer the individual the opportunity to gain "tenure" after a given period of time. Simply put, once tenure is granted, an individual is generally guaranteed a teaching position in the area of hire provided he or she continues to perform at an acceptable level and is not convicted of a felony or like offense, and provided the hiring institution does not declare financial exigency. While a more lengthy discussion of the tenure process is covered in Chapter 7, some discussion needs to be addressed here in terms of seeking appropriate positions for which to apply.

When deciding to which positions you might apply, it is important to keep the issue of attaining tenure in mind in relation to your higher educational interests and the interests of the institution to which you are considering application. Position responsibilities and expectations vary according to university structures. Universities with a heavily research-based focus will expect more research output from their faculty, while universities with a teaching-based focus will expect less research output and will place more emphasis on instruction. Attaining tenure is based on each university's goals and guidelines. Thus, at a research-intensive university, you should expect tenure decisions to be heavily based on research and creative activity output. You need to ask yourself, "Do I want a position in which I need to produce numerous publications or establish a national or international performance venue?" Conversely, in a university where teaching would be valued above research and service in a tenure process, you might ask, "Do I want to work in an institution that places less value on research and creative endeavors?" Every individual has an interest area that is stronger than another. One of your first considerations in applying for any position is to ascertain the type of institution in which you would be employed and then determine whether the goals of that school align with your career and professional goals. Only if that relationship is compatible should you apply for the position.

Let's assume you are applying for positions that are compatible with your career and professional goals. When can you expect to obtain tenure? Individual tenure decisions are made after the completion of annual, two-, or three-year reviews or evaluations. Tenure-track positions, those positions in which tenure can eventually be gained, are offered at any rank from instructor to full professor.

In special cases, tenure can be granted at the time of hire if the individual is being hired at a senior level, has extensive experience, or has gained a national or international reputation in the field. If tenure can be granted at the time of hire, it is referred to as a "tenure eligible" position in the job description. Usually only individuals being considered for senior-level ranks are considered for tenure-eligible status at the time of hire. While there are some exceptions, tenure is generally not offered at the time of hire to individuals entering at the instructor or assistant professor level. Several years of reviews and evaluations will likely follow. Information concerning the various professorial ranks appears later in this chapter.

NON–TENURE-TRACK POSITIONS

Positions can also be offered on a non-tenured basis. Adjunct appointments, renewal or specified contractual positions, and many special appointments are often offered on a non-tenure basis. Adjunct appointments are offered by universities to augment full-time and/or tenure-track faculty. That said, it should be noted that even though adjunct positions are generally part-time appointments, they can be offered as full-time appointments.

Adjunct Positions

Adjunct positions are contractual and are usually offered on a semester-to-semester, quarter-to-quarter, or academic year-to-year basis. Unlike a tenure-track position, there is no guarantee of continued employment once a contract has been completed, nor is there any guarantee of continued employment regardless of the number of years an adjunct professor has held a position. Often adjunct positions are available because of a need to fill a short-term deficiency; however, numerous institutions have adjunct positions that continue year after year.

Adjunct positions can be offered at any rank, but are usually offered at an entry-level rank of instructor or assistant professor. Again, notable exceptions can be found where institutions offer adjunct positions at a senior-level rank. Thus, while adjunct positions are generally not long-term offerings at senior-level ranks, marked exceptions can be found.

Renewal or Term Appointments

Another type of non-tenure-track position is common among institutions of higher education. These positions are "renewal" or "term" positions. These are designed to last for a set or period of time, with the possibility of being renewed each year until the specified period of the appointment has elapsed. Renewal or term appointments are commonly full-time positions, designed to last for a period of one to five years. Unlike an adjunct position, in which the need for the position may exist only for a semester or a year, renewal or term positions are intended to last for a longer period of time. Indeed, the period of time for which the position is to exist is advertised in the position announcement: "An assistant professor, five-year renewal position is being offered." During that time the successful candidate is generally renewed each year, much like professors in tenure-track positions. The individual must perform in a satisfactory manner to continue in the position from year to year. If the renewal or term position were a five-year position, it would be common for the professor to be reviewed after the first year and each year thereafter until the appointment period ended. At that time, the institution would again advertise the position. It may again be offered as a renewal or term appointment, as an adjunct or tenure-track position, or it could be eliminated altogether. The important difference between an adjunct and renewal or term position is that in the latter case, the need for the appointment exists for a specified period of time. Given that there is adequate funding and that an individual's performance is satisfactory, he can be assured of a position for a specific period of time. Adjunct positions do not offer as strong an assurance for continued employment, even though it may occur.

It is generally assumed that renewal or term appointments do not carry the possibility of tenure. However, the rank at which you are hired can differ. Many of these appointments are offered at the introductory level, instructor or assistant professor, but it is not uncommon for renewal or term appointments to be offered at senior-level—associate or full professor—positions. As will be discussed later, salary and work assignment are associated with rank, so it is important to consider the rank of the renewal or term appointment.

Some institutions may offer renewal or term appointments to fill a perceived need for a finite period of time, or until such time that a tenure-track appointment can be secured. Other institutions routinely offer such appointments to augment their faculty. Institutions offering renewal or term positions on a regular basis, especially in specific areas, often seek consistency and flexibility at the same time. By offering a position for a five-year period, for example, the institution receives the consistency an individual can provide by being in that position for five years.

Flexibility is achieved when, at the end of the contractual period, another individual is sought, theoretically bringing in new ideas and approaches to the position and to the department. Some institutions will not rehire an individual who has held a renewal or term position, regardless of how successful that individual has been during the term of appointment, in order to conceivably bring in new approaches, thoughts, and ideas through a "new" hire.

SPECIAL HIRE APPOINTMENTS

There are several types of positions which have not been discussed and which will be referred to as "special appointments." Special appointments can include, but are not limited to, replacement positions, visiting professors or artists, artists in residence, research faculty, "targets of opportunity," and/or distinguished professor appointments. Special appointments can be offered at any rank and can be tenure-eligible, tenure-track, or non-tenure positions.

REPLACEMENT POSITIONS

Replacement positions are most often term appointments, meaning they are contractual and limited to a specified period of time. Replacement positions are most commonly offered when an institution has the need to temporarily "fill in" for a faculty member who may be "on leave" or "on sabbatical," or when there is a tenure-track position that has not been filled but is expected to be filled within a given period of time. Replacement positions are offered on a semester, quarter, or yearly basis. Once the need for the replacement position no longer exists—the faculty member returns from the sabbatical or leave or a tenure-track position is filled—the replacement position ceases to exist.

It is often argued that being in a replacement position can offer an individual a better chance of being offered a tenure-track position or another position in that institution. Being in a replacement position and being offered the "advertised" position is a common occurrence according to Vick and Furlong, who stated "There was a high probability at the outset that an offer would be made to someone who was already within the department." (2008: 15). Given that the replacement hire holds all of the qualifications for the position and has performed in an exemplary manner during the replacement period, she may well have an advantage over other individuals in that the faculty will have had the chance to work with her over the course of a semester or year. The faculty can determine if she would be a good fit for their department or school. It could also be argued that such familiarity can work against a replacement. Because of the position requirements, some conflicts may have arisen within the course of service, such as arguments over funding issues, disagreements on curricular issues, and so on, among the replacement and other faculty. This, then, could weigh against the replacement when she applies for the permanent position. The important point to remember about replacement positions is that they provide valuable university experience, experience that can help candidates obtain "permanent" positions in future job searches.

VISITING PROFESSORS OR VISITING ARTISTS

Visiting professor or visiting artist positions are generally created to add a temporary but important dimension to a department. Visiting professor or artist positions are often targeted appointments that are created so a particular individual or group of individuals may be employed for a given period of time to develop or further enhance a particular departmental interest or program. Professionals on sabbatical from other institutions or professional performers wishing to establish a stronger relationship with a university often are the targets of such searches. However, visiting professor or artist positions need not be targeted appointments and are often open to all qualified individuals. These positions have the advantage of offering individuals seeking such positions the flexibility of focusing on areas of interest while, at the same time, enhancing or expanding a departmental interest or program. Visiting positions can be short term or ongoing positions, and are often contractual or term appointments. They generally do not carry tenure-track or tenure-eligible status and often exist when surplus funds are available from such sources as grants or donations to an institution.

ARTISTS IN RESIDENCE OR DISTINGUISHED PROFESSOR APPOINTMENTS

Artists in residence or distinguished professor appointments are generally permanent positions and often carry with them some type of tenure-track or tenure-eligible status. Artist in residence or distinguished professor appointments are designed to attract individuals who are preeminent in their area of expertise. These appointments are focused on enhancing the image of the institution and bringing a specific expertise to an area, such as bringing an internationally known cellist to the string department to enhance the strings area. Sometimes a wider net may be cast and there be a search to find "the most qualified individual" to join the faculty, whether a performer or an academic. The objective of an artist in residence or distinguished professor position is to bring immediate prestige and eminence to an institution by hiring an individual of noted national *and* international stature.

RESEARCH APPOINTMENTS

Research appointments are more common to disciplines outside of the arts, however, they are infrequently offered in fine arts by larger institutions. Analogous to distinguished professor positions, research appointments are designed to bring to an institution individuals holding specific expertise. These individuals do not necessarily need to have national or international reputations, although they often do; they are brought in to develop or enhance particular research interests in an area. Often research appointments are designed to seek individuals with expertise that transcends one discipline, thus enabling them to secure grants and work with other professors in different disciplines. For example, a university may seek to hire an individual who does research in the area of music cognition, thus expanding the interest and grant-writing capability beyond music into such areas as educational research, psychology, medicine, or other related areas.

Research appointments are generally not tenure-track or tenure-eligible positions, although they often are in the music discipline area. Many research appointments are tied to the ability of the individual to generate funds through grants, encourage cooperative efforts among disciplines within and outside of the university, to secure individual and corporate donations, to effect interest in the creation of research and research publications, and to create and/or successfully facilitate the operations of a research center or enhance a research emphasis in a department. Evaluation decisions concerning continued employment are sometimes based on a plethora of criteria, including the ability to fund positions based on "soft monies" from grants and other such sources. Regardless of the criteria used to assess continued employment potential, the decision on whether to retain an individual in a research appointment often is made only after a period of several years of service has been provided and annual assessments have been conducted.

TARGETS OF OPPORTUNITY AND ENDOWED POSITIONS

There are special funds, not usually within the normal channels for appointment funding, that can become available to departments for hires. Two of these special hiring sources are positions created through "targets of opportunity" and through endowments. Such positions generally augment planned faculty lines and are unique within departments.

Targets of opportunity are positions that can be made available through unique university funding sources. The purpose of such appointments is to attract individuals in unique or underrepresented areas, such as individuals from a minority. Funding sources for these positions are available only if certain criteria are met, fulfilling specific hiring goals a university has established. Such positions offer unique opportunities for those individuals meeting the established hiring criteria.

Endowed positions are those funded by the income generated from assets provided by a donor. Often specific to a practitioner such as an orchestral conductor or an opera director, for example, an endowed position receives all or a major portion of its funding through income generated from the initial donation. Often endowed positions seek individuals of national or international stature to fill such vacancies.

One of your first considerations is to determine the type of position you would like. Tenure-track positions are the most common appointments; however, more and more non-tenure-track positions are appearing as universities attempt to find solutions to staffing issues. Special hires, such as target of opportunity, endowed, one-year replacement, adjunct position and other such hires, are important to consider, especially if you possess the unique criteria being sought. Thus you need to determine whether you would like to become a permanent member of an institution, in which case a tenure-track or like position should be sought, or whether you would like the opportunity of gaining experience at a particular establishment without the guarantee of tenure, in which case a non-tenure-track position would be acceptable.

Rank

The rank at which a position is offered is provided in most higher education job descriptions. The most common ranks are instructor, assistant professor, associate professor, and full professor. The ranks of instructor and assistant professor are customarily considered entry- or junior-level ranks. The rank of associate professor and full professor are considered senior-level ranks. Rank is often based on an individual's education, teaching experience in higher education, experience in the discipline, and/or level of skill or eminence in the field, profession, or area.

While not a hard and fast rule, rank is often correlated with salary level. In general, the salary at an instructor level is lower than that at an assistant professor level, an assistant professor salary less than an associate professor, and so forth. It is important to remember that while rank does not ensure a given salary, universities commonly use rank as one, if not the only, criterion to advertise the salary range for a given position. There are noted exceptions to the notion that individuals in so-called senior ranks receive higher salary offers than those in entry level positions, but rank often does dictate salary range.

Another expectation normally associated with rank is experience. When the rank of instructor or assistant professor is advertised, the general assumption is that individuals will not necessarily have a wealth of teaching or professional experience in the field, comparatively speaking. In entry- or junior-level positions, there is an expectation of growth potential in the areas of leadership and national or international expertise, but not necessarily an expectation that such expertise will already have been acquired. Senior-level positions normally come with the expectation of acquired leadership and national or international expertise. Thus, in senior positions, the following could be expected:

- In a senior position an individual would be expected to be a mentor to the junior faculty in the department, offering guidance and information where and when needed, whereas an entry- or junior-level professor would not necessarily be expected to be immediately familiar with university procedures and policies. The mentor's task is to aid junior faculty in their acquisition and understanding of department, school, college, or university procedures and policies.

- As a senior-level professor, there is an expectation of being a role model, not only to the students, but also to other faculty, especially junior faculty. Senior faculty are commonly perceived to have reached their level of rank and success in university systems by being excellent teachers and outstanding researchers, performers, or composers, and by having been recognized by their colleagues for their level of expertise throughout the nation or world. Hence senior faculty are expected to offer guidance in the enhancement of teaching techniques and skills through formal and informal peer reviews, by critiquing colleagues' research and music manuscripts, or by offering constructive suggestions in performance practices that will enhance the possibility of manuscripts being published and presented or of performances receiving wider acceptance and critical acclaim. Senior faculty are also expected to help colleagues shape and focus their professional research or performance venues, not only through constructive feedback and evaluations but also by offering guidance on the annual review and tenure promotion process, or by providing information on contacts and presentation venues gained through their own professional growth.

- In addition to teaching and service, senior faculty are often looked to for outstanding service guidance, leadership, and direction. Senior faculty are more likely to be asked to serve as coordinators of departments or divisions, chairs of committees, or members of important governance groups. Because of the perception that they have acquired knowledge and skills of university policies and procedures, experience on various committees, leadership role proficiency, and adeptness in the national arena, senior faculty are frequently viewed as excellent chairs and leaders for various university committees, ranging from the departmental to university level. While entry- or junior-level faculty are frequently asked to serve on such committees, they are not normally thrust into positions of leadership.

Position descriptions often define the level of expectation desired in applicants. However, if one understands the function of rank in a university system, he can use this knowledge to more clearly determine his appropriateness for a position. Senior-level position expectations include expertise in the areas of teaching, research or creativity, and service, while entry- or junior-level position expectations allow for such expertise to be gained along the way. Often universities do not include specific dollar ranges in their job descriptions, but rather they state that the salary is based on experience and expertise. Given that, it is valuable to know that rank often frames the salary range of an appointment. An applicant can generally find faculty salary ranges by going to a university's website. Often this information is on public record and available to an inquisitive searcher. It should be noted that salary ranges vary greatly by department and that the average salary of an assistant professor of music is not going to be the same as the average salary of an assistant professor in the school of business, law, or medicine.

Duties, Responsibilities, and Qualifications

Every job announcement has some description of the responsibilities that are basic or essential to the position. Often these are listed as required duties. For example, a school of music may be seeking a cellist primarily to build a studio, hence the duties would include studio cello teaching and recruitment. The school may also be looking for someone who is an active performer, and again, the stated responsibilities might refer to an active performance venue. In both situations, the duties may allow for some flexibility. The area of active performance venue may be flexible. The performance venue could include solo performance, chamber music performance, orchestral performance, and so forth. And while the duty of studio instructor is stated, it does not specify that the individual must provide lessons to students on a weekly basis. Indeed, if an active performance venue is sought from the individual, the cellist may be performing "on the road" and unavailable for instructional guidance. Even though a description of studio cellist and active performer may be delineated in the job announcement, the fulfillment of those duties rarely is specified in detail, allowing for more applicant choices and flexibility in the hiring process.

Along with the basic or essential duties of a given position, a list of other responsibilities, referred to as "recommended" or "desired" tasks, is common. This is a sort of "institutional shopping list" of potential tasks the professor might perform. Using our cello position as an example, the institution is trying to get a studio instructor who is also an active performer. However, within the department or within the school there may be other courses or offerings that require an instructor: freshman music theory or string pedagogy or string techniques class. The individual hired for the position of cellist may well be required to teach additional classes or coach various ensembles as well as teach studio cello and maintain an active performance schedule.

OTHER DUTIES AND RESPONSIBILITIES

In tenure-track as well as non-tenure-track university positions, there are a host of duties that are expected to be performed as part of the position but that aren't necessarily articulated as either required or desired. For example, a studio cellist would be expected to serve on string jury committees, attend string recitals and provide feedback, hold master class sessions for the cello studio, attend string faculty as well as school or college meetings, serve on departmental, school, college, or university committees, and so on. These duties or tasks are so integral to university systems that they often are not mentioned in job descriptions or in job interviews. They become tasks that are basic to the position function and to holding/maintaining the position.

Qualifications

Along with the delineation of job description duties is a section referred to as "qualifications." There are generally two types of qualifications listed in job descriptions. There are minimum qualifications, often referred to as "cut criteria" by committee members, and preferred or desired criteria. Minimum qualifications are those that are required for the position. For example, one minimum qualification for an associate professor of choral music education could be an earned doctorate in music education. Thus, for further or continued consideration for the position, the candidate would need to hold a doctorate in the field of music education. If the candidate did not hold such a degree, she would no longer be considered as a viable candidate for the position and would be "cut" and placed into a group of candidates not meeting minimum qualifications. Hence the term "cut criteria."

Minimum qualifications are listed to ensure that only certain highly qualified candidates with clearly defined interests, experience, and backgrounds may be considered for a position. Thus in the example provided, only applicants whose focus at the doctoral level was in music education would be considered as viable candidates. Other applicants, while being highly qualified in other areas, would not be considered for the position. In most public institutions of higher learning, officers of affirmative action, equal employment opportunity, human resources, and human services oversee the process of applicant review and pay careful attention to those candidates left in consideration after a review for minimum qualifications has been conducted. Remaining candidates form what is considered a final applicant pool from which an individual may be drawn for an on-campus interview. Committee members take great care to ensure that all final pool candidates possess minimum qualifications. If such care is not taken, a search can be stopped by institutional officers of affirmative action, human resources, equal employment opportunity, or the like for failing to provide equal opportunity for all applicants. For example, if we consider our associate professor of music education position minimum qualification of a doctorate in music education, an applicant not yet holding a doctorate in music education would not meet minimum criteria and should be eliminated. However, if a candidate who was "ABD" (that is, who had completed "all but the dissertation" to receive the degree in music education) continued to be considered by the committee, this would be unfair to all those individuals who also were ABD but did not apply because they perceived they did not meet the announced minimum qualifications. Hence, an equal opportunity for those individuals would not have been given and grounds to discontinue the search would be valid.

Preferred or desired qualifications, on the other hand, are those that, should an applicant possess them, might enhance his or her standing for position consideration. These qualifications are desired but not essential to the position. Given our music education position, a preferred or desired qualification could be extensive publications, defined as books, juried research articles, and the like. An individual not having such publications could still be considered for the position as long as she had a doctorate in music education, but preference might be given to a person holding the music education doctorate who had extensive publications.

While the question of being qualified for a position will be discussed in Chapter 2, it bears repeating that unless you meet minimum qualifications for a position, it is not prudent to apply for the position. The majority of public institutions and many nonpublic institutions try to clearly delineate the type of individual they wish to consider by listing minimum qualification criteria, and in such cases, if you do not meet minimum qualifications you will be cut.

There are other qualifications that candidates must fulfill for successful job consideration. These qualifications are generally not listed or may be vaguely articulated, but in general they refer to "fit" within the department, school, college, or university. "Fit" refers to the ability of the candidate to develop excellent and professional working relationships with students, colleagues, other faculty, and administrators at all levels. The ability to develop and maintain professional relationships is essential to the efficient and effective working of a university. Additionally, fit refers to the candidate's ability to support the mission of the department, school, college, or university. In a university that has a strong "in loco parentis" philosophy an individual would be expected to provide students with that kind of support and care and would be a good "fit" for the university.

While these and other fit or mission criteria may not be listed, they are as essential to an applicant's success as are other criteria. It behooves the applicant to read the mission of the institution to which she is applying.

Materials Requested and How to Apply

Higher education positions commonly require applicants to send a variety of materials, depending on the positions themselves. Common to the majority of positions is submission of the curriculum vitae (CV), a letter of application, and references. The CV is an extensive overview of an applicant's education, work, research, and service history. The letter of application acts as the document informing the search committee that you wish to be considered for the position being offered. Written letters of reference may be requested, and if written letters are not requested, then a listing of individuals willing to speak on behalf of an applicant's suitability for a position is solicited.

Additional materials required for position application may include official or unofficial university transcripts, a statement of educational or research goals and/or a philosophy of teaching, examples of current research or creative works, syllabi of courses taught, reviews of concerts presented, books written, and similar types of professional activity, evaluations from colleagues and/or students, evidence of acquisition and current functioning of teacher certification, programs, and so on. In most public and private institutions, documentation concerning citizenship status and other vetting, such as criminal background checks, are required. In addition, private or religious institutions can require materials asking for religious backgrounds or preference, loyalty oaths, and similar information.

Whatever is required for the application procedure, it is important that the applicant consider whether or not he is qualified for the position before sending materials. Copies of CVs, recordings, transcripts, postage, and envelopes can be a considerable expense for the applicant, one that may well be better spent on those positions for which he is eminently qualified. Once the decision is made to make application for a position, all required materials should be gathered, organized, and sent. Often statements will be made in job descriptions asking that only certain materials be sent initially and that other materials, if any, be sent only upon request.

Job position announcements uniformly provide information concerning the manner in which materials should be sent. While some universities still ask that paper copies of materials be submitted to a certain individual at a certain university locale, many universities are now using electronic material submission. Electronic document submission provides a paperless manner in which to submit all or perhaps just initial application items. Whether they are submitted electronically or nonelectronically, it is imperative that the highest-quality product be sent. The topic of application material preparation and submission will be discussed in detail in Chapter 2, but it can not be overstated that well-presented and organized applications are generally received with more enthusiasm than those that are ill-prepared or of poor quality.

Materials should be sent in a timely manner to ensure they reach the designated destination or individual by, or before, the application review date. Some university application receipt deadline procedures will not allow for review of materials received after a certain date, while others allow for more flexibility. It is safe to say that materials received by the designated review deadline will receive careful and considerate review. Thus, it is important that materials be sent in time to reach the review committee on or before the initial review date indicated. If there is no specified review date, a rare occurrence, it is suggested that the applicant send the materials as soon as they are ready.

Type of Institution

Often, especially in job advertisements that are listed on an institution's website or sent through the postal service (NASM-participating schools routinely send other NASM schools job announcements), a position announcement description will contain information on the university or college itself. Such descriptions provide information on the institutional setting within a city, the size of the campus, the number of students attending, the size of the city in which the university or college is located, its locale within the state, a breakdown of the climate, industry, public and private K-12 schools systems, and so on. These narrations may also provide the university mission and classification in terms of the Carnegie Foundation for the Advancement of Teaching (2001).

Classifications, found in the Carnegie publications or websites are "time-specific snapshots of institutional attributes and behavior based on data" (http://www. carnegiefoundation.org). According to McCormick and Zhao, these classifications were "not intended to be the last word on institutional differentiation" (2005: 52). However they go onto explain that "the higher education research community readily adopted the new system, and it soon became the dominant—arguably the default—way that researchers characterized and controlled for differences in institutional mission.". Carnegie classifications provide a snapshot of the institution's mission as viewed both internally and externally and provide the potential applicant with more bits of information concerning the institution. To understand the categorical distinctions given to various colleges and universities, take a closer look at the Carnegie classifications.

The Carnegie classifications have recently been revised to better identify and to describe institutions of higher learning. The initial classification framework was mentioned in an analysis of higher education demands in 1971 and was published in an article released by the Carnegie Commission in 1973 (Carnegie Commission on Higher Education 1971, 1973). The basic framework of these classifications (Carnegie Commission on Higher Education, 1971) were:

1. **Doctorate-granting institutions:**
   a. Heavy emphasis on research,
   b. Moderate emphasis on research,
   c. Moderate emphasis on doctoral programs,
   d. Limited emphasis on doctoral programs.
2. **Comprehensive colleges:**
   a. Comprehensive colleges I,
   b. Comprehensive colleges II.
3. **Liberal arts colleges:**
   a. Liberal arts colleges—selectivity I,
   b. Liberal arts colleges—selectivity II.

4. **All two-year colleges and institutes and Professional schools and other specialized institutions:**
   a. Theological seminaries, Bible colleges, and other institutions offering degrees in religion,
   b. Medical schools and medical centers,
   c. Other separate health professional schools,
   d. Schools of engineering and technology,
   e. Schools of business and management,
   f. Schools of art, music, and design, and so on,
   g. Schools of law,
   h. Teachers colleges,
   i. Other specialized institutions.

Since these beginnings, the Carnegie Classification has been revised and updated four times to account for changes in institutions and their offerings.

A recent revision now includes some significant changes from previous editions of the basic classification. While greater detail on the Carnegie classification can be found on its website at http://classifications.carnegiefoundation.org/, the following provides a brief summary of the current Carnegie classification.

1. **Associate's colleges**: These include institutions in which bachelor's degrees account for less than 10 percent of all of the undergraduate degrees or where all degrees are at the associate's level. There are fourteen levels of associate's college categories.
2. **Doctorate-granting universities**: These include institutions that grant at least twenty doctoral degrees per year, not including those that qualify for entry into professional practice, such as the JD, MD, and so on. Doctorate-granting universities are differentiated by the amount of research activity, national federal and nonfederal grant funding, and, as stated above, the number of doctoral degrees awarded. There are three levels of doctorate-granting universities: (1) research universities with *very high* research activity; (2) research universities with *high* research activity; and (3) doctoral or research universities.
3. **Master's colleges and universities**: These include institutions that grant at least fifty master's degrees per year. There are three levels of master's-granting universities: (1) master's colleges and universities with *larger programs*; (2) master's colleges and universities with *medium programs*; and (3) master's colleges and universities with *smaller programs*.

4. **Baccalaureate colleges**: These include institutions that award fewer than fifty master's or fewer than twenty doctoral degrees, and programs in which the baccalaureate degrees represent at least 10 percent of degrees granted per year. There are three levels of baccalaureate colleges: (1) baccalaureate colleges, arts and sciences; (2) baccalaureate colleges, diverse fields; and (3) baccalaureate or associate colleges.

5. **Special focus institutions**: These include institutions that grant degrees at the baccalaureate or higher levels in a concentration of single field or set of related fields. There are nine levels of special focus institutions, divided into (1) Spec/Faith: theological seminaries, Bible colleges, and other faith-related institutions, and (2) Spec/Medical: medical schools and medical centers, and so on.

6. **Tribal colleges**: These are colleges and universities that are members of the American Indian Higher Education Consortium.

All levels and types of higher education institutions are included in the Carnegie classifications: public, private, community, special focus such as denomination-affiliated, conservatory, and tribal colleges or universities that offer associate through doctoral degrees. The importance of knowing what the institutional Carnegie classification is for any given college or university is that the potential applicant can summarize the institutional focus and mission. Given this information, applicants can then decide the degree of fit that may exist between the focus and mission of any given college or university and their training, background, and interest. That college's or university's focus and mission directly affect positions in every department, school, or college within the institution. If it is a doctorate-granting university and is classified as a research university, very high in research activity, indicating an emphasis on the attainment of grant funding, on producing research, and on granting doctoral degrees, it would stand to reason that any faculty position within such a university would place strong emphasis on obtaining grants, producing research, and working with doctoral programs. Applicants would logically be expected to be interested in such endeavors, as they would support the university's mission and Carnegie classification.

One final item that is often included in job descriptions is the beginning date or the date faculty must "report." This is the time faculty are expected to be on campus and available for meetings, advising, and other such duties. In Figure 1.1 a fictitious example of a job description is shown.

DUDLEY STATE UNIVERSITY

NOTICE OF FACULTY VACANCY
Assistant Professor, Tenure-track

Position:	Teach applied clarinet, perform in faculty ensembles, and teach other classes depending upon the background of the successful candidate.
Qualifications:	Required: Masters Degree in Music and University Teaching Experience Preferred: Doctorate or ABD in Music
Rank and Salary: competitive	Assistant Professor, full-time, tenure-track, salary
Starting Date:	August, 2009
School and College	The School of Music, within the College of Fine Arts, has 45 full-University time and 21 part-time faculty. A full member of the National Association of Schools of Music, the School has 440 music majors and offers the Bachelor of Arts degree, the Bachelor of Music degree in Music Education, Performance, and Music History/Literature, the Master of Music degree in Music Education and Performance degree in Music. The School is housed in the Fine Arts Center that contains studios, rehearsal rooms, classrooms, a concert hall, a recital hall, and also houses the School of Art. The University was founded in 1864, is located on the northeastern edge of metropolitan Boston, and has a student population of 37,000.
Applications:	Candidates should submit a letter of application, curriculum vitae, official transcripts, CD demonstrating clarinet performance, and three current letters of recommendation related to this position.
	Review of files will begin November 3, 2008 and end when the position is filled.
	Send all materials to:
	Dr. Glen Clark, Chair School of Music Dudley State University 3640 John Wright Lane Boston, MA 02101

Dudley State University is an equal opportunity-affirmative action employer.

FIGURE 1.1 Job description announcement

Summary of Position Announcement Descriptions

The Position Announcement Description is the informational tool that is provided by the hiring institution to inform interested applicants of potential position openings. These descriptions contain such information as type of position and position rank, potential duties and responsibilities, minimum qualifications, application materials, a review timeframe, starting date, and often brief descriptions of the hiring institution, information on the department, school, or college, and a depiction of the institution's locale. Positions can be offered as tenure-track or tenure-eligible, non-tenure-track, including adjunct and renewal or term appointments, or special hire appointments, including replacement, visiting professor or artist, artist in residence or distinguished professor, research, target of opportunity, or endowed positions.

Rank is also an important item provided in job descriptions. Entry-level ranks, often viewed as instructor to assistant professor, and senior-level positions, generally assumed to be associate or full professor positions, are common rank categories in higher education institutions. The rank at which a position is offered is often associated with the expectations for the position in terms of experience, duties, and visibility, as well as salary and tenure or tenure-eligible status. The potential or acquired ability to assume leadership positions, to offer guidance in the areas of faculty and student development, provide local and national research expertise, to be recognized for national and international expertise, to develop curriculum, and to support mission guidelines are key components of faculty rank function and are strong determinants in position selection.

A function of the job description is to detail the basic, required, or essential expected duties as distinct from recommended or desired duties. The basic position duties are those that are essential to the functioning of the position and to the fulfillment of departmental expectations for that position. The basic duties are generally not subject to change appreciably over the term of the appointment and are not subject to change during the hiring process. If, for example, the basic advertised duties of a position were to "teach freshman music theory classes and conduct the orchestra," it would be highly unusual for those duties to be morphed into a position in which the emphasis would be upon "teaching jazz pedagogy and conducting the wind ensemble." Recommended or desired duties, on the other hand, are often a "shopping list" of skills a department may like the candidate to possess to some degree. Desired duties are not essential to an applicant's qualification for a position, but if the candidate possesses the ability to teach or provide skills in one or more of the desired areas it may enhance her employment opportunity.

The qualifications portion of a job description distinguishes between those criteria that must be met by all candidates for continued consideration as opposed to those criteria that are preferred or desired. Minimum job qualifications are referred to as "cut criteria." Applicants not meeting minimum job qualification are eliminated from further consideration, or are "cut" from the pool of potential candidates. Preferred or desired qualifications may include a host of items such as specific administrative experience, degrees, enhanced teaching or performance experience, or extensive publication.

Application materials requirements vary, but the submission of the curriculum vitae, letter of application, and references are commonly required items necessary for application consideration. Additional materials, such as transcripts, statements of educational or research goals and/or a philosophy of teaching or education, examples of current research or creative works, recordings, course syllabi, concert reviews, publications, student or colleague evaluations, and other such items, while not required initially, may be requested later. It perhaps "goes without saying" that materials should be received by the hiring institution no later than the stated initial review date for optimum consideration.

Many position announcement descriptions will contain the starting date as well as information on the university or college, including the setting of the institution within the city, campus size, student numbers, city population, climate, and industry, public and private K-12 schools systems within the area. Often these narrations contain the institution's Carnegie Foundation for the Advancement of Teaching classification, which can help delineate a university's mission. For a checklist of job preparation information see Job Search Checklist.

References

American Association of University Professors. 2012. 1940 statement of principles on academic freedom and tenure. *Policy documents and reports 3*. http://www.aaup.org/AAUP/pub-sres/policydocs/contents/1940statement.htm (accessed April 3, 2012).

Carnegie Classification Web pages: www.carnegiefoundation.org/

Carnegie Commission on Higher Education. 1971. *New students and new places: Policies for the future growth and development of American higher education*, New York: McGraw-Hill.

Carnegie Commission on Higher Education. 1973. *A classification of institutions of higher education*. Berkeley, CA.

Carnegie Foundation for the Advancement of Teaching. 2001. *The Carnegie classification of institutions of higher education* (2000 ed.). Mento Park, CA. http://www.carnegiefoundation.org.

McCormick, A. C., and C. Zhao. 2005. Rethinking and reframing the Carnegie classification. *Change* (September–October): 51–7.

Vick, Julia. M., and Jennifer S. Furlong. 2008. *The academic job search handbook*. 4th ed. Philadelphia: University of Pennsylvania Press.

Wilson, Robin. 2010. Tenure, RIP: What the vanishing status means for the future of education. http://chronicle.com/article/Tenure-RIP/66114/ (accessed April 3, 2012).

ADDITIONAL JOB LISTING RESOURCES

Academic Careers Online: http://www.academiccareers.com/ Global academic job search listings.

Academic Keys: http://finearts.academickeys.com/seeker_search.php Global academic search listings.

Affirmative Action Register: http://www.aar-eeo.com. Numerous listings.

College Music Society's *Music Vacancy List*: www.music.org. Subscription required.

Conductor's Guild: *Conductor Opportunities*: http://www.conductorsguild.org. Subscription required.

Higher Ed Jobs: http://www.higheredjobs.com/Faculty/search.cfm?JobCat=124. Music position listings.

Inside Higher Ed: http://www.insidehighered.com/ Academic search listings.

Musical Chairs: www.musicalchairs.info. Music position listings.

My Auditions: http://www.myauditions.com/. Music position listings.

Peabody Institute Job Vacancy Bulletin: http://www.peabody.jhu.edu/jvb. Numerous listings.

Society for Music Theory Listserve: http://smt.ucsb.edu/smt-list/smthome.html. Subscription required.

Bienen School of Music at Northwestern University: . Lists additional sources for positions in various music areas.

2

PREPARING YOUR APPLICATION MATERIALS:

APPLYING FOR THE JOB

WHILE IT MAY seem to be an easy task initially, preparing and making an application for a position is time-consuming and challenging. The steps to job application include preparing your curriculum vitae; constructing a cover or application letter; developing, obtaining, or gathering materials such as CDs, transcripts, articles, and syllabi; and organizing these materials for the application process. You should be ready to provide statements of a teaching or research philosophy, a teaching portfolio, reviews of concerts, and programs. You should also be preparing presentations and/or music for at least one recital for onsite interviews.

The focus of this chapter will be on the preparation of your application materials. Later in this book a discussion of the preparation needed for a telephone or Skype interview and the on-site interview will be undertaken. However, this chapter will focus on your CV, cover or application letter, references, and supporting materials. The task of organizing your materials and customizing them for each position, even after your initial materials have been prepared, can in itself become a full-time task. We will begin with the preparation of the CV, for it is and will be one of the critical documents that is needed for job applications and will continue to be needed in the tenure and promotion processes, consideration for grants, honors, awards, national offices and boards, and a host of other venues.

Curriculum Vitae

The curriculum vitae, often referred to by its acronym CV, is derived from Latin, meaning "course of life"—the word *curriculum* is the singular second-declension neuter Nominative meaning "course," while *vitae* is the singular first-declension feminine Genitive meaning "of life," hence "course of life." While not a reflection of their personal life, the "higher education" CV is a detailed inventory of an individual's professional life. The CV is considerably longer, more inclusive, and more comprehensive than the résumé. A résumé (re´sum´e) is defined as "a summing up or summary" (Morris 1969: 1109) and normally does not exceed two pages in length, while the CV should literally provide the course of one's professional life. While the term "curriculum vita" is frequently seen, the proper term for this document is "curriculum vitae."

The two basic requirements of a well-constructed CV are that is easy to read and that it has quality materials laid out in a fashion that clearly and concisely presents the individual's professional achievements. A discussion of CV appearance will be undertaken followed by the general construction of the document. A more detailed discussion of CV construction will then be presented.

CV PREPARATION APPEARANCE

The CV is one of the key documents in the candidate selection process. The CV is used by the review committee to recommend applicants, by directors and deans to select candidates, and by provosts and presidents to approve the nominee. The CV is one of the most important documents you will prepare for your application portfolio. Unlike the traditional business résumé, which varies from one to two pages, the CV can be limitless in length and is a comprehensive and comparatively detailed document of your educational, employment, and scholarly or creative history. Due to the amount of information you are providing, it is very important that you use a format that satisfies the following criteria:

1. It is professional looking:
   a. Use quality paper if a "hard copy" of the document is sent.
   b. Have an appropriate amount of "white space" in your document: let it breathe.
   c. Use a header containing your name and the page number. The header should be flush right with your name and the acronym CV on the first line (Dr. Donald L. Hamann, CV) followed on a second line by the page number. There should be at least two spaces following the header and the content on the page. If you would rather paginate in a footer, I suggest centering the information.

2. It is easy to read: Use fonts that are at least 12 point and professional in appearance. Times, Times New Roman, and Courier are some of the more commonly used fonts.

3. It is easy to comprehend:

   a. Use spacing for clarity purposes.

   b. Organize materials in a logical fashion; use headings, subheadings, bullets, indentations, underlining, bold type, italic, and other such devices to allow the reader to easily grasp and remember the information you are providing.

   c. Try inserting an extra line of spacing between major headings.

   d. If you have a long list of bulleted items, ascertain whether you can use additional subheadings to further categorize or clarify the information. The use of indentation, line separation, and so forth can also help add clarity.

   e. All information provided should be as brief as possible while conveying the appropriate message.

   f. A general rule to follow is organize your information so that important material/items/points *always* stand out.

4. It provides comprehensive information: Your CV entries should provide enough information to adequately convey the importance of items listed without providing excess information that clutters or detracts from that goal.

5. It is well written: Proper grammar is critical in the preparation of your CV. Verb tense, word choice, and so forth, are important in transmitting the proper image you wish to convey. Of utmost importance is spelling. The importance of correct spelling in a CV cannot be overstressed.

6. It uses a consistent format or style: Whether you are listing information as citations or entering information under headings, consistency of format and style will help the reader more quickly comprehend the information you are sharing.

CREATING YOUR CV: GENERAL DOCUMENT CONSTRUCTION

The material you present and the manner in which you present your professional information can help or hinder you in the job review process. Reviewers look to the CV as one measure of a candidate's suitability and "fit" for a position. Thus a candidate's task is to highlight and illuminate those informational items that may be most meaningful to reviewers. CV preparation is a process of gathering pertinent and meaningful information and presenting that information in a format that is eminently easy to read, comprehend, and synthesize. The first step to CV preparation is gathering pertinent information for inclusion in your document and categorizing those materials.

Through the years, you have amassed information relating to your professional career and development. You must organize this information into an easily comprehended format that allows for expansion. It is perhaps best to present, and then discuss, the different categories under which you will list your information. Universities are familiar with the categorization of professional experiences using three broad categories: Teaching, research and/or creative activities, and service. While these headings are augmented in your CV, it is useful to think about these three categories as you prepare your CV.

You begin your CV by providing your personal information, followed by your educational background. The next most common category is your employment history, under which you discuss your teaching experiences. Following employment history is research and/or creative activity, which is often followed by grants received. Service, honors and awards, and references conclude the basic sections of a CV. Other sections, such as repertoire lists, reviews, and so forth, can be added to these basic components, but the initial emphasis will be on the construction and content of the eight basic categories listed.

1. Personal information and contact details
2. Educational background or experience
3. Employment history or professional career experience
4. Research and/or creative activity
5. Grants
6. Service
7. Honors and awards
8. References

The eight categories outlined above are common headings seen in CVs, but they are not exclusive. If you find you need to add categories to your CV to best convey your professional history, do not hesitate to include them. Given these caveats, let's begin the process of creating your CV. The following steps should assist you in this process.

Step 1: Begin by making a list of all of your accomplishments, starting with your initial college experience.

Step 2: Organize these materials under meaningful, and yet accepted, recognizable categories, under the larger framework of educational background, employment history, research or creative endeavors, grants, service, and honors and awards. Remember also that your organizational format will need to be flexible enough so it can be expanded in the future and revised at any given moment.

Step 3: Once items have been placed in appropriate categories, organize them by subcategories, where appropriate, and chronologically from most recent to least recent under each heading and subheading.

Step 4: Identify additional subheadings (subheadings under subheadings) that further define your information.

Step 5: Review the materials to make sure they are accurate and that they are not repeated in another section of your CV

Step 6: Consider removing items:
   a. with which you are not comfortable,
   b. that you do not feel are worthy of mention in the CV, or that
   c. others have questioned as to their appropriateness, for example, performances in college groups that were part of a degree requirement, participation in high school groups, and so forth.

Step 7: Consider adding materials that would add clarity and understanding or would eliminate time periods otherwise unaccounted for in your professional history.

Step 8: Shorten or lengthen materials under individual headings to provide adequate detail and eliminate materials that hide important information.

Step 9: Present your materials so:
   a. they are easy to read (large enough fonts: 12 point),
   b. they present the reader with a clear sense of the message you are trying to convey, and
   c. important information stands out and other materials are presented but do not dominate or cover important items.

Step 10: Consider the CV as a document that expresses you, the person. This is a composite picture of you as a professional and you need to feel comfortable with that picture. Determine whether your CV adequately and appropriately reflects your accomplishments and conveys your strengths as an individual and as a candidate for the position.

Step 11: Once you have completed Step 10, have as many people as possible review your CV. Have them *be as critical as possible* pointing out:
   a. any confusion or lack of clarity in any item or category,
   b. spelling or grammatical errors,
   c. lack of attentiveness to layout issues (font type, font size, indentation issues, breathing/space, organizational concerns, and so forth), and/or
   d. questionable entries.

Use this feedback to revise your CV as you deem appropriate. Everyone has his/her opinions and those opinions often conflict. Remember, you are the final judge of your CV's content and appearance.

Step 12: Begin to consider individuals to serve as your references. Initiate the process of asking individuals to serve as your referees. As they agree to do so, add them to your reference list, should you choose to include one at the end of your CV.

In general, the idea behind the CV is to include detailed yet, paradoxically, concisely presented information, chronologically arranged, that articulates the individual's professional life. It should be presented in such a manner that it is reviewable in a minimum of time with maximum information being acquired. A CV is like a lengthy sales booklet—you are highlighting your skills, achievements, and experiences in hopes of convincing others that you are the best choice for the position. The more convincing your CV, the better are your chances of continued candidacy consideration. As you prepare your CV, you need not be concerned about its length but rather about its clarity and comprehensiveness. Remember, you are highlighting your skills, achievements, and experiences and your goal is to be thorough.

We will now look more closely at the information presented under each category of your CV and discuss various manners of presenting that material, with an eye to style, spacing, and other presentation considerations, important to the overall effect and impact of your CV. We begin with your contact or personal information.

CV CATEGORIES

Personal Information and Contact Details

Obviously you want hiring committee members or administrators to be able to contact you easily and quickly should they have additional questions or seek supplementary materials, or should they wish to set up a telephone or Skype interview or have you come to their campus for an interview. It is customary to reveal the following information at the beginning of your CV:

1. your full name, excluding any descriptive titles,
2. your mailing address—this can be your home, work, or both addresses,
3. home, work, and/or cell telephone numbers,
4. email addresses, and
5. websites.

Brian E. Compthecon   *Composer • Theorist • Conductor*

343 52nd Street NW
Canton, OH 44709
Email: composer@yahoo.com
Telephone: 330-333-1111
Cell: (330) 222-1211

FIGURE 2.1 CV: Applicant information illustration #1

Your full name should appear on the CV. Avoid using titles such as Dr., EdD, PhD, DMA, MFA, and so on. If you hold a doctoral or master's degree, this will be reflected in the educational background section of your CV. The use of Mrs. or Miss is also discouraged, as it can reveal marital status. You should also avoid listing information such as race or religious or political affiliation. Affirmative action guidelines protect an individual from divulging information that does not pertain to the applicant's ability to perform the duties of the position. Your marital status, gender, race, religious or political affiliation, and other such information have no bearing on your qualifications for a position. Therefore it is recommended that you not include such information in your CV. Examples of applicants' information follow. Note the different style and manner of presentation in each of the three (Figures 2.1, 2.2, and 2.3).

Educational Background or Experience

The next most common heading to appear in a CV is educational background or experience. Listed from most recent to least recent, your educational background is in essence a chronological hierarchy of degrees. Each degree has a separate entry with the following information pertaining to educational background:

1. the type of degree or type of study completed (i.e., PhD, DMA, postdoctoral study, MFA, MM, etc.),
2. the institution that awarded the degree, and

Personal

Name:	Compthecon, Brian E.
Home Address	343 52nd Street NW Canton, OH 44709
Telephone:	Home: (330) 333-1111 Cell: (330) 222-1211
Email:	composerplus@yahoo.com

FIGURE 2.2 CV: Applicant information illustration #2

Brian E. Compthecon
Curriculum Vita

Professor, School of Music
College of Fine Arts
University of Northern Ohio
Canton, OH 44708
(330) 343-2222
www.music.northernohio.edu
composer@yahoo.com
Faculty website: http://web.cfa.northohio.edu/netid=bcomptheon

Home Address
343 52nd Street NW
Canton, OH 44709
(330) 333-1111
Cell: (330) 222-1211

FIGURE 2.3 CV: Applicant information illustration #3

3. the years in which study began and was or will be completed.
   a. In the case of dissertations or theses, many individuals list the titles of these documents under the degree listing.
   b. Academic grade point average and honors (e.g., "graduated summa cum laude") can also be listed under each entry if desired.
   c. When applicants are in the process of pursuing a doctoral degree and have completed all requirements necessary with the exception of completing the dissertation, this is referred to as "all but dissertation" or ABD.
      1. It is useful to list this status under the doctoral degree study entry. Individuals who have ABD status often list the date in which all degree requirements, excluding the dissertation/dissertation defense, were completed (usually indicated by the passing of some type of comprehensive or doctoral candidacy exam) along with an anticipated dissertation completion date.
      2. The anticipated completion date of the doctoral dissertation or master's thesis is often provided, when, if "all goes as planned," the document will be completed and successfully defended. It is understood that when an anticipated completion date is listed it is subject to change.
      3. Individuals who are not ABD but have completed all course work for the degree, but have not yet taken and passed their comprehensive exams, may indicate the same; for example: "Coursework completed July, 2012—comprehensive exams scheduled for August 13, 2012."

One final item that is often found in the "Educational background or experience" section of CVs, especially of individuals applying for studio teaching, applied composition positions, and so forth, is a listing of master teachers with whom they have studied, in master class situations, private studio settings, or other professional venues. The settings, such as master class or private study, for example, are used as headers. While it is not as common, individuals in other discipline areas, such as music history, music education, or music theory, can list study with individuals they consider to be major professors. If such listings are desired, they should appear after the educational background information following each degree, or after all educational background has been provided. An example of fictitious CV information appears in Figure 2.4.

There are various formats that can be used when presenting your educational background and studies with individuals of note. The examples that follow, Figures 2.5, 2.6, and 2.7, display three different approaches that convey similar information.

Each of these formats has individual appeal and clearly conveys the author's intent. Once you have determined the information you deem important to include, provided you have the time, you may wish to experiment with different presentation formats. Experimenting with various formats does not need to be limited to any one section of your CV. The previous examples hopefully have provided some ideas that you may wish to carry through your CV, not only in this section, but also

---

Dr. Brian E. Compthecon, Ph.D.   *Composer • Theorist • Conductor*

343 52nd Street NW
Canton, OH 44709
Email: composer@yahoo.com
Telephone: 330-333-1111

<u>Education</u>

2003   **Kent State University**
       Ph.D. in Music Theory & Composition
       Dissertation:
       Part I: Analysis of Vincent Persichetti's Mass for Mixed Chorus
       Part II: Original Composition: Edward's Mass for Chorus and Organ
       Composition Studies: Thomas Janson, Frank Wiley, & James Waters
       Theoretical Studies: Thomas Janson and Richard Devore
       Music Education Studies: Donald Hamann

1988   **New England Conservatory of Music**
       M.M. in Composition
       Composition Studies: Robert Ceely, Orchestration: William Thomas McKinley
       Theoretical Studies: Robert Cogan & Gerald Zaritsky
       Conducting Studies: Lorna Cooke DaVaron & David Hodgkins

1985   **Baldwin-Wallace College**
       B.M. in Composition
       Composition Studies: Loris Chobanian
       Theoretical Studies: James Feldman, Walter Winzenberger, & Lawrence Hartzell
       Conducting Studies: Stuart Raleigh & Warren Scharf
       Piano Studies: George Cherry, Organ Studies: Warren Berryman
       Vocal Studies: Charles Smith, Joyce Koch

FIGURE 2.4 CV: Educational background sample

R. Cyril Morress
5555B Eastern Court
Tucson, Arizona 85708
(620) 954-0075
morress@email.arizona.edu

<u>**Education**</u>

Master of Music in Choral Conducting   Anticipated May 2011
‣ University of Arizona, Tucson, AZ
    Current GPA: 4.0

Bachelor of Music in Sacred Music   2009
‣ Westminster Choir College of Rider University,
    Princeton, NJ
    GPA: 3.7 (*Magna cum laude* Graduate)

Primary Conducting Instructors:
‣ Dr. Bruce Chamberlain
‣ Dr. James Jordan
‣ Dr. Elizabeth Schauer
‣ Dr. Joe Miller
‣ Gerald Custer
‣ Ruth Ochs

Private Voice Instructors:
‣ Dr. Kristin Dauphinais
‣ Guy Rothfuss

Sacred Music Professors:
‣ Kathy Ebling-Thorn
‣ Dr. Robin Leaver
‣ Dr. Steven Pilkington

Private Piano Intructors:
‣ Miriam Eley
‣ Marilyn Shenenberger
‣ Dr. Stefan Young

FIGURE 2.5 CV: Educational background format #1

in the "professional career experience" section that follows, as well as all the other CV components.

Employment History or Professional Career Experience

Your teaching experience, professional performance career, or similar musical employment experience is the next area normally found in CVs. This information should again be chronologically listed from most to least recent. This section should be viewed as your work history.

Academic Positions

If you are applying for an academic post in, for example, music education, theory, or history, your teaching experience should be listed first, even if you have

R. Cyril Morress
5555B Eastern Court
Tucson, Arizona 85708
(620) 954-0075
morress@email.arizona.edu

Education

Master of Music in Choral Conducting   Anticipated May 2011
    ▸ University of Arizona, Tucson, AZ
        Current GPA: 4.0

Bachelor of Music in Sacred Music   2009
    ▸ Westminster Choir College of Rider University,
        Princeton, NJ
        GPA: 3.7 (*Magna cum laude* Graduate)

Primary Conducting Instructors:
    ▸ Dr. Bruce Chamberlain (choral/orchestral)   2009-Present
    ▸ Dr. Elizabeth Schauer (choral)   2009-Present
    ▸ Dr. James Jordan (choral)   2006-2009
    ▸ Dr. Joe Miller (choral)   2009
    ▸ Ruth Ochs (orchestral)   2008-2009
    ▸ Gerald Custer (orchestral)   2007-2009

Private Voice Instructors:
    ▸ Dr. Kristin Dauphinais   2010
    ▸ Guy Rothfuss   2005-2009

Sacred Music Professors:
    ▸ Kathy Ebling-Thorn   2005-2009
    ▸ Dr. Robin Leaver   2005-2009
    ▸ Dr. Steven Pilkington   2005-2009

Private Piano Intructors:
    ▸ Dr. Stefan Young   2009
    ▸ Marilyn Shenenberger   2007-2008
    ▸ Miriam Eley   2005-2008

FIGURE 2.6 CV: Educational background format #2

professional performance experience. A heading as simple as "teaching experience" can precede this section.

Under each teaching situation the following should appear:

1. the year(s) of employment,
2. the employing institution, and
3. your duties and responsibilities in the position.

The amount of description provided to explain your duties and responsibilities can vary, but information that is too lengthy or is not presented in such a fashion that it can be easily grasped is often overlooked in a cursory viewing of a CV. Thus the information provided should be as brief as possible and should be organized so important points stand out. The use of bullets, indentation, line separation, and

R. Cyril Morress
5555B Eastern Court
Tucson, Arizona 85708
(620) 954-0075
morress@email.arizona.edu
murpr@email.arizona.edu

Education

Master of Music in Choral Conducting   Anticipated May 2011
> University of Arizona, Tucson, AZ
  Current GPA: 4.0

Bachelor of Music in Sacred Music   2009
> Westminster Choir College of Rider University,
  Princeton, NJ
  GPA: 3.7 (*Magna cum laude* Graduate)

Primary Conducting Instructors:
> Dr. Bruce Chamberlain (choral/orchestral)   University of Arizona
> Dr. James Jordan (choral)   Westminster Choir College
> Dr. Elizabeth Schauer (choral)   University of Arizona
> Dr. Joe Miller (choral)   Westminster Choir College
> Gerald Custer (orchestral)   Private
> Ruth Ochs (orchestral)   Private

Private Voice Instructors:
> Dr. Kristin Dauphinais
> Guy Rothfuss

Sacred Music Professors:
> Kathy Ebling-Thorn
> Dr. Robin Leaver
> Dr. Steven Pilkington

Private Piano Intructors:
> Miriam Eley
> Marilyn Shenenberger
> Dr. Stefan Young

FIGURE 2.7 CV: Educational background format #3

so on, all aids the clarity and ease of reading and understanding of your CV. The following example, Figure 2.8, is from a fictitious individual named Susan Hanes who is a flutist and theory instructor and has applied for a music theory position.

For an equally effective way to format these experiences, see "An Academic-oriented CV" by Paulis under Academic CVs.

If you are applying for an academic position and you have professional performance experience, the performance experience information should appear after your teaching experience. The thinking behind this is that as an academician your teaching interest should be strong and is of utmost importance, thus your teaching experience should appear first. A listing of professional performance

SUSAN HANES
6431 N. Tierra de las Catalinas #49, Winder, WI 54451
(595)235-2222 home, (595)623-7001 office
hanes@aol.com

TEACHING EXPERIENCE

2002-2004	**University of Central Wisconsin,** School of Music and Dance
	Professor, Flute and Music Theory
	• Music Theory – undergraduate majors
	• Flute Studio—graduate and undergraduate flute majors
	• Director—UCW Flute Ensemble Festival
	• Flutist with the UCW Wind Quintet
1993-2002	**Yoder State University,** Danish School of Music
1999-2002	*Associate Professor, Flute and Music Theory*
1993-1999	*Assistant Professor, Flute and Music Theory*
	• Music Theory – undergraduate majors
	• Flute Studio—flute majors and minors
	• Founder and Director—Danish Flute Ensemble and Danish Flute Festival
	• Flutist with the Danish Wind Quintet
1988-1991	**Julliard Conservatory**
	Graduate Teaching Assistant in Music Theory
1987-1988	**State University of New York College at Fredonia**
	Graduate Teaching Assistant in Flute and Music Theory
1984-1987	**Radford University,** Richmond, Virginia
	Instructor of Flute and Music Theory

FIGURE 2.8 CV: Academic post application illustration #1

experience(s) should have a separate heading such as "professional performance experience." Items should be chronologically listed from most recent to least recent. The year(s) of employment, the employing organization, and the duties performed should again appear under each entry. Figure 2.9 is an example of such an entry.

Other examples of academic-oriented CVs can be found under Academic CVs.

Performance Positions
If you are applying for a studio, applied, or conducting position, it is often suggested that your professional performance employment should appear before any teaching experience. Your first category would then be "Professional experience," followed by a second category of "Teaching experience," if applicable. However,

Curriculum Vita

Douglas E. Thoonsoon

3333 North Crest Sextho Drive
Tucson, AZ 85719
(520) 232-8523
dougthoon@email.arizona.edu

Teaching

University of Arizona

Summer 2008	MUSIC 109 "Popular and Rock Music in the United States"
	Instructor of Record
2007-2008	GTA for MUSIC 109 "Popular and Rock Music in the United States"
2006 – 2007	Assisted with Fundamentals of Choral Conducting Class
	Assisted on a volunteer basis
2006	GTA for MUSIC 103 "The History of Jazz"
2000	MUS 13 "Beginning Classical Guitar," University of Missouri
	Instructor of Record

University of Missouri

1998 – 2000	MUS 12 "Elementary Folk Guitar,"
	Instructor of Record
1999 – 2000	Occasional Guest Lecturer in Music History, University of Missouri

Other

Spring 1998	Student Teaching at White Bear Lake High School, White Bear Lake, MN
Fall 1997	Student Teaching at Hopkins Elementary School, Hopkins, MN
1987-1991	Numerous teaching experiences with children and adults, in both large and small settings, within the context of professional ministry

PROFESSIONAL EXPERIENCE

Conducting

University of Arizona

Spring 2008	Arizona Choir, 32-voice highly select mixed ensemble
	D. M. A. Lecture-Recital
Fall 2007	University Singers, a 100-voice mixed ensemble
Spring 2007	Recital Choir, a 32-voice mixed graduate ensemble
Fall 2006	University Singers, a 90-voice mixed ensemble
Spring 2006	Honor Choir, a 50-voice auditioned women's ensemble
Fall 2005	*Kantorei,* a 30-voice auditioned mixed ensemble

Festivals/Symposia

February 2007	Vancouver Chamber Choir, Vancouver, B.C., Canada
	Canada's National Conducting Symposium
2002	Western National Conducting Festival, Akon, MO
2001	Oregon Bach Festival, Eugene, OR

Church

2000 - 2005	Sanctuary Choir, Nativity Episcopal Church
2000 - 2005	Nativity Bells, Nativity Episcopal Church
2000 - 2005	Contemporary Worship Ensemble, Nativity Church
1997 - 1998	Sanctuary Choir, Holy Trinity Lutheran Church
1997 - 1998	Bell Choir, Holy Trinity Lutheran Church
1997 - 1998	Contemporary Worship Ensemble, Holy Trinity Church
1995 - 1997	Sanctuary Choir, Lake of the Isles Lutheran

FIGURE 2.9 CV: Academic post application illustration #2

another approach equally recommended is to list your teaching experience first regardless of your performance background. The idea behind this approach is that the position for which you will be applying at the collegiate level will probably be primarily oriented toward a teaching assignment and thus teaching should be acknowledged first. The decision to list your teaching experience before or after your professional experience is yours, of course. Obviously if you have no teaching experience, this becomes a moot point. In many situations, the fact that an individual has been a member of a distinguished group or orchestra or has participated in noted recital venues is paramount to teaching experience. Thus, depending on the wording of the position announcement, it might behoove the applicant to prepare two CVs, one with professional experience listed before teaching experience and visa versa. The applicant can then decide which CV might best be submitted for any particular position.

Regardless of the order of the materials, the information in both your teaching and professional employment sections should be chronologically listed from most to least recent. A heading as simple as "Professional experience" can be used to highlight those experiences, just as the heading "Teaching experience" can be used to feature this involvement. Performance experience subheadings could include employment in a full-time orchestra or orchestras, solo chamber music experience, and so forth. The Professional Experience section reflects your gainful employment as a musician and is used to delineate your avocation. As in an academic CV, the teaching experience portion should contain the year/years of employment, the employing institution, your duties and responsibilities in the position. Other examples of performance oriented CVs can be found under Performance CVs.

Non–Music- and/or Music-related Experiences

Non–music- or music-related employment can be listed separately from the "Professional experience" or "Teaching experience" headings. Listing non–music-related job items, especially when individuals are developing their CVs early in their careers, provides the reviewer with a continuous picture of the candidates' activities. Individuals who have had experiences in nonmusic positions may have been required to demonstrate leadership and so on. Such skills may be sought in the job position for which the candidate is applying. For examples of such listings see "A Performance-oriented CV" by Meez under her heading of "Additional Employment History" and "A Performance-oriented CV" by Jones under her heading of "Special skills" under Performance CVs.

The same holds true for positions outside the "normal" academic circles. Working in the music industry, in church settings, as a private studio instructor, or as a recording studio engineer, for example, gives experiences that can potentially be viewed as valuable to a hiring institution. It is important to note employment-related experiences, especially when you are beginning to develop your CV and your career. These experiences help convey the types of skills you have acquired in various situations. Often these experiences can be of primary interest to a hiring body. A listing of such experiences can efficiently be completed under a separate heading, such as "Non-music- or music-related experiences." An effective way to format these types of experiences can be found in Mallig's CV, see "An Academically Oriented CV" by Mallig, under "Academic CVs."

Continuity and consistency are important when developing your chronological listing of developmental activities in your CV. When there are periods that are not accounted for in one's career development, these are referred to as "gaps." An example of a gap would be a period of time after receipt of a degree and before acquisition of employment. If an individual received a degree and then could not attain pertinent employment for a year, this would be considered a gap. The reason for the lapse of time between the receipt of a degree and the attainment of music employment could have been due to employment in an area outside of music for that period of time. Because search committee members usually question gaps in CVs, it is important to account for all activities during your career, whether they are related to music or not. Since certain types of related activities might not logically seem to belong under the Teaching or Performance headings, the separate heading of "Non–Music- or Music-related Positions" is created to list such experiences. Usually, as an individual advances his/her career, the elimination of non-music- and/or music-related listings might be considered. For an effective way to handle a "gap" see "A Performance Oriented CV" by Mansilver (pages 3 and 4) under "Performance CVs."

There are situations in which a "gap" occurs and you were not pursuing educational study, teaching, performing, exhibiting, producing shows, or gainfully employed in another profession or area. Some of these gaps may be due to personal health issues, family obligations, extensive travel, participation in an organization such as the Peace Corps or in a religious mission, and so forth. Listing extensive personal information should be avoided, but you may briefly mention events, such as those already listed, that identify activities that appear during gap time periods. A cautionary note is in order, however. There is a fine line between revealing pertinent information concerning your employment history and revealing personal information. Your level of comfort and professional adroitness should be used as guidelines in your decision to include or not to include personal information and to determine the extent of the personal information provided in your CV, should you deem such information important to a clearer understanding of your professional history.

Thus far we have discussed and described the presentation of your educational background and your employment history in the CV. Both are important to prospective employers as the information provides the hiring institution with a glimpse of your potential in given job settings. However, more detailed information is needed to help hiring committee personnel make decisions concerning your potential for the position being sought. The remainder of the CV can be viewed as providing this detail and information and typically begins with a section detailing your performance, composition, or research efforts. For ease of presentation, the discussion of this section will be divided between two types of CVs: an academic- and a performance-oriented CV.

Research and Creative Activity: An Academic-oriented CV

As an academician, the next major section of your CV is the "Research and/or creative activities" section. Simply stated, research activity is viewed as an academic activity whereas creative activity is viewed as an artistic endeavor. Thus research activity is that pursuit which generally results in the writing, presentation, and subsequent publication of research articles, books, monographs, and other such scholarly manuscripts. Creative activities are those endeavors that result in artistic outcomes such as recitals, productions, films, concerts, CDs, TV or radio broadcasts, and so forth. The two activities are similar in that they reflect a level of professional adeptness, acuity, activity, interest, adroitness, and ability in the applicant's field of focus.

Whether activities are research oriented or creative endeavors, each undertaking is perceived in a different light depending on various factors. As you construct your CV, you need to account for the various weightings and perceptions of each venture. In so doing, various subcategories will be formed in order to highlight the importance of each activity, making sure that the most important endeavors are not overlooked because they are "buried" among less important undertakings.

If we were to look at a CV in which the major research activities were publications and presentations (an academically oriented CV), we would most likely find several subheadings under the major heading of "Research." Under the "Research" heading we would likely find a subcategory of "Publications," and that subdivided as follows:

Publications: books, chapters in books, or monographs,
Publications: juried or reviewed research journals,
Publications: juried or reviewed professional magazines, and
Publications: nonjuried sources.

Under the heading of "Presentations" it would be common to find the following subheadings:

International presentations: juried or reviewed,
National presentations: juried or reviewed,
Regional or state presentations: juried or reviewed,

and perhaps even several categories of nonjuried presentations;

International presentations: nonjuried,
National presentations: nonjuried, and
Regional or state presentations: nonjuried.

The subcategories indicate the hierarchy of importance afforded to each item. For example, an article that is published and has gone through a juried, reviewed, or blind-review process is viewed as more important, esteemed, and prestigious than an article that has not gone through such a process. (The juried, reviewed, or blind review is a process whereby a manuscript is sent to a panel of editorial reviewers who themselves have been selected for their abilities to assess a manuscript for publication consideration. The reviewers read the document and weigh the merits of the manuscript and will recommend: [1] publication with minor or minimal changes, [2] publication only if major concerns are addressed, or [3] rejection of the article for further publication consideration. This process is completed with neither the author(s) nor reviewers knowing who wrote or reviewed the manuscript.)

Within each of these subcategories, individuals reviewing the various publications and presentations will also note the journal in which an article appears, the publisher of a book, or the venue at which a presentation was given. Some journals are perceived to be more notable than others because of the rigorous review process manuscripts go through (Hamann and Lucas 1998). Likewise, books published by major publishing houses are viewed as more prestigious than those produced through small, desktop, or what is known as "vanity" publishing companies. Presentations that are given at international sites are often viewed more highly than state presentations. When listing the various publications and presentations, it is important to consider the weight of each endeavor. Juried publications and presentations should be listed separately from nonjuried publications and presentations. Items should appear in chronological order from most recent to least recent under each subheading.

The criteria for determining whether or not you should create a subheading under a major heading, for example, a subheading of international juried presentations under a major heading of presentations, is usually decided by the number of events you have to put under a subheading. For example, if you have given two or more international juried presentations, you could and probably should consider creating a subcategory under the heading "International presentations: juried or reviewed" to highlight those presentations. Highlighting publications and presentations through subheadings helps the reader quickly note the number of events you have achieved in your career in a hierarchical format that is clear and easy to comprehend. The use of subheadings prevents important events from being lost or "buried" among less important events.

Finally, if your major focus is as an academician but you are also an active performer, these creative activities should follow your scholarly endeavors. A discussion of what to consider when listing creative activities is presented in the discourse on performance-oriented CVs. In Figure 2.10 an example of scholarly endeavors as listed in a CV is provided.

Research and Creative Activity: A Performance-oriented CV

In the academically oriented CV, publications and presentations are featured and subcategories and hierarchal distinctions are made; creative endeavors should be organized in the same way for a performance-oriented CV. The performance-oriented CV is often preferred by individuals in the areas of performance, composition, conducting, studio work, performing or creating music in film production, and similar specialization emphases. Just as an academically oriented approach does not preclude the inclusion of performance or creative endeavors, the performance-oriented CV does not preclude the inclusion of publications and similar activities. However, the performance- or creative-oriented CV focuses on those ventures that are not normally viewed by "the outside world" as research oriented but as "creative pursuits."

If we were to look at a CV in which the major activities were performances, creation of compositions, performing or creating music for films, conducting appearances, and other such creative activities, we would most likely find several basic subheadings. Examples are: "Performances: orchestras, chamber music, solo, accompaniment: orchestral, chamber, etc." Under these subheadings, other

Refereed Research & Professional Publications:
Refereed & Invited Research Presentations

Refereed Books/Chapters in Books

Hamann, D. L., & Gillespie, R. (2009). *Strategies for teaching strings: Building a successful school orchestra program.*(2nd Edition). Oxford University Press, NewYork, NY.

Hamann, D. L.,& Gillespie, R. (2004). *Strategies for teaching strings: Building a successful school orchestra program.* Oxford University Press, New York, NY.

Cutietta, R., **Hamann, D. L.**,& Walker, L. (1995). *Spin-offs: The extra-Musical advantages of a musical education.* United Musical Instruments U.S.A., Inc., Elkhart,IN.

Hamann, D. L. (1991).*Creativity in the music classroom.* (Editor & Contributor) Music Educators National Conference, Reston, Virginia.

Etc.

Refereed Articles
National/International

Cooper, S, **Hamann, D. L.**, & Frost, R. (2012).The effects of stretching exercises
during rehearsals on string students' self-reported perceptions of discomfort. *Update: Applications of Research in Music Education, , .* DOI: 10.1177/8755123312438720

Hamann, D. L, Frost, R., &Draves, T. (2011). Factors influencing high school string students' selection of string teaching as a career. *String Research Journal, 2,* 17-24.

Russell, J. & **Hamann, D. L.** (2011).The perceived impact of string programs on K-12 music. *String Research Journal, 2,* 49-66.

Cooper, S. &**Hamann, D. L.** (2011). Perceived articulation uniformity between trumpet and violin performances. *Contributions to Music Education*, 37(2), 29-44.

Etc.

Refereed Professional Publications

Hamann, D. L. (2002). Wanted: 5,000 future string teachers! *American String Teacher,* 52(1), 72-78.

Hamann, D. L. (2002). Member2Member: Student knowledge of the care and maintenance of their instruments. *American String Teacher,* 52(2), 41-44.

Hamann, D. L. (2000). Getting the big picture. *Music Educators Journal,* 87(3), 17-18.

Hamann, D. L., & Gordon, D. (2000). Burnout: An occupational Hazard. Music Educators Journal, 87(3), 34-39.

Hamann, D. L. (1990). Burnout: How to spot it, how to avoid it. Music Educators Journal, 77(2), 30-33.

Hamann, D. L. (1985). Musical performance and anxiety: The other side of stage fright. *Music Educators Journal, 71*(8), 26-28.

Etc.

FIGURE 2.10 CV: Scholarly publications/presentations illustration

Refereed Research Paper/ Research Presentations

National/International

Cooper, S. & **Hamann, D. L.** (2010). Perceived articulation uniformity
　　Between trumpet and violin performances. Presented at the poster session
　　for the 2010 American Educational Research Association (AERA) Annual
　　Conference: Denver, CO.

Cooper, S. & **Hamann, D. L.** (2010). Perceived articulation uniformity
between trumpet and violin performances. Presented at the poster session
　　for The 2010 National Association for Music Education (MENC)
　　Research Conference: Anaheim, CA.

Gillespie, R. **Hamann, D. L.** (2010).An investigation of new string programs
　　established in American schools between 1999 and 2009. Poster presented
　　at the 2010 American String Teachers Research Poster Session: Santa
　　Clara, CA.

Etc.

Refereed Research Paper/ Research Presentations

State/Regional

Hamann, D. L., Frost, R., &Draves, T. (2009). *Imagine a career with
　　strings attached.* Poster presented at the Research Poster Presentation
　　at the Arizona Music Educators Association, Mesa, AZ.

Russell, J., & **Hamann, D. L.** (2009). *Perceived Impact of String
　　Programs.* Poster presented at the Research Poster Presentation at the
　　Arizona Music Educators Association, Mesa, AZ.

Hamann, D. L., & Ebie, B. (2008). Students' perceptions of university
　　method class preparation for teaching across music disciplines. Poster
　　presented at the Research Poster Presentation at the Arizona Music
　　Educators Association, Mesa, AZ.

Etc.

Invited Research Paper Presentations
National

Hamann, D. L. (2008).*Collegiate Roundtable Keynote Address:
　　Preparing for P&T Evaluation.* Session presented at the 2008 ASTA
　　National Conference: Albuquerque, NM.

Hamann, D. L. (2008).*Current Trends in String Research.* Session
　　presented at the 2008 ASTA National Conference: Albuquerque, NM.

Hamann, D. L. (2005).*Enhancing right-hand techniques with internal
　　and external aids.* Session presented at the 2005 Minnesota Music
　　Educators Association 78th Annual Midwinter In-Service Clinic:
　　Minneapolis, MN.

Etc.

FIGURE 2.10 Continued

common categories are found, such as "International, national, regional, state, or local," indicating the level of recognition of each activity. Subheadings under these designations further define the creative endeavors and frequently include such distinctions as "Invited," "Exchange," or "Tour or series." Additional subheadings may include "Reviewed or juried" and "Not reviewed or not juried." A review is a critical assessment of a performance, for example, by an individual hired to perform such assessments for newspapers and so forth.

Thus, under the major heading of performances, you could have the following subheadings, again organized from most recent to least recent under *each* subheading:

Performances
Solo: International performances, exhibits, productions
  Tour, series, performances
    Reviewed
    Not reviewed
  Invited performances
    Reviewed
    Not reviewed
  Exchange performances
    Reviewed
    Not reviewed
Solo: National performances
  Tour, series, performances
    Reviewed
    Not reviewed
  Invited performances
    Reviewed
    Not reviewed
  Exchange performances
    Reviewed
    Not reviewed
Solo: Regional performances
  Tour, series, performances
    Reviewed
    Not reviewed
  Invited performances
    Reviewed
    Not reviewed
  Exchange performances
    Reviewed
    Not reviewed
Solo: State or local performances
  Tour, series, performances

Reviewed
Not reviewed
Invited performances
Reviewed
Not reviewed
Exchange performances
Reviewed
Not reviewed

These or other subcategories can be used to delineate the other fine arts or discipline-oriented activities in which you participate. Further considerations for categorical distinctions can also be considered.

Orchestra, chamber music members, conductors, and opera singers often identify their roles in a group or a production, such as "Principal or section leader," "Assistant director or director," and in opera, for example, which role was performed or sung. When the position held was permanent or full time, as opposed to a one-time or part-time position, it is also common to state the length of the performance season, as well as the number of services provided in a season, rather than to list each performance separately. For CV examples of these events see "A Performance-oriented CV" by Jones and "A Performance-oriented CV" by Witski under "Performance CVs."

Individuals who perform as soloists alone or who are featured soloists with groups may wish to further delineate their performance by indicating whether it was a concerto or a concertino experience, if it was part of a larger musical event, such as a festival, or even as part of a nonmusical event such as a performance given at a prominent dedication ceremony, the kind of group, and the location at which it was held. When listing solo recitals, the equivalent type of information should be provided for each performance. Similarly, accompanists should specify the circumstances of their performances, the caliber of the individual with whom they performed, and the venue of the performance. The same type of description would be valuable for the conductor who appears as a guest with a variety of groups. Composers whose works are performed by groups or artists should provide details of the performances or exhibits by describing the group or sponsor, venue, and situation. See "An Academic-oriented CV" by Janson under Academic CVs.

Finally, as mentioned previously and if applicable, the nature under which performances are held should be stated: Was a performance the result of winning a competition? Was it an invited or exchange performance? Did you audition for a group and become an alternate or permanent substitute for that group? Are you "under management"? And so on.

CDs, DVDs, broadcast (radio, television, etc.) performances, and the like should appear separately in the CV. Again, concise yet consummate information should be provided for each listing under this category, including the audience, both size and type, that was reached through the venue, the nature of the production (who produced the recording, the play, the broadcast, etc.), the setting in which the performance took place (local, national, international), the number of times the event was played or shown, and any other information that would convey the significance of the recording, broadcast, or video (DVD).

In the performance-oriented or creative CV, it is also important not only to highlight performance experiences but also to accentuate publication or presentation activities. These activities should be broken down into appropriate categorical distinctions, including but not limited to such subcategories as: regional, state, national, international; invited reviewed, exchange, juried, and so on. The more precise and concise information that can be provided concerning the activities, the clearer your professional contributions become.

As in the academic-oriented CV, the creative or performance-oriented CV should describe professional experiences in as clear and easily understood fashion as possible, providing precise yet descriptive information about events and activities. You want to highlight your creative experiences, put them in the best possible light, and convey the significance of each event in as easily grasped fashion as possible. An example of a performance CV listing of such items appears in Figure 2.11.

Grants

While the academic- and creative- or performance-oriented CVs tend to differ when listing publication or creative activities, the sections of the CV that include grants, service, and awards or honors tend to be similar. The receipt and description of grants generally follows one's publications or presentations or creative or performance activities.

When listing your grant activity, you can consider listing grants that were funded as well as grant applications submitted but not funded. Individuals who are constructing CVs early in their careers may want to list grants that were both funded and not funded. National grant proposals, for example, involve a tremendous amount of organization, time, and effort to prepare for submission. Even

CHAMBER MUSIC PERFORMANCES, 1993-2003

• **CLEVELAND WIND QUINTET—University of Cleveland (UC)**

Nov	2003	Concert at the Cleveland Senior Academy
Nov	2003	Faculty Artist Series Recital
April	2003	UC "Sparks" Concert
April	2003	Faculty Artist Series Recital
April	2003	School Concerts UC
Jan	2003	Southwest Honor Band Concert
Dec	2002	Faculty Artist Series Recital
Dec	2002	Concert at the Cleveland Senior Academy

• **DANISH WIND QUINTET—Yoder State University (YSU)**

Institutes of Art Concert Series

Feb	2000	Muller Institute of Art Concert Series
Nov	1999	Tober Institute of Art Concert Series
Apr	1999	Muller Institute of Art Concert Series
Apr	1998	Muller Institute of Art Concert Series
Jan	1998	Tober Institute of Art Concert Series
Nov	1997	Tober Institute of Art Concert Series
Feb	1997	Tober Institute of Art Concert Series
Oct	1996	Muller Institute of Art Concert Series
May	1996	Muller Institute of Art Concert Series
Apr	1996	Tober Institute of Art Concert Series
Jan	1996	Muller Institute of Art Concert Series
Oct	1995	Hintz Institute of Art Concert Series
Mar	1995	Tober Institute of Art Concert Series
Feb	1995	Hintz Institute of Art Concert Series
Mar	1994	Tober Institute of Art Concert Series
Jan	1994	Muller Institute of Art Concert Series

Recital Series

Apr	1999	Danish Recital Series
Oct	1998	Danish Recital Series
Feb	1998	YSU Fine Arts Recital Series
Jan	1998	Danish Recital Series
Jan	1997	Danish Recital Series
Nov	1996	Friends of Flute Music Recital Series
Nov	1995	Danish Recital Series
Apr	1995	YSU Recital Series

SOLO PERFORMANCES, 1993-2003

• **CONCERTOS**

Feb	2002	Danish Wind Ensemble, Keith Gates *Concertino*
Aug	2002	**Gala Evening Concert, NFA Convention in Dallas, Keith Gates**

Concertino

Nov	1997	Smith Chamber Orchestra, Kent Kennan *Night Soliloquy*
Mar	1996	Smith Chamber Orchestra, Charles Griffes *Poem*
Jan	1996	Smith Chamber Orchestra, J. S. Bach *Suite No. 2 in B Minor*
Feb	1995	Danish Wind Ensemble, Daniel Bukvich *Surprise, Patterns, and Illusions*

• **NATIONAL AND INTERNATIONAL RECITAL APPEARANCES**

Mar	2003	Wisconsin Flute Association, Guest Artist Recital
Oct	2002	Tony PIECE Symposium Gala Concerts, Boswil, Switzerland
Aug	1996	World Premiere, Dan Cage *All the Winds in the World*, NFA Convention, New York, NY
Jan	1996	Georgia Flute Association, Guest Artist Recital
Sept	1993	Northeast Ohio Flute Association, Guest Artist Recital

FIGURE 2.11 CV: Performance/creative activities illustration

· FACULTY SOLO RECITALS

Sept	2003	YSU Faculty Artist Series, "Flute and Friends"
Apr	2002	Danish Concert Series
May	2000	Danish Concert Series
May	1999	Danish Concert Series
Apr	1998	Danish Concert Series
Oct	1996	Danish Concert Series
Feb	1996	Danish Concert Series
Jan	1996	Muller Institute of Art Concert Series
Oct	1995	Danish Concert Series
May	1995	Tober Institute of Art Concert Series
Nov	1994	Danish Concert Series
Feb	1994	Danish Concert Series
Feb	1994	Hintz Institute of Art Concert Series

FIGURE 2.11 Continued

though a grant of this type is not funded, it shows the CV reader that you are, and have been actively interested in, pursuing outside funding sources, and that even though you may not have been successful, the effort may be extremely noteworthy to prospective hiring institutions, especially in these days of shrinking state funding. Individuals interested in seeking alternative funding sources may be considered stronger candidates for positions. If you do list unfunded grant attempts, you may wish to delete these attempts later, as your grant funding award success improves.

Grants that are funded and not funded should both include basic information.

1. The major grant writer should be listed, and if you were assisted, those individuals should also be listed.
2. The percentage of coauthors' contributions to the grant-writing effort should be identified, as should the percentage of your contribution. For example, if you completed 80 percent of the work for a grant and another individual contributed 20 percent, that should be indicated.
3. The amount of the award received, or in the case of nonfunded grants, the amount of the award sought, should be indicated.
4. The funding source should be identified.
5. The title of the grant and the date submitted and/or funded should be provided.

It is important to list the significance of each grant. Again this can be done through categorical distinctions, using headings such as "international," "national," and so on, or by using categories such as "Grants funded: Over $500,000"—"Grants funded: $100,000–$500,000," and "Grants funded: Under $100,000," for example. Again, the idea is to show the type, amount, and importance of the grant activity you have

Funded Grants and In-Kind Funding (selected samples)

Combined Totals: Over $300,000 at the University of Arizona (UA) and over $370,000 at Ball State University (BSU)

> National Association of Music Manufacturers (NAMM) Foundation Program Grant: *Effective applications of technology in the music classroom: An action research model* ($30,752)
> > • TIME Research Committee member
> > • Also served as research mentor throughout period of grant (2008-2010)
> UA: In-Kind Music Building Renovations (Painter, plumbers, electricians) (over $300,000 value)
> BSU: Lilly II Grants to increase retention for music theory and music engineering technology students ($30,000)
> BSU: Music Faculty, CFA Computer Competency Plans (over $200,000)
> BSU: Ball Grant "Redefining Music Education" ($15,000)

FIGURE 2.12 CV: Grants illustration

pursued. Obviously, large national grants are important to institutions, but any type of grant-writing activity indicates a certain interest on an individual's part. The willingness of an individual to pursue grants may be of interest to a hiring institution. The following is an example (see Figure 2.12) of funded grants as listed in a CV.

Service

The next major heading in a CV is often "Service." Service includes those items that do not fall under teaching, performance, and the like. Service includes such activities as being a member of a committee, holding an office in a professional organization, chairing a search committee, assisting with the writing or preparation for a National Association of Schools of Music (NASM) or a National Council for Accreditation of Teacher Education (NCATE) review, among others. Service includes those activities that are related to your position, such as service on university committees, related to your professional organizations, such as being the president of your local flute society, or are related to service in your community, such as being the conductor of a community orchestra or the director of your church choir.

Service is a broad category that allows for recognition of casual service activity, such as membership in professional organizations, as well as more active roles such as being the chair of the faculty senate at your university. Each event is meaningful. It is your task to convey that meaning by using subheadings, such as "Professional service at the university level," "Professional service at the college level," or "Professional service at the school or departmental level," for university service, or "International or national service," "Regional, state service," or "Local service," for professional organizations. Each mention of service should provide the length of your role, the nature of the activity, your involvement in the group, organization, or committee, and the importance of that involvement. Service is an important component of university positions, and hiring committees like to be reassured that the person they hire will be willing to undertake his/her "fair share" of service activities within the department, school, or college.

The importance of subheadings, again, is for clarity and hierarchical distinction. For example, if you were listing your professional service at the school or departmental level, you could have many subheadings under this category, including "Committees" (with a further subheading under this category, such as "Service as the chair of the committee" or as a "contributing member"), graduate student committees (again with subheadings such as "Dissertation committees," and distinctions under this heading, such as "Major adviser" or "Committee member," or "Master's committees": "Major adviser" or "Committee member"), undergraduate student committees, and so forth. Figure 2.13 gives an example of CV service listings.

Honors and Awards

Another category that is often listed in the CV is "Honors and awards." This category is one that can highlight significant events that may not have appeared in other sections of the CV. For example, if you were awarded first place at a major performance competition, if your dissertation was selected for the "Outstanding dissertation of the year award," or if you received an honor from a community group, a university, or a professional group, these would be considered worthy of being placed under the category of "Honors and awards." As with other listings, the year the honor or award was given, the nature of the award, and the significance of the award should be provided. In Figure 2.14 an example of "Honors and awards CV" listings is shown.

References

A final, general category that has appeared more frequently in CVs within the last several years is a listing of individuals who provide references. This listing is commonly titled "References." It is customary to see the term "reference" used to identify an individual from whom a recommendation is sought. However, the correct term for an individual writing or providing a recommendation is "referee." In this book, the term referee will be used to identify the individual providing a reference. Please note that the term reference is often used interchangeably, albeit not correctly, to convey the same meaning as the word referee in many job announcements throughout the United States, since its use has become commonplace. While the topic of references and referees will be discussed in more detail later in this chapter, the entry of "References" in your CV will now be discussed.

Service Activities

Service to the Institution

University of Arizona Only (Select Committees)

2003 – present	Member: University Undergraduate Research Awards Committee
2003 – present	Member: College of Fine Arts Education Committee
2007 – present	Member: University Undergraduate Research Awards Committee
2010 – 2011	Member: Choral Music Education Search Committee
2009 – 2010	Member: School of Music Director's Assessment and Review Committee
2006 – 2007	Member: Choral Music Education Search Committee
2005 – 2007	Member: Cello Search Committee
2005 – 2006	Member: College of Fine Arts Promotion and Tenure Committee
2004 – 2005	Member: School of Music Promotion and Tenure Committee
2003 – 2004	Chair, Director of the School of Music Search Committee
Etc.	

Professional Appointments and Recognitions (Select)

2011	Outstanding Achievement in String Research Award — ASTA 2011 National Conference in Kansas City, MO
2010	National Citation for Leadership and Merit — ASTA 2010 National Conference in Reno, NV
2009 – 2010	Contributing Editor: *String Research Journal*
2008 – 2009	Chair: ASTA National Research Committee
2008	National Citation for Leadership and Merit ASTA 2008 National Conference in Albuquerque, NM
2004 – 2006	President: Arizona String Teachers Association
2000 – 2006	Member: *Journal of Research in Music Education* National Editorial Committee
2000 – 2002	President: Arizona Collegiate Music Educators
1999 – 2009	Editor: *Journal of String Research*
Etc.	

FIGURE 2.13 CV: Service activities illustration

The requirements for job application reference information vary from institution to institution. Hiring institutions may require that:

1. letters of reference be sent with application materials;
2. letters of reference be sent independently of application materials (under separate cover);
3. the applicant provide a list of referees who can be contacted;
4. that both letters of recommendation and a list of referees be provided.

Honors, Awards, and Special Recognitions (selected samples)

Invited for membership on UA HeadsUp Steering Committee (2010); Not able to accept due to SPBAC meeting time conflicts on campus

Nominated for UA Vice-Provost for Academic Affairs and Associate Provost for Faculty Affairs positions (2008); Declined both position nominations

Excellence in Music Administration Award: Arizona Music Educators Association (AMEA) Convention, January 2008

Selected for inclusion in various "Who's Who" publications, including: America's Registry of Outstanding Professionals (NY); Who's Who Among America's Teachers (TX): Who's Who Millennium Editions (NY); International Who's Who of Information Technology (NC): Who's Who In America (NJ)

Nominated by Ball State University VP for the 2000 Cyberstar Award "Outstanding IT Educator," Indiana Information Technology Association, Indianapolis (IN)

Teaching Award, Research Award & Dissertation Award (1995), Graduate Student Senate, Kent State University (only student in KSU's history to be awarded all 3 awards in the same year)

Cover Photo & Feature Article on the Donald Wilson & Peter McAllister Classical Guitar Duo: "Two is Better than One" by Lynne Harting. In Guitar Canada national magazine, Toronto (October 1988 issue)

FIGURE 2.14 CV: Honors and awards illustration

Given the variety of requests, it has become an increasingly common practice to provide a list of references at the end of the CV. Thus, should the hiring institution require that only a list of references be provided, the information is available in the CV.

There are certain basic informational items contained in reference listings. Reference listings should provide as much information as possible concerning your referees and should include the following basic information:

1. Name of the individual, along with titles, if appropriate.
2. The position the individual holds or fulfills in his/her professional career such as: director of the School of Music, coordinator of conducting, graduate coordinator, dean of the College of Fine Arts, professor of music education, assistant director of choral activities, director of research, principal viola, and so on.
3. Business address of the individual, including the institution or organization at which the person is employed, or, in some cases (for example if a referee has retired), the home address.
4. Contact information, including if possible home, business, and cell phone numbers, email addresses, and so forth. This section should be as complete as possible, as it is generally an important and sometimes the sole means used to contact your references.

Job candidates may additionally list individuals who are willing to provide letters of reference "upon request" or individuals who have been asked to send letters of recommendation on behalf of the applicant. Reference information may often be duplicated in other documents, such as in letters of application or the personal applicant information forms required by the hiring institution; nonetheless, reference information is still commonly provided in the CV. Figure 2.15 shows a reference listing in a CV.

REFERENCES: Dr. Donald L. Hamann
Professor of Music
Director, Institute for Innovation in String Music Teaching
University of Arizona
School of Music and Dance
Tucson, AZ 85721-0004
(520) 621-3231
dhamann@u.arizona.edu

Dr. William K. Wakefield
Director of Bands/Coordinator of Wind Conducting
University of Oklahoma
500 W. Boyd
Norman, OK 73071
(405) 325-2731
wkwakefield@ou.edu

Dr. Dan Stiffler
Director of Fine Arts and Foreign Languages
Wichita Public Schools
201 N. Water
Wichita, KS 67202
(316) 973-4440
dstiffler@usd259.net

Dr. Thomas Cockrell
Music Director, University of Arizona Symphony Orchestra
Nelson Riddle Chair
University of Arizona
School of Music and Dance
Tucson, AZ 85721-0004
(520) 621-7028
cockrell@u.arizona.edu

Mr. Gene Thrailkill
Professor Emeritus
Director of Bands
University of Oklahoma
1907 Oakhurst Circle
Norman, OK 73069
(405) 364-4296
gene@genethrailkill.com

Mr. Gregg I. Hanson
Director of Bands
University of Arizona
School of Music and Dance
Tucson, AZ 85721-0004
(520) 621-1683
hansong@u.arizona.edu

FIGURE 2.15 CV: Reference illustration

OTHER CV INCLUSIONS

Depending on the type of position you are seeking, you can consider adding additional information at the end of your CV. For example, it is not uncommon for conductors to list as part of their CVs the following:

1. works that they have conducted with orchestras, wind ensembles, choirs, and so on,
2. works they would be able to conduct at a moment's notice, or
3. works they have studied in private studio or master class situations and would be able to conduct with some additional preparation.

A more accomplished and active conductor may wish to limit her repertoire list to active performances and then perhaps only to conducted performances with a limited timeframe, such as the past three to five years.

Performers too should consider listing works performed by various categories such as the following:

1. works that have been performed with various ensembles including orchestral, wind, choral groups,
2. works that have been performed in solo recitals, chamber works performed in concert, concerti, solos, and so forth, or
3. works that they are ready to perform at a moment's notice, or
4. works that they have studied in private studio or master class situations and would be able to perform with some additional preparation.

A more accomplished and active performer may wish to limit his repertoire list to only publicly performed performances and then perhaps only those publicly performed within a limited timeframe, such as the past three to five years. Additionally, sample programs may also be considered for inclusion in a separate document. An example of such listings can be found in "A Performance-oriented CV" by Barren under "Performance CVs."

The decision to include additional material in your CV, as opposed to submitting it under separate cover, is a personal choice. The advantage to the inclusion of these materials in the CV is that the materials can be reviewed as part of the CV. (The materials should appear at the end of your CV after the major heading categories.) A disadvantage of including them in the CV is the task of updating or reorganizing these materials along with other information in the CV each time the document is submitted. Whether you choose to include additional materials in your CV or submit them as separate documents, the clarity of your organizational presentation is paramount, along with correct spelling and grammar, neatness, and precision. The following example, Figure 2.16, is from a vocalist who has organized repertoire in his CV.

REPERTOIRE LIST

OPERATIC ROLES:

OPERA	ROLE	COMPANY	DATE
La Bohème	Marcello	Southern Arizona Opera Guild	02/2010
Madama Butterfly	Sharpless	La Musica Lirica	07/2009
Chin Chun Chan (A Zarzuela by Lius G. Jorda)	Ladislao &Charamusquero	University of Arizona	01/2009
La Périchole	Paquillo	University of Arizona	11/2008
Il trionfodell'onore (By Alessandro Scarlatti)	Rodimarte Bombarda	Oakland University	04/2008
Amahl and the Night Visitors	Page	Southern Great Lakes Symphony	12/2007
Meanwhile, back at Cinderella's (By Dennis Arlan)	Filbert Nabgratz & Fairy Godfather	Oakland University	04/2007
The Magic Flute	2nd Priest & Papageno Cover	Loyola University	01/2004

OTHERS ROLES PARTIALLY PERFORMED OR STUDIED:

Rinaldo	Argante
Giulio Cesare	Giulio Cesare
Le Nozze di Figaro	Conte Almaviva
Così fan tutte	Guglielmo
L'Elisird'Amore	Belcore
Don Pasquale	Malatesta
Hamlet	Hamlet
La Traviata	Baronne
La Bohème	Marcello
Midsummer Night's Dream	Bottom
The Old Maid and the Thief	Bob

COMPLETE SOLO CANTATAS:

Johann Sebastian Bach	Ich will den Kreuzstab gerne, BWV 56
	Ich habe genug, BWV 82
	Amore traditore, BWV 203
Georg Philipp Telemann	Meine Liebe lebt in Gott, TWVW: 1095

INDIVIDUAL CANTATA ARIAS:

Johann Sebastian Bach	Liebster Gott, wann werd' ich sterben, BWV 8	Doch Weichet, ihr tollen vergeblichen Sorgen
	Schauet doch und sehet, BWV 46	Dein Wetter zog sich auf von weiten
	Selig ist der Mann, BWV 57	Ja, ja, ich kann die Feinde Schlagen
	Auf Mein Herz, des Herren Tag, BWV 145	Merke, mein Herze, beständig nur dies
	Ich lasse dich nicht, du segnest mich denn, BWV 157	Ja, ja, ich halte Jesum feste
	Schweigt stille, plauderte nicht, BWV 211	Hat man nicht mit seinen Kindern

FIGURE 2.16 CV: Repertoire illustration

oratorio arias:

Johann Sebastian Bach	*Magnificat*, BWV 243	Quia fecit mihi magna
	Mass in B Minor, BWV 232	Quoniam tu solus sanctus
		Et in Spiritum sanctum
	Mattäus-Passion, BWV 244	Mache dich, mein Herze rein
	Weihnachts Oratorium, BWV 248	Grosser Herr und starker König
		Erleucht' auch meine finstre Sinnen
George Frideric Händel	*Messiah*, HWV 56	Thus saith the Lord...But who may abide
		The people that walked in darkness
		Why do the nations
		The trumpet shall sound
	Samson, HWV 57	Honor and arms
	Semele, HWV 58	More sweet is that name
		Where 'er you walk
	Belshazzar, HWV 61	Oppressed with never ceasing grief
	Judas Maccabeaus, HWV 63	Arm, arm ye brave
	Joshua, HWV 64	See the raging flames arise
	Alexander Balus, HWV 65	Thrice happy the monarch
		Virtue, thou ideal name
		O sword in thou all-daring hand
	Alexander's Feast, HWV 75	Revenge, Timotheus cries
	Dettingen Te Deum, HWV 283	Vouchsafe, O Lord
Franz Joseph Haydn	*Die Jahreszeiten*	Schon eilet froh der Ackermann
		Seht auf die breiten Wiesen hin!
Felix Mendelssohn	*Elijah*, Op. 70	Itisenough!
Gabriel Fauré	*Requiem*, Op. 48	Hostias
		Libera me

CONCERT ARIAS:

Wolfgang Amadeus Mozart		Mentre ti lascio, o figlia, K. 513
		Rivolgete a lui lo sguardo, K. 584

OPERATIC ARIAS:

George Frideric Händel	*Alcina*, HWV 34	Verdi prati, selve amene
	Rinaldo, HWV 7°	Sibillar gli angui d'Aletto
	Floridante, HWV 14	Alma mia, sì tu sol sei
	Giulio Cesare in Egitto, HWV17	Empio dirò tu sei
		Va tacito e nascosto
		Se in fiorito ameno prato
		Quel torrente, che cade dal monte
	Berenice, HWV 38	Sì tra i ceppi
Wolfgang Amadeus Mozart	*Le Nozze di Figaro*, K. 492	Se vuol ballare
		Non più andrai
		Hai già vinta la causa...Vedrò mentr'io sospiro
	Don Giovanni, K. 527	Ho Capito, Signor sì
		Deh vieni alla finestra
	Così fan tutte, K. 588	Rivolgete a lui lo sguardo, K. 584
		Non siate ritrosi
		Donne mie, la fate a tanti
	Die Zauberflöte, K. 620	Der Vogelfänger bin ichja

FIGURE 2.16 Continued

		Ein Mädchen oder Weibchen
		Papageno's Suicide Aria
	Zaide, K. 344	Nur mutig mein Herze
Gaetano Donizetti	*L'Elisir d'Amore*	Come paride vezzoso
	Don Pasquale	Bella siccome un angelo
Vincenzo Bellini	*I Puritani*	*Ah! per sempre io ti perdei*
Richard Wagner	*Tannhäuser*, WWV 70	O! du mein holder Abendstern
Charles Gounod	*Roméo et Juliette*, Op. 17	Mab, la reine des mensonges
	Faust, Op. 20	Avant de quitter ces lieux
Ambroise Thomas	*Hamlet*	Ô vin, dissipe la tristesse
Peter Illyich Tchaikovsky	*Eugene Onégin*, Op. 24	Onégin's Aria
Engelbert Humperdinck	*Hänsel und Gretel*	Ach wir armen leute!
Ernest Korngold	*Die Tote Stadt*	Mein Sehnen, mein Wähnen
Ruggero Leoncavallo	*Zazà*	Zazà, piccola zingara
Giacomo Puccini	*Edgar*	Questo amor, vergogna mia
Carl Menotti	*The Old Maid and the Thief*	When the air sings of summer

VOCAL ENSEMBLE WORKS:

Johann Sebastian Bach	*Weihnachts Oratorium*, BWV 248	Herr, dein Mittleid
George Frideric Händel	*Rinaldo*, HWV 7°	Al trionfo dell nostrofuore
	Giulio Cesare in Egitto, HWV 17	Caro! Bella! Più ama bilebeltà
	Israel in Egypt, HWV 54	The Lord is a Man of War
Franz Schubert		Der Hochzeitsbraten, D. 930
Peter Cornelius	*Dreizweistimmige Lieder*, Op. 6	1. Liebesprobe
		2. Der Beste Liebesbrief
		3. Ein Wort der Liebe
Leonard Bernstein	*Songfest*	Opening Hym: Tothe Poem

COMPLETE SONG CYCLES:

Ludwig van Beethoven	*An die Ferne Geliebte*, Op. 98
Franz Schubert	*Die schöne Müllerin*, D. 795
Robert Schumann	*Dichterliebe*, Op. 48
Gabriel Fauré	*Poèmes d'un Jour*, Op. 21
Maurice Ravel	*Don Quichotte à Dulcinée*
Francis Poulenc	*Chansons Gailardes*, F.P. 42
	QuatrePoèmes de Guillaume Apollinaire, F.P. 58
Ralph Vaughan Williams	*Songs of Travel*
Elie Siegmeister	*Elegies for Garcia Lorca*
Paul Bowles	*Blue Mountain Ballads*
William Presser	*Six Songs of Autumn*

SELECTED ART SONGS BY LANGUAGE:
ITALIAN:

Giachino Rossini	Mi lagnerò tacendo (Versions II & IIIIII)
	L'ultimo ricordo
Vincenzo Bellini	Vaga luna, che inargenti
Gaetono Donizetti	Occhio nero incendiator
	Sull'onda cheta e bruna

FIGURE 2.16 Continued

Carlotta Ferrari	Non t'accostare all-urna
Alfredo Catalani	La Pescatrice
Ruggero Leoncavallo	Mattinata

GERMAN:

Wolfgang Amadeus Mozart	An Chloë, K. 524
	Warnung, K. 433
Ludwig van Beethoven	Mailied, Op. 52 No. 4
	Neue Liebe neues Leben, Op. 75 No. 2
	Es war einmal ein König, Op. 75 No. 3
	Mit einem gemalten Band, Op. 83 No. 3
	Ich liebe dich, WoO. 123
Franz Schubert	Auf der Bruck, D. 853
	Das Lied im Grünen, D. 917
	Der Musensohn, D. 764
	Der zürnende Barde, D. 785
	Der Zwerg, D. 771
	Des Sängers Habe, D. 832
	Die Forelle, D. 550
	Du bist die Ruh, D. 776
	Erlkönig, D. 328
	Geheimes, D. 719
	Im Frühing, D. 882
	Lachen und Weinen, D. 777
	Sehnsucht, D. 636
	Über Wildemann, D. 884
Johann Carl Gottfried Loewe	Edward, Op. 1 No. 1
	Die Wandelnde Glocke, Op. 20 No. 3
	Der getreue Eckart, Op. 44 No. 2
	Kleiner Haushalt, Op. 71
	Tom der Reimer, Op. 135
Johannes Brahms	Der Gang zum Liebchen, Op. 31 No. 3
	Wie bist du meine Königin, Op. 32 No. 9
	Sonntag, Op. 47 No. 3
	Entführung, Op. 97 No. 3
	Ständchen, Op. 106 No. 1
Gustav Mahler	Liebst du um Schönheit
	Wer hat dies Liedlein erdacht?
	Das Irdische Leben
Richard Strauss	Heimliche Aufforderung, Op. 27 No. 3
	Morgen!, Op. 27 No. 4
	Nichts, Op. 10 No. 2
	Zueignung, Op. 10 No. 1

FIGURE 2.16 Continued

FRENCH:

Wolfgang Amadeus Mozart	Oiseaux, si tous les ans, K.307
	Dans un bois solitaire, K. 308
Camille Saint-Saëns	Aimons-nous
	Danse Macabre
	Violons dans le soir
Gabriel Fauré	Au bord de l'eau, Op. 8 No. 1
	Nell, Op. 18 No. 1
	Mandoline, Op. 58 No. 1
	En Sourdine, Op. 58 No. 2

ENGLISH:

Henry Purcell	If Music be the Food of Love
	I'll Sail Upon the Dogstar
	Man is for the Woman Made
	Since from my Dear
Charles Ives	At the River
	Charlie Rutlage
	Slugging a Vampire
	The Circus Band
	The Greatest Man
	The Things Our Fathers Loves
	Two Little Flowers
Peter Warlock	Mr. Belloc's Fancy
	Captain Stratton's Fancy
	Peter Warlock's Fancy
Aaron Copland	The Dodger
	Simple Gifts
	I Bought Me A Cat
	The Little Horses
	Zion's Walls
	The Golden Willow Tree
	At the River
	Ching-A-Ring Chaw
William Bolcom	Fur (Murray the Furrier)
	Song of Black Max

MUSICAL THEATRE/OPERETTA:

Arthur Sullivan	*Pirates of Penzance*	I am the very model
Victor Herbert	*Fortune Teller*	Slumber On, My Little Gypsy Sweetheart
Cole Porter	*Kiss me, Kate*	Brush Up Your Shakespeare
Richard Rodgers	*Oklahoma!*	Oh What a Beautiful Mornin'
Carousel		If I Loved You
		Soliloquy

FIGURE 2.16 Continued

SUMMARY: CV PREPARATION AND APPEARANCE

Your CV is a unique reflection of your professional career that necessitates a unique combination of creative effort with ordered and careful precision to best convey your professional experiences. The saying that every journey begins with the first step is certainly applicable when creating your CV. The above steps are offered as a means for you to begin your creative journey into putting together your CV, with the caveat that first steps of any endeavor are there to begin the process but not to end it. Thus, as you work on your CV, remember that you must feel comfortable with your CV, and as your professional growth and path are embellished and/or changed, your CV should reflect that natural progression. Remember, your audience is looking for an individual to best complement their faculty. They are seeking individuals who can serve as excellent models, mentors, and teachers for students, ones who will work well with the current faculty, will be seen as leaders in their area, and will be able to maintain a consistent and high level of productivity throughout their tenure. Your CV is a document that can support a hiring committee's perception of your abilities.

Other Application Materials

While your CV is understandably one of the most important components of your application, it is not the only item needed for a complete application. A cover letter or letter of application, statements of teaching philosophy, and materials such as transcripts, CDs, articles, syllabi, reviews of concerts, programs, a teaching portfolio, and the like may also be required. Additionally, while not necessarily required, there has been a growing interest in Facebook listings, YouTube postings, websites, and other such electronic information discrimination vehicles.

COVER LETTER, OR LETTER OF APPLICATION

A key component of your application is a well-constructed cover letter, or letter of application. There are two schools of thought concerning cover letters. Some believe that the letter of application will be reviewed before the CV is examined, and if the cover letter encourages further review of a candidate's materials, the CV will then be read (Dehne 2009). Conversely, some believe that the CV will be reviewed first, and then, if warranted the cover letter will be reviewed. In either case it points out the importance of both the CV and the letter of application ("The reality of cover letters" 2009).

The cover letter provides the search committee with a snapshot of you as a potential colleague. It is a brief statement of introduction in which you plant the seeds of expectation. Your letter of application should endorse the perception that you are a most appropriate candidate for the position and that you are a candidate who can bring a host of skills and expertise to the position that will enhance student learning and departmental growth. Your cover letter should be specific and personal and address the needs of the position. Your goal is to entice each committee member to learn more about you after reviewing your letter of application. In essence your cover letter is encouraging the search committee members to consider taking valuable time from their schedules to review your materials and consider you for the position. You not only want to inform the committee of your experience and expertise but to let them know how you would use your skills to enhance student learning and development, fulfill goals and objectives of the music department, and address the mission of the university. Indeed, some university job announcements actually direct the potential candidate to specifically address the candidate's qualifications and abilities in relation to the announced position. The following was taken from a University of Kansas music position announcement in 2010, in which the following were listed for application materials:

1. A letter of application that describes how the candidate's experiences and accomplishments relate to the required and preferred qualifications listed above,
2. a curriculum vitae,
3. a list of three references complete with contact information,
4. a one- or two-page statement of the applicant's teaching philosophy within a comprehensive university music school, including your objectives and means of achieving those objectives.

Note that the university is directing the candidate, in her letter of application, to describe how she would address the needs of a comprehensive university music school. (You may also have noted that there was a requirement for a teaching philosophy statement, which will be addressed later in this chapter.) Hence the letter of application is a key component in your application portfolio and needs to address specific criteria to be as effective as possible. These will be discussed.

We shall look at the basic sections of a cover letter, but before we do, it can't be stressed enough that the letter of application will exhibit your written communication skills. Your letter of application, like your CV, should be checked for grammar, spelling, and clarity. It should be read by at least one individual, if not several, skilled in proofreading such materials.

First, the format of your letter should follow a basic or typical business letter design (Doyle 2009). One effective business letter format is the block design. In the block design all information begins flush left. The layout of a block business style letter typically adheres to the following:

1. The date and the address to which you are sending the information. The date is separated from the address.

   Month, day, year
   Professor/Dr. First name Last name
   Title
   Name of Organization
   Address
   City, state zip code

This certainly is not the only business form style you can use, however, it does provide some idea of the type of formatting seen in a cover letter/letter of application. Other examples of business style formats can be found at: http://writing. wisc.edu/Handbook/BusLetter_Block.html, http://owl.english.purdue.edu/owl/ resource/653/01/, or try Googling "business letter format."

2. Whenever possible, the salutation, or greeting, should be addressed to an individual.

   Dear Dr. Singleberg:
   When this is not possible or such information is not provided, address your salutation to the members of the particular search committee:
   To the Members of the Trumpet Search Committee:
   To the Chair of the Trumpet Search Committee:
   To Whom it May Concern:

3. The body of the letter consists of three to five paragraphs, single spaced, with each new paragraph separated by a double space. In your opening sentence you should indicate you are applying for a particular available position. State the position for which you are applying and list any identifying information provided, including position numbers, to delineate that particular position. Often universities have several openings in one school or even one department. To avoid any confusion, you should identify the position for which you are making application as succinctly as possible. Your first paragraph should inform the readers as to the purpose of the letter and, if applicable, indicate where you learned of the position. If an individual recommended that you apply for the

Dear Dr. Moore:

I write to apply for the faculty position of Assistant Professor and Choral Conductor at Gustavus Adolphus College, a vacancy I became aware of through the College Music Society posting. As a native Minnesotan and Lutheran college alumnus, it is with utmost enthusiasm I submit this letter of application. I am currently finishing a Doctor of Musical Arts degree at The University of Arizona and anticipate a final defense of my document in the spring of 2011. My research project examines twenty-first century choral music as "parable-art," with focus on compositions by two Minnesota composers, Stephen Paulus and Ralph M. Johnson.

FIGURE 2.17 Cover letter: Opening paragraph illustration

position, especially if it was a faculty member from the institution to which you are applying, indicate this. Finally, the first paragraph should express your enthusiasm and the perceived match of your credentials to the position qualifications. Often a brief overview of what you will present in the remainder of the letter will be outlined in this first paragraph as well. In Figure 2.17 an example of an opening paragraph is presented.

Your middle paragraphs should detail what you have to offer the institution in terms of your expertise and experience. You should illustrate how your skills, experience, and expertise relate to the specific position for which you are applying. Focus on the employer's needs and explain how you will be able to address those needs. Highlight need statements in the position announcement and describe how your experience would fulfill their wants. Offer evidence of your knowledge of potential institutional needs gleaned through your research of the organization. You should emphasize your skills in problem solving, recruiting, and working as a team member, your collegiality, leadership, mentoring and guidance, and your ability to display continued growth and to gain national exposure through your research and/or creative activity. Explain how these skills and abilities will transfer and be relevant to the position for which you are applying—to the needs of the institution. This can sometimes be best accomplished through short narratives or stories of personal experience. Interpret important points in the CV as they relate to the job requirements—focus on what you can bring to the position.

One way to think about the construction and content of your middle paragraphs is to focus on the three areas on which most faculty are evaluated: (1) teaching, (2) research/creative activity, and (3) service, not necessarily in this order. If you address these three areas and how your expertise and experience in them relates to the advertised job position, it will give the hiring committee some needed insight and information with which to more completely evaluate your appropriateness for the position. See Figure 2.18 for an example of middle paragraphs.

The responsibilities of this position seem tailored for someone with my pedagogical goals, expertise, and ideology. Educating the whole person *through* music is the foundation of my teaching philosophy. In the choral rehearsal, this process is rooted in the daily pursuit of excellence and the shared value that the whole is greater than the sum of its parts. When all involved are dedicated to offering the very best of themselves, artistic achievements can be transformative. It is my hope that the pursuit of excellence and discipline fostered in the choral rehearsal will result in my students pursuing excellence in other areas of their lives.

As a role model and mentor for students at Gustavus Adolphus, especially those pursuing careers in choral music education, I would draw upon my experience as a public school teacher, as well as my continued study of music education at The University of Arizona. My ability to offer the necessary insight and guidance necessary for future teachers would also be supported through prior public school and university teaching experiences. It would be a delight to advise and supervise music education students, as well as teach methods courses, conducting, and choral literature.

As a graduate of Concordia College in Moorhead and former Concordia Choir member, I am vested in the Lutheran choral tradition and understand its distinctive role in the greater choral community. It would be an honor to serve as a steward of the strong musical heritage at Gustavus Adolphus. I believe strongly in a liberal arts education and understand the value and importance of an academic environment that enriches the spiritual lives of its students. If selected to fill this position, I guarantee my highest commitment to the Department of Music and the College as a whole and will work tirelessly to uphold its reputation of excellence, while continually striving to inspire students to realize their full academic and artistic potential.

FIGURE 2.18 Cover letter: Middle paragraphs illustration

Your final paragraph should reiterate your interest in the position. You can also indicate your interest in providing any other information or materials that may be desired by the committee. Use a formal valediction for your closing. If you did not include your contact information at the top of the letter it is acceptable to include such information in block form after your name, which follows the valediction. An example of a closing paragraph can be seen in Figure 2.19.

Overall, your cover letter must not only provide evidence that you are qualified for the position but it should also detail how you would use your expertise to provide exemplary student guidance and appropriate collegial support and compatibility were you to be offered the position. Your cover letter should address how you would contribute to the institution as well as to the faculty and students. What is it you have to offer and how would you use those abilities to better the school, faculty, and students? As you prepare your letter, a presentation or discussion of these two elements—your skills and how you would use them in the position for

I would welcome the opportunity to visit Gustavus Adolphus and interview with the search committee, faculty, students, and administrative team. I have enclosed my curriculum vitae, statement of teaching philosophy, and undergraduate transcripts. Three letters of recommendation and additional transcripts will follow. Please feel free to contact me for any additional information or materials. Thank you for your consideration of my application.

Sincerely,

FIGURE 2.19 Cover letter: Closing paragraph illustration

which you are applying—must be evident. While talking about one's background and experience is relatively easy to do, addressing needs of a school can be more challenging.

It is often suggested that applicants circle all of the action verbs in a job announcement and then proceed to use those action verbs in their cover letter. By using those action verbs when constructing your cover letter, you are more likely to think about and address the position needs. In essence you will be more aware of the institutional and student needs as highlighted in the position announcement and will be more likely talk about those needs as they relate to your skill base. Additionally, you should strive to remove the emphasis from yourself and focus on what your contribution could be to students and faculty, as well as to the department, school, and university. Thus, the word "I" should be used sparingly. Sell yourself, but do so in a manner that is supportive of fulfilling the needs of the institution and the needs of students and faculty.

Given these general guidelines, your letter might look like the example that appears in Figure 2.20.

March 15, 2011

Professor George Plumpton, Chair
String Music Education Search Committee
School of Music
PO Box 210004
University of Arizona
Tucson, AZ 85721-0004

Dear Dr. Plumpton:

Please accept my application for the position advertised in the May issue of the *Chronicle of Higher Education* advertised as Assistant Professor, String Music Education, in the School of Music at the University of Arizona, Position #345897. Initially your position came to my attention when Dr. Hamann, the former Professor of String Music Education, called and encouraged me to apply. After several years as a public school orchestra director, and having had my groups successfully play at such venues as the Mid-West Band and Orchestra Clinic and American String Teachers Association National Conferences, I pursued and completed my Ph.D. in Music Education. Interest in research during my graduate training led to a published book and several juried articles. After reading your job description, talking with Dr. Hamann, and reviewing your on-line program and curriculum, my interest intensified. While having been very successful in my current position at Georgetown University, the possibility of working with your students in string techniques and string methods classes, helping them augment their expertise as teachers and musicians, and further developing their skills, is appealing. The opportunity to expand students' research interests and collaborate with faculty in and across departments is most exciting. Hopefully you will find my experience, background, and interests compatible with your programmatic goals.

Based on your job announcement, it appears that your position involves work with graduate student committees, mentorship of student associations, and service on a variety of committees. While at Georgetown State University, I actively sought to contribute to the profession at all levels and have continued to develop and refine my skills as a mentor and facilitator. Being an advisor for the American String Teachers Student Association, serving as both a committee member and a major advisor on masters and doctoral committees, and contributing to numerous school, college,

FIGURE 2.20 Cover letter: Sample letter

and university level committees, has been rewarding. The challenge and opportunity to contribute in any way possible to foster student growth and facilitate development through work on university committees is welcomed.

Your position involves working with undergraduate string music education and performance majors. As a public school orchestra director and university professor, my objective was to create classroom atmospheres in which students could explore their potential, discover their unique talents, enhance their skills, and embrace new experiences. This remains my self-assigned charge. The prospect of working with your undergraduate and graduate students in venues such as the string techniques and string methods classes, the UA String Project, graduate research, statistics, and higher education courses opens a wealth of possibilities for creating real life experiences for students and for building bridges leading to greater interaction among university colleagues as well as with community supporters.

The University of Arizona has always been noted for its leadership in the field of music research and publication. I also understand the need to provide research leadership to fulfill promotion and tenure requirements at major research-intensive universities such as the University of Arizona and would relish the opportunity to work in this environment and contribute to the goals of the institution. As noted in my CV, my recently published string method book with Oxford University Press, along with my other published or edited books/chapters, the 65 juried national/international research sessions, and the 54 juried research articles, in such publications as the *Journal of Research in Music Education, Contributions to Music Education, Journal of String Research, String Research Journal, Update: Applications of Research in Music Education, Psychology of Music*, and the *Bulletin for the Council of Research in Music Education*, attest to my interests in maintaining a high level of involvement in music research and publication. It would be a privilege to share my interests in research and publication in both classroom and collaborative settings with your students and colleagues.

The prospect of joining the dedicated faculty of musicians, scholars, and educators in the School of Music at the University of Arizona and working with your students is exciting. I look forward to consideration of my candidacy for your string music education position. Please feel free to contact me should you wish any additional information or materials.

Sincerely,

Dr. Shirley Needajob
10475 Waiting Lane Drive
Colby, Wisconsin 54451
SN@wisdom.net
(715) 782-9898

FIGURE 2.20 Continued

Note that the opening paragraph in this hypothetical letter of application briefly outlines the applicant's history to date. Dr. Shirley Needajob, the applicant, indicated how she was drawn to the position. She added that the former professor in this position encouraged her to apply for the position, indicating, perhaps tacitly, his support of her candidacy. Note also how Shirley begins to address the needs of the University of Arizona as she points out some of the responsibilities in the position announcement.

The second paragraph outlines Dr. Needajob's service experience commitment and she again makes reference to the University of Arizona's interest in the service component, "Based on your job announcement it appears that your position involves work with graduate student committees, mentorship of student associations, and service on a variety of committees." In the next two paragraphs, Dr. Needajob provides information in the area of teaching and research, while in the final paragraph she reiterates her interest in the position. In the third paragraph, Dr. Needajob articulates her teaching experience and presents her basic philosophy. She speaks to the University of Arizona's need in the area of teaching, "in venues such as the string techniques and string methods classes, the UA String Project, graduate research, statistics, and higher education courses opens a wealth of possibilities for creating real life experiences for students and for building bridges for greater interaction within university colleagues as well as community supporters."

And so, too, in the fourth paragraph, Dr. Needajob acknowledges the university's eminence in the area of research and then outlines her expertise and publication record. The final paragraph in Dr. Needajob's application letter articulates her interest in the position.

While each application letter is unique and every applicant has his own approach to addressing this part of the application process, a letter that addresses the areas of teaching, research, and service will provide any committee with a broad overview of a candidate's abilities. Each position will have unique needs. It behooves the applicant to first acknowledge those needs and then state how his background will be of value to the university in addressing those needs. By doing so, committee members will know first that you are not just sending out a "boiler plate" application letter, but that you have thought about their needs in relation to your abilities. Such personalization also affords committee members the opportunity to visualize you in that position. For other examples of cover letters see "Cover Letters."

Writing an excellent letter of application presents many challenges. You may wish to read Noble (2007). Vick and Furlong (2008) also provide several cover letter samples. Further cover letter preparation ideas and samples can be found in works by Yate (2008), Kennedy (2009), and Hansen (1998), to name a few.

The basic purpose of your cover letter is to generate interest in you as a candidate, as a colleague. Thus your cover letter is intended to assist you in the following:

1. formally applying for a particular announced position;
2. introducing yourself;
3. acknowledging the university's needs in relation to your expertise and experience by providing an overview of your most important and relevant background, knowledge, experiences, accomplishments, philosophy, and skills as they relate to the position;
4. presenting a glimpse of the resources you have to share with students and faculty;

5. encouraging further study of your CV and other materials; and ultimately

6. prompting an invitation to an on-campus interview.

To this point, a discussion of perhaps the two most critical pieces of information, the CV and the cover letter, has been conducted. There are, however, other items that may be requested of you either when you initially submit an application or later in the review process. Some of these materials will most likely include a statement of teaching or educational philosophy and/or a research statement, transcripts, letters of recommendation, CDs, DVDs, articles, performance reviews, discographies and other such lists of performances, roles, works performed or conducted, and perhaps a teaching portfolio, none of which were included in your CV.

TEACHING OR EDUCATIONAL PHILOSOPHY AND RESEARCH STATEMENT

Your "philosophy of teaching" or "philosophy of education" statement is often requested in job applications. While a philosophy of education statement is technically different than a philosophy of teaching statement, they are often used interchangeably and are commonly asking for the same information. Your teaching or educational philosophy statement should be brief, generally one to two pages in length, should be written in the first person, should avoid technical language, and should be a narrative explicating your values and beliefs about teaching and learning. In essence, it's a statement on how you approach teaching.

The Duquesne University Center for Teaching Excellence (2010) and Haugen (1998) are two of many sources available that provides information on writing a teaching philosophy statement. The Duquesne University Center for Teaching Excellence suggests that there are six commonly found dimensions in faculty teaching philosophies, which include:

1. your purpose for teaching and learning,
2. your role as teacher,
3. your view of the student in the learning process,
4. the methods you use to encourage the process of teaching and learning,
5. the assessment you use in that process, and
6. a "framing device," which can be a critical incident about teaching that can provide a context for your prior statements.

Kuther (2010) suggests you conceptualize your teaching philosophy by first stating what your view of learning is: How do you perceive the learning process? What is meant by learning? How do you conceptualize it? Is there a particular educational or philosophical approach that characterizes how you view the process of teaching and learning (Piaget, Dewey, Gestalt, and so forth)? How does learning occur? (How is it facilitated in the studio or classroom?) What experiences have influenced your view of learning? This would comprise a paragraph.

Next, define teaching and explain your role as instructor in the teaching-learning process. Explain how you challenge students, facilitate learning, and accommodate different learning styles and abilities. And explain how your life and teaching experiences have influenced your view of teaching.

Your third task is to address student goals. What goals do you set for your classes and why, and how do you help your students achieve these goals? What outcomes and expectations do you have of your students (writing, problem solving, critical thinking, knowing content, acquiring skills and technical facility, and so forth)? And how do you determine when you've reached or fulfilled those goals—in other words—what are your assessment or evaluation tools, rubrics, or methods?

In a final paragraph you should explain how you would implement your philosophy. Thus far you've defined and described the teaching and learning process; now you want to explain what you would *do* to implement and operationalize your philosophy. What would students be doing, what kinds of course materials, assignments, and projects could we expect to see? What might we see you doing in the classroom? How might you interact with students? Would we see lectures, small group discussions, one-on-one interactions, student presentations, or other such teaching-learning exchanges? Discuss your experiences: How have they reinforced or modified your philosophy and goals? And finally, how does your teaching make a difference in the lives of your students, in your own personal growth, and in the profession? In Figures 2.21 and 2.22 examples of teaching philosophy statements are presented.

Additional teaching philosophy statements can be found under "Teaching Statements."

Your teaching philosophy is your conceptual thoughts about the teaching and learning process as applied in realistic settings. If you need additional information or assistance in writing your teaching philosophy, one of many excellent guidelines for doing so was compiled by Dr. Ciara O'Farrell (2010). Another such guideline has been produced by Montell (2003) Sample teaching philosophies can be found on the website of the University of Central Florida (2010).

STATEMENT OF TEACHING PHILOSOPHY
Bradley A. Miller

Educating the whole person *through* music is the foundation of my teaching philosophy. To facilitate this process, I strive to cultivate a learning environment that 1) encourages the continuous growth of musical skills and knowledge, 2) empowers musicians to connect to something greater than themselves, and 3) inspires lifelong participation in, and advocacy of music.

Many of my teaching practices are drawn from a constructivist approach, as I believe that people learn best when actively engaged in the learning process. I seek new strategies, within a traditional rehearsal model, to encourage critical thinking. These strategies include both discussion and reflection regarding musical concepts, meaning of texts, and artistic interpretation. Though opportunities exist to encourage students to think independently, it is imperative that the ensemble maintains a unified vision, through the lens of the conductor. These precepts result in heightened musical experiences and increased musical knowledge and skills.

My teaching approach is rooted in the continued development of a series of relationships. First, a transparent relationship between conductor and ensemble creates an environment in which trust and vulnerability enable a deeper connection to the repertoire. Second, ensemble members must come together as a united community of musicians, respectfully working toward a common goal. Finally, the ensemble must develop a deep relationship with the music itself. Paul J. Christiansen stated, "You don't begin to understand good choral music until it goes beyond the technical and into the emotions." This process begins with my own knowledge of the score, preparedness, and ability to devise successful rehearsal procedures. Through the course of uncovering the many layers of a musical work, the art that lies beneath the printed page is ultimately revealed.

It is my goal to send forth into society young adults brimming with passion for the choral art and committed to sharing their musical gifts. Having embraced the values of hard work, dedication, community, and service, these young people will feel compelled to continue their musical journey, as well as advocate for musical opportunities within their communities.

FIGURE 2.21 Teaching philosophy statement illustration #1

Research Statement

The research statement differs from the teaching or educational philosophy in that it is directed toward your research or creative efforts. It provides a summary of your achievements to date and some insight into your possible future endeavors. Strong research or creative statements are eminently readable and provide the reader with a realistic view of your research or creative agenda. The most compelling statements are those that also address the needs, facilities, and goals of the school to which you are applying. Thus, the research statement allows a hiring committee to assess your: area(s) of research or creative interests, potential to secure grants, academic ability, possible research needs, compatibility with the department or school, and if applicable, your potential for being promoted and/or receiving tenure.

Background

The research statement should first provide a background of work completed and current work being undertaken. In this opening statement, indicate the importance of your research, how your research contributes to your field—its relevance, distinctiveness, and importance, including key findings and promising lines

Statement of Teaching Philosophy
Heather Zosel

I believe that students can be engaged in every facet of the choral rehearsal. They can be active singers, decision makers, and listeners. This in turn prepares them to be energetic performers with ownership of the ensemble and the performance. The conductor should not be the only ears in the choir, but should gradually teach the students to listen and make appropriate stylistic and vocal decisions in the rehearsal. With these skills, students will be able to be life-long learners and performers of music.

I believe in preparing students to be life-long learners and performers of music. Preparation takes place through understanding of our musical heritage, score study, and appreciation of others. Through the study of our musical heritage, we gain insight into the history and trends of music composition and performance. It is important, especially as a conductor, to make stylistically and historically informed decisions in order to represent every genre and composer accurately. Score study gives insight into the composers' intentions, and also prepares the student for the podium. The basic gestures of cueing, breathing, entrances, and cut-offs come to life as the student understands the form, style, and historical significance of the piece. The choral classroom is the most important place to appreciate and look for the best in others. The voice is such a personal instrument, being a part of our body, and our students must learn a deep respect for each individual. This will in turn aid their relationships in every facet of their lives.

The most detrimental thing a teacher can do is to think for her students. Each student must be actively engaged and able to think critically about each decision. My job is to guide students through the decision-making process, by providing visual and auditory materials to expand their knowledge, asking thought-provoking questions, and creating a safe environment for them to experiment and explore their developing concepts. When students leave my classroom, I want them to be confident on the podium, in the classroom, and in their relationships with others.

FIGURE 2.22 Teaching philosophy statement illustration #2

of inquiry for future endeavors—and in what direction you hope to take your research in the future. If you are just entering the profession and have limited research background other than your dissertation, it will be expected that you have begun to think about research beyond the dissertation itself. How do you plan to use your dissertation research line in future projects? What future questions do you hope to answer based on your dissertation findings? Has that line of research been promising and do you hope to continue within that field or perhaps a related or different field of inquiry? You need to generate a sense of excitement about your line of research. What excites you about your research? How will your past and current efforts follow logically and yet provide different, important, and innovative findings?

Research Agenda

This section of your research statement should flow logically and naturally from your opening statement/paragraph. In this section you should provide a realistic three- to five-year research plan that should be credible and provide potential outcomes. You might wish to state some of the major problems you hope to attack and the approach you plan to use to accomplish that goal. Do you have a funding source in mind to assist you with your research? If you know a particular agency that funds your line of research, you can name the agency and briefly outline how you would or perhaps have and will continue to receive funding. This will underscore your interest in grantsmanship and support the preposition that you are an able, independent researcher, knowledgeable about key issues in your area or field. At the same time, you should have research goals that are broad enough so that if one topic doesn't get funded there are other areas of investigation you could pursue. In summary, this section should outline your three- to five-year career research goals, describe your research specialty interests, and provide plans to obtain funding.

Relevance

In this section of your research statement you should further detail how your line of research will be and is compatible with that of the unit to which you are making application. What lines of research has the unit produced in the past? Show how your research complements and enhances those lines of inquiry. In addition, mention the types of research resources you will need to be successful in your new job. You may wish to provide some insight into your plans and methodologies for addressing questions to show both the need for your research resources and to provide additional support for the importance of your line of inquiry within the unit, the school, the university, and the profession.

A research statement is a brief summary of your work, written in the first person and generally not exceeding one or two pages. Your statement should orient the reader to your specific interest within the broader discipline and describe how your research fits the context of developments in the field and how it will correspond with and contribute to the unit, department, school, and university. Additional sources for assistance in writing your research statement include the following:

Research statements
http://studentaffairs.duke.edu/career/graduate-students/academic-career-preparation/research-statement (provides sample statements)
Developing a winning research statement http://career.ucsf.edu/pff/assets/ResearchStatementHandout.pdf
Assembling your application materials http://serc.carleton.edu/NAGTWorkshops/careerprep/jobsearch/application.html
Writing a research plan

http://sciencecareers.sciencemag.org/career_development/previous_issues/
articles/1820/writing_a_research_plan

TRANSCRIPTS

There are basically two types of transcripts: official and unofficial. Official transcripts are those that are sent by the university to another institution. Official transcripts are never to be given to the individual student. Unofficial transcripts are those that have been issued to the student, do not carry a university seal, are copied, and so forth. While many universities do not require that official transcripts be sent as part of the application, eventually you may need to have an official transcript sent from each of the universities you attended to confirm that you indeed did graduate and receive a degree from the institution or institutions you listed as attending. Thus you should maintain transcript contact information for all universities you attended.

Official transcripts are generally not required on an initial application, however, unofficial or student-issued transcripts can be requested. It would behoove you to order and have at the ready several sets of transcripts to include in an application when requested. Sometimes a copy of a student-issued transcript is adequate for application submission. Some universities do not require transcripts as part of their application process.

LETTERS OF REFERENCE

As was mentioned earlier in this chapter, it is becoming a more common practice to list individuals who are willing to serve as your "providers" or "referees" in the CV. Whether you are simply providing a list of referees in your CV, having your referees submit letters on your behalf, or submitting letters of reference yourself, the choice of individuals you choose to serve as your referees is crucial. Candidate references, whether they are presented verbally or in written form, are *expected* to be positive and supportive.

There are several considerations that should be carefully addressed when choosing your referees. Below is a discussion of these items, including the selection of referees, your responsibility to referees, and additional items for reference consideration.

Selecting Individuals to Serve as Referees

When you ask an individual to serve as one of your referees or to provide a letter of recommendation for you, it is very important that you ask that person several questions. First, ask the person if s/he is willing to serve as a referee for you and/ or if s/he would be willing to write a letter of reference for you. Next, determine whether or not the potential referee is willing to positively support you. You need to find individuals who are honest and fair and truly support you and your endeavors. You want a referee to write you a very positive and supportive letter when needed and/or to speak highly of you if contacted by telephone or email. How then do you determine whether a referee will support you in such a manner?

Listen carefully to an individual's response when asked if s/he would serve as a referee for you. If a person responds, "No," to your inquiry about providing a reference, thank the person for her honesty and candor and find another individual to serve as a reference. Some individuals may not be as "forthcoming" about saying "No" to the request to serve as a referee. They may make comments such as, "I really don't know that much about your progress in your program," or "I don't know that much about you," or "I've only had you in one (two, three) courses," and so on. Statements such as these generally indicate that the person is uneasy about serving as a referee for you. It doesn't matter whether or not the person does or does not know you that well, has or hasn't had many classes with you, or does or doesn't know about your progress in your degree program, what she is trying to tell you is she doesn't feel comfortable being a referee for you for some reason. Again, your course of action should be to thank the individual for her consideration and tell the person that you understand her concern. Don't try to convince a person to serve as a referee for you if they do not wish to do so, as that individual may have concerns about your qualifications. Also, don't be offended by being rejected by someone to serve as your referee. Be thankful that the individual was honest with you about her ability to support you. Applicant's references are *expected* to be very supportive and when there is any kind of doubt about that support, search committee members "negatively note" such lack of support.

The decision on who to ask to serve as your referees is certainly another issue that demands some planning on your part. You will want to select individuals who will of course support you, but you also need to consider the impact of the reference upon a potential committee. A stellar recommendation from a lay person, let's say an individual from the clergy who knows you very well, may be influential, but wouldn't a stellar recommendation from the head of the area in which you are receiving your degree be even more influential? Will an individual from another music department be able to address critical issues in your discipline as well as someone in your discipline? Also, consider the impact your references might have on a hiring committee. A reference from an individual who has tremendous local charisma, respect, visibility, and credibility may not have as much impact on a hiring committee as a reference that comes from an individual who has tremendous national or international visibility, respect, charisma, and credibility.

You also need to consider balance when selecting referees. While this may seem to contradict the previous statements, it does not. You want to have referees who can completely and thoroughly address your abilities and competence in your area, but you also need to have referees address other areas of importance, such as collegiality, character, work ethic, potential, flexibility, and ability to work as a team member or to take a leadership role.

Finally, in choosing your referees, you need to consider selecting individuals who have the ability to write an impressive reference letter and to speak eloquently on your behalf. Perhaps the last consideration could be titled "There are reference letters and there are reference letters—there is support and there is support!" Different individuals have different talents. A wonderful conductor may also be an outstanding reference-letter writer while an eminent music historian may not have impressive skills at writing reference letters. There are a few ways to determine the "ability" of your referee's reference-writing skills.

1. If you are fortunate enough to know someone on a hiring committee who has seen your letters of reference or has spoken to your referees, he may be willing to let you know if there are any "problems" with any of your references. Of course, confidentiality is always maintained in these situations and names are not shared, but a comment such as, "You may want to consider a reassessment of some of your referees" is a clear indicator that the level of support you want does not necessarily exist among *all* of your referees. A reevaluation of your referees would be in order at this point.

2. If asked, individuals may be willing to provide you with copies of reference letters sent to hiring committees. Note, however, that some individuals feel that such requests are an encumbrance and the requests may temper their view. Conversely, some reference writers will, as a matter of course, provide such letters without request. If secured, you can evaluate the perceived "impact" your referees' letters might have on a hiring committee.

3. Asking other colleagues or students about their referee selections can often trigger an informative discussion. If your colleagues are getting telephone/Skype or on-campus interviews, their referees must be writing and providing strong support. You may wish to consider these individuals for your references.

Selecting the best individuals to serve as your referees deserves careful consideration and thought. The referee selection process should not be delayed, but the more thought and consideration put into this decision-making process the better your chances are to receive the optimum amount of support from your referees in your job search.

Your Responsibility to Your Referees

When an individual does agree to be your referee, you have an obligation to that individual as much as they have an obligation to you. Your obligation is to provide your referees with all of the information they need to successfully write letters of recommendation and support you when contacted by telephone by a committee.

1. Give your referees a copy of your CV. This will enable them to draw on items from your CV when composing letters of reference and will also help them better describe your qualifications for a position when talking to hiring committee members.

2. Provide your referees with a copy of the job description, the address or email to which their letter should be sent (often with electronic application submissions the university will notify referees that they should upload their reference letters to an electronic application material gathering site, rather than send them), the deadline for receipt of the letter, and any other important information. You should also highlight, on a separate page, pertinent information you feel is important for your referees to address. The more information you can provide your referees the better your letters of recommendation will be.

3. It is not uncommon for referees to submit individual letters of recommendation on your behalf on institutional letterhead. Letters of recommendation are generally kept in computer files and many individuals are happy to revise various bits of information to individualize their letter of recommendation for you. Don't abuse this privilege. Do not ask a referee to submit numerous letters on your behalf. Be selective in your application process and apply only for those jobs that you feel strongly match your qualifications. Allow ample time for the writer to submit a letter on your behalf. There may, however, be times when the "turnaround" time for a letter of recommendation is short. Such requests should be kept to a minimum. Even with computers and improved modes of communication, providing letters of recommendation is time consuming. Be sure you are qualified for positions for which you apply to insure that your reference-letter writers' time is well spent on your behalf.

Additional Reference Consideration Items

How many references do you need? The minimum number of references or letters of reference required for most positions is three. Many applicants will have more than three individuals listed on their CVs, along with their contact information, and will generally have three or more individuals who are willing to write letters of recommendation on their behalf. Having more than three individuals willing to be contacted or to supply letters of recommendation insures that a minimum of three letters will reach a hiring committee when requested. Listing more than three referees on your CV for contact possibilities also increases the chances of the hiring committee reaching at least three individuals within the time frame they have been allowed.

Often individuals *other than those listed on your reference list* will be contacted for information concerning you. This is an increasingly common practice among hiring committees, as they feel they can get an "unbiased" opinion from individuals not listed on an applicant's reference list. Individuals contacted who are not on reference lists fall into several categories. Those not on a reference list who are often contacted include the following:

1. Individuals from the university you attended who are known by a hiring committee member. These individuals are usually faculty members or administrators, and may or may not be associated with the department in which you have completed major work. Hence, faculty members in theory, education, strings, voice, brass, woodwind, percussion, conducting, composition, or history departments could be contacted regarding your suitability for a position. Often administrators, especially those from smaller schools, are contacted for similar informational feedback.

2. Major professors, coordinators, and/or division heads in your major area of study are often contacted, even though you have not listed them. If, for example, you are a choral conducting major in a DMA program and you list the assistant director of the choral conducting department as a referee, the director of the department will often be contacted as well, even though they were not listed.

3. Former employers can be contacted. Because a large component of any position involves collegiality and work ethic, committee members are keenly interested in obtaining as much information as possible in these areas (Schoenfeld and Magnan 1994). Talking to former employers often helps committee members obtain this type of information about you.

There are several important factors to note concerning references. First, make sure that the referees you ask to represent you are *truly* willing to do so. Listen carefully to what you are told by an individual when you ask him to serve as a referee for you. Second, select individuals who can best address the questions posed by a search committee. If you are a doctoral music studio student, for example, it is advantageous for you to have a prominent music studio professor as one of your referees. Third, remember that all individuals with whom you come in contact during your course of study may one day be asked to critique your fitness for a position or, for that matter, recommend you for a position. Collegiality should be first and foremost in importance when dealing with colleagues, faculty, and administration.

AUDIO OR AUDIOVISUAL RECORDINGS

If you are applying for a performance position, you can be certain that you will be asked to produce recordings of recitals, concerts, or produced CDs. Composers are often requested to send recordings of works composed and performed, and conductors, too, are asked to send DVDs of a rehearsal or performance. It is not unheard of for individuals applying for academic positions (music education, theory, musicology, etc.) to produce DVDs of teaching episodes. Regardless of the position, you need to be prepared to send in quality recordings of your art form. Let's first address the issue of recordings of performances.

If you are a performer, you can be assured that somewhere in the application process you will be asked to send in a recording. Today, with digital technology prevailing, the most common recording format is the CD. Additionally, YouTube has become a growing vehicle from which a performer's skills can be investigated; however, playback quality of YouTube performances varies widely and such presentations must be considered carefully for playback appropriateness. Regardless of the format, you need to be aware that quality and perfection is your goal in these recordings. While every member of a search committee realizes that missed notes and mistakes do occur in performances, in reality committee members generally prefer to hear flawless and aesthetically inspired performances. If a committee member is listening to two performances, both equally inspiring, but one performance has some performance flaws, which do you think the individual would choose as the superior performance? Like a letter of recommendation, the expectation is that anything submitted for application consideration should be perfect. Why would anyone submit anything less than that? Hence, the expectation of any recording you send is that it will be perfect, flawless, and reflective of the highest level of performance you have to offer. Perfection is the standard, perfection is the expectation, and with today's technology, this is entirely possible.

If you are a performer, one task that you should complete as soon as possible is to produce a flawless CD of your playing. If you are associated with a university, that institution may have a recording studio that you can use, inexpensively or at no cost, to help you produce a flawless CD. A CD produced in this manner will generally require repeated "takes" and numerous editing sessions that will involve a serious time commitment on the part of you and the recording engineer. So plan ahead; this is not a task that can be completed on short notice. If you know you will be entering the job market in a given year, you should be preparing and planning your CD recording at least six months to a year ahead of your actual application deadline.

If you can't offer a CD produced in a studio and must use "live" performances, you should also have these edited. Do not include works on your "live" CDs that show flaws or weaknesses. Often, even with live performances, if the recital or concert was recorded digitally, editing of minor errors can be accomplished in a studio in a short amount of time. If a movement of a work is seriously flawed, DO NOT include that selection on your CD. Remove that movement from CD consideration. In addition to editing live performances, some mixing can also be done to enhance the blend and balance of your CD. The order of performances on your CD is also important, and your best performance should be the first one on your CD as it is frequently the most heard. A wonderful CD can get you to the next step in the application process. It is a critical part of your application package. Remember, a committee wants and expects perfection; give it to them.

There are times when an unedited CD performance is specifically requested. If such is the case, you must honor that request; but again, this does not necessarily dictate that you include all recital selections performed at a particular concert. You may decide to provide a live CD performance of select works or partial works (select movements) or perhaps a selection of works from several recitals. Whatever the procedure, make sure that your recording is of the best quality possible through utilization of the highest-quality recording equipment and engineering available.

We know that performers will be asked to submit a CD of their playing initially or as they advance through the application screening process, but as mentioned earlier, it is not uncommon for composers, conductors, and even at times, academicians to be asked to produce audio or audiovisual recordings of their performances, conducting, or teaching. For example, composers will often be asked if they have a recording of one or more of their composed works. Thus, if you are a composer and your works are being performed in concert or rehearsal, plan to have them professionally recorded and later edited. Conductors, too, are asked for audiovisual recordings of performances they have conducted. If you are a conductor, it would behoove you to professionally record your performances in an audiovisual format. Even individuals who are applying for academic positions should consider having segments of teaching episodes professionally recorded. Teaching DVDs can positively influence search committee members if prepared professionally and with care.

How important are audio and audiovisual recording? If you are a performer, recordings are essential—plan on them being requested as part of the application screening process. Even conductors and composers should plan on submitting recordings as part of an application screening process. It is becoming more and more common for conductors and composers to be asked to provide audio and/or audiovisual evidence of their craft. Thus, the quality of your recording often determines whether you continue to be considered a viable candidate for a position. Your application planning must include the preparation of high-quality, professional audio and/or audiovisual recordings.

ARTICLES, PERFORMANCE REVIEWS, WORKS PERFORMED OR READY TO PERFORM, AND OTHER

In addition to audio and audiovisual recordings, other materials may accompany a CV and cover letter. Such materials can include copies of published articles and/or books and performance reviews. If not previously listed in your CV, you should have a prepared list of works performed, ready to perform, or studied, roles played in operas or theater selections, and so forth.

While an inventory of published books, chapters in books, and juried and nonjuried articles will appear in your CV, you may be asked to send representative samples of these works to support your application. Correspondingly, scholarly works based on written articles that have been presented at learned meetings but are not yet published may also be considered as support materials for your application. If such materials are sent, they must represent your finest publications or written examples and reflect the type of writing and/or research that you would be conducting at the institution to which you are making application. For example, if you are primarily a quantitative researcher, you should consider sending your finest quantitative research efforts. Any documents you submit are generally viewed as reflective of the kinds of research that are of interest to you, that you would like to continue to conduct, and that you would best assist others in producing.

Similarly, if you are an editor of a journal, magazine, or book, or if you write a column in a local/state professional association newsletter or journal, you may wish to include samples of these publications as supporting application materials. Many individuals list only juried articles and presentations in their CVs, even though they may have written numerous nonjuried/referred articles for professional magazines at the national, regional, state, or local levels or have presented at several nonjuried venues. For such works, not listed in your CV, a folder of such resources can be compiled, listing the works written or presented, along with representative samples of them and sent as a document supporting your application.

Often, performances, CDs, DVDs, première works, books, films, productions, and so forth receive reviews in newspapers, magazines, and other such sources. These are important outside critiques of your works. The importance of such reviews can't be overstated. While some individuals choose to add such critiques or reviews to their CVs, this can become cumbersome, especially if a listing of repertoire is also included as a CV addendum. Thus, a well-constructed, indexed folder of press releases, critiques, and reviews of works may be the most appropriate format to use to display such materials. Your review/critique/press release folder can be sent as a supporting document to your application.

Finally, if you haven't already included works performed, ready to perform, or studied, roles played in operas or theater selections, and so forth in your CV, you should consider doing so in a supplemental folder. As your portfolio grows, it becomes challenging to present and delineate the multifaceted professional tasks you have undertaken and completed. A listing of such events using clearly articulated and systematic headings can help a committee member quickly and clearly grasp a complex professional career. With any such listing your goal is to have the reviewer, as quickly and comprehensively as possible, view and retain salient highlights of your career that will positively contribute to your candidacy.

TEACHING PORTFOLIO

A teaching portfolio is useful to construct and to send as additional material for job candidacy consideration; while it is not often required, it is on occasion asked for as supplementary information (Seldin 1991). The teaching portfolio includes items that are dependent on one's experience and one's preference for its usefulness. It consists of materials from oneself, materials from others, and teaching outcome assessments or evaluative statements.

Some self-generated materials you could include in your teaching portfolio are listed below.

1. If you have had teaching responsibilities you can include the following:
   a. A listing and a brief description of courses you have taught.
   b. Course syllabi with detailed content, goals and objectives, methodology, assessment rubrics, texts, and so forth.

    c. A description of evaluation and improvement procedures implemented in one's teaching.

    d. Information pertaining to the direct supervision or participation of direction of student theses, dissertations, honors projects, research group activities, and so forth.

    e. An overview of curricular revisions, new course development, and other such activities.

2. If you have had limited teaching responsibilities, such as graduate assistantships and so forth, you may wish to include the following:

    a. A personal statement of your teaching philosophy, strategies, and objectives.

    b. A statement of your teaching goals in the next one or two years, five years, and/or ten years.

You can also consider a section that contains materials from individuals other than yourself. These can include the following:

1. If you have had teaching responsibilities:

    a. Statements from colleagues within and outside of your department, chairpersons, or other outside sources pertaining to your: syllabi; in-class teaching effectiveness; out-of-class activities, such as curricular development or instructional research; student course and teaching evaluations or the actual evaluations themselves; your role in and contribution to the department; your performance as a faculty advisor; honors and teaching awards from internal and external sources; professional exchanges with other colleagues concerning teaching approaches and methodologies; and invitations to other departments and/or other institutions to demonstrate teaching-learning approaches.

    b. A DVD or other such recording of actual teaching episodes in diverse settings and in various classrooms.

2. If you have had limited teaching responsibilities, such as graduate assistantships and so forth:

    a. An invitation from outside sources to present a paper in your teaching discipline at local, state, regional, or national conferences and workshops and other venues.

    b. Participation in local, state, regional, or national teaching organizations in your discipline.

c. Involvement in research that contributes directly to the enhancement of teaching.

A final section in your teaching portfolio can reflect your students' accomplishments. These are student outcomes predicated on good teaching. Such outcomes presume some teaching experience and longevity. This section can include the following:

1. Student conference or workshop presentations or publications.
2. Nonpublished student essays, compositions, performances, and so forth from course-related work.
3. Student career choices as influenced by your guidance and/or advisement.
4. Student honors, awards, and other acknowledgements as a result of course-related work and/or teaching/advisement.
5. Statements from alumni about the quality and effect of your teaching on their careers and lives.
6. The effect of your influence on your students' success in positions taken after graduation.
7. Positions held by your students at other teaching institutions, learned societies, professional organizations, and so forth.

A teaching portfolio is one way in which you can highlight the teaching component evaluated in most university positions. The research and service components are more transparent and easily understood than teaching. A simple listing of publications, performances, exhibits, presentations, compositions, and so forth, in various venues and in different settings can convey accomplishment in the area of research, just as a listing of committee service at local, state, regional, and national or international venues can do the same for that component. However, a simple listing of classes taught does not provide the necessary depth of involvement or concern for student progress that one would hope for—hence a teaching portfolio may be considered an essential component of your application materials.

SENDING UNSOLICITED MATERIALS

The decision to send unsolicited materials must be carefully considered. Increasingly, universities are using "electronic" application submissions, some of which preclude conveyance of any, other than requested, materials. While numerous universities accept "paper" application submissions, the protocol for receipt of unsolicited materials is often unclear. Some universities use a centralized campus office, such as a human resources office, for receipt of materials. It is often questionable whether unsolicited materials would be accepted through such an office. By the same token, application materials sent directly to an individual at an institution are most frequently cataloged by a staff member who may or may not be allowed to put unsolicited materials in your file. These materials may be relegated to a supplemental file, of which committee members may not be aware and to which they may not have convenient access.

Reproducing and sending unsolicited materials can be costly, especially if you are doing so frequently. So the question of whether or not to send unsolicited materials is one of both cost and of effectiveness. If committee members won't or can't review your "extra support" materials, should you send them? While there are two approaches to which most people adhere—the "it couldn't hurt school" and the "wait until asked" approach—sending unsolicited materials can unintentionally send the message that you can't follow directions or don't like to cooperate. It is best, for several reasons, not to send materials until requested to do so. However, it will befit you to have supplemental materials carefully and thoughtfully prepared in anticipation of a search committee request. In this case, the motto "always be prepared" would be a good one to adopt.

ELECTRONICALLY SHARED INFORMATION SYSTEMS

The growth of electronically shared information systems is changing how we learn about others. Social networks, such as Facebook, Myspace, and Twitter, along with other Internet systems, such as YouTube, personal websites, and other electronic information dissemination vehicles, are making a wealth of information available almost instantly. Individuals seeking positions in higher education are increasingly considering these vehicles as potential outlets for dissemination of their information, profiles, and creative efforts, and institutions have, in many sectors, been turning to such systems to gain additional information about prospective candidates. Whether you choose to disseminate information through these systems is of course your choice, but should you choose to do so, the astute individual would be wise to insure that all information posted on such systems is of the highest quality and has a professional demeanor.

Perhaps one of the more common means to share biographies, CVs, headshots or professional photographs, teaching philosophies, portfolios, and such creative efforts as compositions, sound clips of performances, professional writings, and so forth is the personal website. Accessed through a Uniform Resources Locator (URL), a website is a set of web pages consisting of text, image, video, audio, jpeg, and other media and is hosted on at least one web server. As with any resources that are open to public perusal, the quality of the website layout itself, as well as the materials on the website, must be of the highest quality. For example, a "headshot" provides a lasting impression of an individual and conveys personality traits (intelligence, sensitivity, etc.). By carefully selecting a photographer who can capture those elements you want conveyed, your headshot can have a positive impression on a viewer or prospective employer. By the same token, a CV, a music performance, or a carefully crafted biography can make a positive impression on the viewer. Professional websites need to be artfully, tastefully, and professionally constructed; they can serve as a host for your professional materials and can be linked to other social networking systems, such as Twitter, Facebook, Myspace, and hi5, as well as video-sharing websites such as YouTube.

Facebook, Myspace, hi5, and others are social networking systems that provide the capability of sharing photographs, contact information, interest, and personal information. LinkedIn, another networking system, is basically used for professional interaction and is considered a business-related social networking site. Such systems provide ways to control information through privacy settings and by selecting those who can see specific parts of profiles. They are accessed separately, but such systems can be linked to each other and accessed from a central location, such as a website, thus making them useful to the individual who wishes to store various information items in different places and have the capability of responding to different venues via social networking systems. Another useful website for sharing videos is YouTube. Designed to share user-generated content, such as music performance videos, YouTube allows uploads of up to fifteen minutes with larger uploads allowed, when certain criteria are met, for up to twelve hours.

These and an ever-increasing host of social and professional as well as personal websites are now available to the individual seeking alternative venues for dissemination of their professional information. Interest in various networking and electronic-sharing systems has allowed individuals to market themselves through a plethora of avenues. With the advancement of technology such websites are constantly enhancing audio and visual quality and allowing for enriched environments for displaying one's efforts. Again, the choice to present oneself through such forums is an individual choice and has not yet become a mandatory component of the higher education application process. As in all application materials, quality and professional integrity are keys words to consider when using electronic-sharing systems.

Making Application for a University Position

With the preparation of your application materials, your CV, your cover letter focused to reflect the specific position and university being offered, and additional requested materials, you are now ready to make your official application for a position. If you are making a paper application, one which is not electronically submitted, the manner in which you submit your materials can have a lasting positive or negative impression on committee members. Materials submitted, especially your CV, should be presented in the most professional manner possible. If you are not submitting your CV electronically choose a high-quality "white" bond paper for your document. If sent nonelectronically, consider professionally binding your CV. Not only will this convey concern for organization and professionalism, your CV will also stand up to repeated viewing and even more importantly, it will not be subject to pages being lost or placed out of order. Other materials, such as transcripts, teaching philosophy statements, letters of review, and so forth, if not conveyed electronically, can also be organized and bound in a folder with a cover or cover page. Thus, your application portfolio, when viewed, will convey a professional image and will be viewed positively.

Online or electronic applications are becoming increasingly common as universities become "paperless." More than likely you will be asked to download or scan your application materials and, as mentioned previously, reference or recommendation writers are also being requested to email or upload their letters. Materials are generally sent to a distribution center and are then made available to committee members for review. When submitting online applications, make sure that what you are sending is the correct file. It is not uncommon for candidates to send files that have not been edited or that were intended for another institution. Keep an application file with corrected and updated CVs, cover letter(s), and so forth, apart from "working" files. This will help avoid confusion later. Also, carefully read submission directions. Some applications require various documents to be submitted separately to different files. Once you submit a file, especially if it is not the correct one, it may be difficult if not impossible to retrieve or delete it.

Carefully read and follow application directions. You do not want to be unique because you did not follow application guidelines; in fact, such uniqueness at this point reflects poorly on your application and candidacy. Committees don't generally view individuals positively who don't or can't follow basic guidelines. Requested materials should also be sent in a timely manner. While some committees are allowed to look at incomplete files after the closing date, many are not. If your file is not complete, not only will the committee not have the same information from you as for others for review consideration, your file may not even be reviewed. Be aware of the closing date stated on the application and adhere to it. Committees often want to review materials as soon as possible, and applications received after a closing date, even if they can be reviewed, may not receive the same time, attention, or consideration.

The goal of your application materials is to get you to the next step of the application process, whatever that step may be: a request for additional materials, telephone calls to your references, a telephone or Skype interview, or an on-site interview. Remember: YOU ARE YOUR APPLICATION MATERIALS. The materials you submit become the summation of your professional efforts and in essence are a validation of your professional merit as documented through your competitions, recordings, articles, written reviews, and so forth.

It is paramount that you carefully prepare *all materials* with attention to professionalism. Attention to spelling, grammar, neatness, clarity, appearance, precision, integrity, and perhaps a touch of salesmanship can help candidates present those informational items that are most meaningful to reviewers.

References

Dehne, Selena. 2009. Connecting your resume and cover letter. http://www.jist.com/shop/web/career-central/resumes-and-cover-letters/connecting-your-resume-and-cover-letter (accessed September 3, 2009).

Doyle, Alison. 2009. Job searching: Cover letters. http://jobsearch.about.com/od/coverletters/a/aap3p401b.htm, accessed September 4, 2009.

Duquesne University Center for Teaching Excellence. 2010. The statement of teaching philosophy. http://www.duq.edu/cte/academic-careers/teaching-philosophy.cfm, accessed November 10, 2010.

Hamann, Donald L., and Keitha V. Lucas. 1998. Establishing journal eminence in music education research. *Journal of Research in Music Education* 46 (3), 405–413.

Hansen, Katharine. 1998. *Cover letters for new graduates*. Berkeley, CA: Dynamic Ten Speed.

Haugen, Lee. 1998. Writing a teaching philosophy statement. http://www.celt.iastate.edu/teachng/philosophy.html, accessed November 10, 2010.

Kennedy, Joyce L. 2009. *Cover letters for dummies*. 3rd ed. Hoboken, NJ: Wiley.

Kuther, Tara. 2010. Writing your statement of teaching philosophy. http://gradschool.about.com/cs/teaching/a/teachphil.htm, accessed January 3, 2010.

Montell, Gabriela. 2003. How to write a statement of teaching. http://chronicle.com/article/How-to-Write-a-Statement-of/45133, accesed November 3, 2010.

Morris, William, ed. 1969. *The American heritage dictionary of the English language*. New York: American Heritage and Houghton Mifflin.

Noble, David F. 2007. *Galley of best cover letters: A collection of quality cover letters by professional resume writers*. 3rd ed. Indianapolis: JIST Works.

O'Farrell, Ciara. 2010. Writing a teaching philosophy statement. http://www.tcd.ie/CAPSL/assets/pdf/Philsophy_Statement.pdf, accessed November 10, 2010.

Schoenfeld, Clay and Robert Magnan. (1994). *Mentor in a manual: Climbing the academic ladder to tenure*. 2nd ed. Madison, WI: Atwood.

Seldin, Peter. 1991. *The teaching portfolio: A practical guide to improved performance and promotion/tenure decisions*. Bolton, MA: Anker.

The reality of cover letters. 2009. http://www.collegegrad.com/jobsearch/best-college-cover-letters/the-reality-of-cover-letters/, accessed September 8, 2010.

University of Central Florida. 2010. Sample teaching philosophies. http://www.fctl.ucf.edu/facultysuccess/professionalportfolios/philosophies.php, accessed November 1, 2010.

Vick, Julia Miller, and Jennifer S. Furlong. 2008. *The academic job search handbook*. 4th ed. Philadelphia: University of Pennsylvania Press.

Yate, Martin. 2008,. *Knock 'em dead cover letters*. 8th ed. Avon, MA: Adams Media.

3

APPLYING FOR THE JOB: THE PROCESS

The Application Submission and Review Process

In this chapter we will discuss the application review process. There is perhaps nothing more agonizing for candidates than waiting to hear back from a university concerning their application and of course, whether they are being considered for an on-campus interview. What this chapter will do is outline and discuss the processes conducted by search committees when reviewing position applications. Hopefully, after reading this chapter, you will better understand the search procedure and subsequent time lag between application submission and university notification concerning your position candidacy status.

Consideration To Make Application

Before we begin the discussion of the application review process, we need to examine the consideration of submitting an application. Generally, most individuals apply for a position for one of three reasons: (1) they are encouraged to do so, (2) they believe they have a chance at being hired for the position because of their appropriate qualifications, or (3) they feel they have the qualifications a university *would like* to have in a faculty member.

Let's first discuss the process of applying for a position when encouraged to do so. A number of universities regularly contact and encourage individuals to apply for positions that will be, or currently are, open. This practice is generally referred to as "recruitment," and if you have been contacted and encouraged to apply, you would have been recruited. A university will conduct a recruitment campaign either to enhance the applicant pool or to ensure that individuals perceived to have particular skills or talents are aware of the position opening and will consider submitting an application.

At this point, a few questions must be asked: What happens to an application from an individual who is not recruited? Will it receive equal consideration as compared to an application from someone who has been recruited? Should an individual not recruited even bother to apply? The good news is that all applications are to receive equal treatment. By law, institutions receiving state and federal funding must consider all applicants equally. This is a practice also followed by many privately funded institutions, even though it may not be mandated. Quality institutions follow established applicant review guidelines. Equality and fairness are paramount within these guidelines. So, even if you weren't recruited, you should still apply if you fit the job description criteria. The search committee's task is to find the most qualified individual for the open position regardless of whether s/he was recruited.

Often your adviser, other faculty members, or colleagues will encourage you to apply for a particular position. When encouraged to apply for a position, it is important to recognize that this individual acknowledges your qualities and sees them as fulfilling those of the job description. While you may not ultimately apply for that particular position, it would be of value to ascertain what qualities others see in you that led them to their endorsement. Your strengths are those perceived by yourself and by others. The way others view your abilities will offer insight into how you are perceived in the field.

A final application consideration is to ascertain whether you are truly qualified for a position. While this topic has already been broached briefly, it is certainly worth repeating. Each position offered by public institutions includes the job description minimum criteria, or "cut" criteria. Applicants must meet the minimum criteria to be considered for candidacy. Public universities and private institutions that receive any type of federal funds, including research grant monies, must adhere to guidelines provided by affirmative action, human services, human resources, or equal employment opportunity offices. Failure to follow these guidelines can result in serious negative ramifications for the department, school, college, or university. It bears noting that while many private institutions follow such guidelines, some do not; some private institutions can consider an applicant, even if they do not meet minimum criteria.

Some individuals feel that even though they don't meet minimum criteria, they might have a chance at securing the position, and therefore submit an application. This may be a feasible strategy if you are applying to a private university; however, it is highly unlikely that candidates will be considered for positions for which they are not even minimally qualified. As an overall strategy, it is best to focus your attention on positions for which you are clearly qualified and meet minimum criteria. By doing so, you will have more time to prepare your cover letter and other materials for a limited number of positions that, hopefully, will help you create a stronger application packet. As we discuss the application submission and review procedure, we will operate on the premise that each candidate must meet all *cut criteria* to be considered for the announced position.

The Application: The Clock Begins

Let's assume you have received a job announcement for a position for which you qualify and would like to be considered. You have submitted your materials a month before the announcement deadline or best consideration date. If your application was not submitted electronically, it most likely was directed to some office that maintains submissions for all schools or for that particular department. If your application materials were submitted electronically, your submission would most likely be electronically housed at a central university location, and you would have received an automated generic email indicating receipt of those materials. Provided your application was complete when you filed electronically, you most likely would not receive any further correspondence until after the position consideration date.

If your materials were not submitted electronically, you likely sent copies of your CV and other documents via USPS, UPS, FedEx, or a similar carrier. For this "paper" application procedure, you would have been directed to send application materials to either a university office—such as the human services or human resources office or the office of personnel—or perhaps an office in the department in which the position is being offered (most likely the director's office). In some cases, applications are sent to the search committee chair but are housed in another location within the department or school. Rarely are applications held in faculty offices, for security and access reasons. Smaller colleges and universities tend to have all paper applications for faculty—regardless of discipline—sent to a central office for processing, while larger universities tend to handle paper applications within the respective department or school. Regardless of where paper applications are sent or held, they usually undergo one or more of the following procedures:

1. Application materials are placed in labeled files, categorized, and separated by position. (This becomes necessary when more than one position search is being conducted by the same school or department.)

2. Each file is verified for completeness using a check-off sheet on which the receipt of required items is noted by date.

3. The applicant's contact information is recorded.

4. Letters of receipt are sent to each applicant.

5. Applicants with incomplete files are notified of the materials still needed to complete their applications.

6. As applicants send additional materials to complete or supplement their applications, these items are added to their files.

7. Usually application submission triggers an automatic form sent by an affirmative action, human services, human resources, or equal employment opportunity office. To complete the form, you are requested to provide basic demographic information such as gender, race, and so forth. While this response is often perceived as a positive indication that the search committee is specifically interested in your application materials, the search committee is often unaware of when or if the form is sent. The information you provide is not shared with the committee, and whether or not you elect to complete and return the form, it has no bearing on your application. More discussion on the use of information gathered by this office is discussed in Chapter 6.

FORMATION OF A SEARCH COMMITTEE

Generally, prior to the application process, a search committee is formed. The head of the school or department usually chooses the search committee members. These individuals most often represent members of the department that is offering the position, such as music education, strings, conducting, and so forth, plus select faculty from other departments who are perceived to be able to provide additional input and perspective. From this pool of individuals one member is chosen to chair the committee. Typical chair duties can include: calling and organizing meetings, contacting applicants, assisting in formulating search criteria, writing the job announcement itself, and so forth.

Once a search committee is formed, it receives a "formal charge," most often from the director, chair, or head of the school (hereafter the leader of the school will be referred to as "director"). The charge generally includes a review of the position and, if already formulated, a review of the advertised criteria for the position. It is not uncommon for the search committee to formulate criteria for the position as one of its first tasks. In either case, the criteria for the position are discussed or reviewed and the members are charged to strictly follow guidelines set forth by their affirmative action, human resources, human services, or equal employment opportunity office. Guidelines are given to the search committee chair prior to the first meeting of the full committee or are presented by a member of the Affirmative Action, Human Resources, Human Services, or Equal Employment Opportunity office during one of the first meetings. Guidelines are reviewed with committee members before looking at any applications. The search committee is informed as to the number of candidates they can bring in for an on-site interview. Procedures regarding reimbursement of committee costs incurred during the search are reviewed, such as meals during on-site interviews, travel expenses, and so forth.

The search committee tasks prior to on-site visits, in addition to initially assisting in the job description formation, normally include, but are not limited to the following:

1. The formation of a checklist of minimum or mandatory *and* desired position criteria. Candidate criteria can be determined and assessed through check-off and rating scales with specific categories and either nominal check-off or assigned point values assigned to each category. Open-ended comment sheets are often used either singly or in combination with other assessment forms to evaluate candidates;

2. Establishing procedures for the review of applications. Generally with electronic submissions committee members have access to all files at any time. With paper submissions, checkout procedures are necessary to provide committee members access to application files;

3. The discussion and formation of a projected calendar of events. The events generally include, but are not limited to, the initiation and completion of the applicant reviews, reference reviews, calls or contacts, telephone or Skype interviews, on-campus interviews, and the final meeting at which the committee recommendation is formulated and then forwarded to the director;

4. The formation of questions to be asked: of references pertaining to the candidate, during telephone or Skype interviews, and during search committee meetings with candidates during on-site visits.

5. The creation of on-site interview activities and schedules or timetables, generally including:
   - a research presentation or recital performance,
   - a teaching presentation or master class or studio teaching presentation,
   - meetings with students (undergraduates or graduates separately or together),

- meetings with faculty at large,
- entrance and exit search committee meetings,
- meetings with the director of the school and dean or assistant dean of the college,
- meetings with external personal such as teachers, performers, artists, directors, and so forth from the community,
- meal gatherings,
- attendance at concerts, exhibits, plays, or other university functions,
- time to spend with a real estate agent, especially if there is a senior hire involved.

THE COMMITTEE'S REVIEW OF APPLICANTS' MATERIALS

The search committee is often very active prior to the position's application closing date. While some activities may not occur until the closing of a position, an active search committee is gearing up for the review process. During the first meeting, in which the actual applicant review process begins, the chair conducts a review of the position criteria and procedures. This meeting is usually held immediately after the position's closing date and often occurs prior to that date.

Often, especially if applications are submitted electronically, committees begin discussing candidates during this first meeting. Electronic submissions are generally available for individual committee member review immediately upon receipt, once access codes are available to committee members. The purpose of the first applicant review meeting is to review and establish procedures in order to narrow the field of candidates for further consideration. The narrowing of candidates from a large pool to a smaller pool is completed in various ways. All use, to some degree, the minimum position criteria as cut criteria to help refine the candidate pool, along with other criteria that appear in the job announcement. Once a group of individuals has been identified as qualified according to the position criteria, it is referred to as a "final pool."

GETTING TO THE FINAL POOL

The process of an individual securing a place in the final pool involves the review of the advertised position criteria in relation to each applicant's qualifications. It is essential that candidates meet the minimum qualification requirements for the position. Cut criteria are usually clearly stated in the job announcement and may be worded as, for example, "The candidate must have...," or "The candidate will hold a degree in..." There may be more than one cut criterion for any position.

Search committees review applicants' materials to determine whether or not minimum qualification requirements are met—a process that usually can be completed expeditiously. The remaining applicants, noted as having met minimum qualifications, are considered for final pool candidacy.

After initial applicant cuts have been made, a more thorough review of materials is conducted for the remaining submissions. In this review, the search committee members are looking for various criteria (teaching or performing experience, international or national exposure, and so forth) to reveal candidates that would be strong contenders for the position. This is where having materials that are well organized, that clearly identify salient elements of your career, is crucial.

Committee members will review each portfolio as thoroughly and quickly as possible. Some committees produce sheets that detail ideal candidate qualities. Members work from such sheets making comments during their review of materials. Others use criteria sheets or check lists that are either provided by the search chair or created by each committee member. As committee members review materials, they formulate positive and negative impressions of applicants within a short time frame. Time is of the essence, as numerous files often need to be reviewed and evaluated in a relatively brief period.

One fact remains constant, top candidates' materials are organized in such a manner that important criteria are highlighted, easily identified, provide carefully selected and categorized information, and reflect professionalism and quality. While perhaps not stated in the job position posting criteria, it would be rare indeed for any search committee not to consider applicant professionalism and quality as reflected through their materials. A manuscript submitted with typing errors or a recording in which numerous rhythmic or technical errors exist will be viewed as careless and unprofessional and reflect poorly on the applicant. All materials submitted are *expected* to be of the *highest quality*. The assumption is that "if submitted, it's your best." It is your task to insure this is the case.

It is unusual that, initially, any committee member has the time to listen to all selections on a CD, read every line in a manuscript, digest each category on a CV, or remember every comment within letters of recommendation. Listening to select sections of a performance, skimming or speed-reading manuscripts or CVs, cover letters, or letters of recommendation is not uncommon at this stage of the candidate review process. While every committee member probably wishes he had more time to devote to each applicant's portfolio, reality dictates otherwise. Therefore, it is *your* task, *not* the committee's, to organize materials so your best qualities are easily and quickly identified. You are in essence "selling yourself" through your portfolio contents and the manner in which those materials are presented.

As the committee continues to review candidates' portfolios, each member begins to form ideas of whom she believes would best fill the position. Once all files have been reviewed, the committee meets to begin the process of selecting the top candidates from the pool. Depending on the number of applications, a final pool may be decided during the first meeting or by the second meeting, although sometimes a third or fourth meeting is needed. Each additional meeting is typically called within a week of the previous meeting when possible, dependent upon the committee members' accessibility. Top final pool selection generally results in a list of between five and fifteen candidates, which is dependent upon the quantity and quality of the applicant pool. Each committee member has a vote in the pool reduction process. While there are various ways to achieve a final pool, the premise is to select top candidates, from all of those who are qualified, for an intense review.

The top final pool candidates—individuals identified by their materials as outstanding candidates—are those who appear highly qualified to perform the position duties. Technically at many institutions, any person in a final pool can be hired and/or interviewed even if the committee does not choose to recommend them. The director, most typically the dean, or any other head, can select an individual from the final pool without committee recommendation for continued review and/or interviewing. Thus, if you are one of the individuals in the final pool, you are considered a viable candidate for the position until the position is filled. Generally, only when a contract is signed will final unsuccessful pool applicants receive a letter informing them that the position has been filled.

Once the final pool has been identified, the next committee task is to narrow that pool further to identify candidates for telephone or Skype interviews or on-site interviews. In order to accomplish this task, committee members are normally assigned to do at least one—if not more—of the following:

1. Contact final pool candidates and request additional review materials when needed to further assess candidate qualifications. Such requests may include recordings, documents, publications, and so forth.
2. Review additional materials already sent or requested and received.
3. Call referees to find out more about the candidates.
4. Call individuals who might know this person at a professional level even if not listed as references.

Generally it is not until after the above procedures have been conducted that a telephone or Skype interview would be conducted. A telephone or Skype interview is not always completed or necessary, but if conducted, it is one of the final steps before determining who should be contacted for an on-site interview.

THE TELEPHONE OR SKYPE INTERVIEW

With the advent of computer communication programs such as Skype, more and more "telephone interviews" are becoming video interviews. And while Skype is only one of many such videoconferencing systems, it will be used in this book to represent all such platforms. The convenience of having both visual and aural exchanges between a candidate and committee members provides advantages a telephone exchange can't offer. Whatever system is used, the purpose of the telephone or Skype interview is to glean additional information or to corroborate data previously submitted.

The purpose of the telephone or video interview such as a Skype interview then, like the call to referees, is to further screen applicants for an on-campus interview. At this point, reference calls have most likely been made and additional materials, if any, have been reviewed. The committee has met and discussed the results of the reference calls and review of materials. Telephone or Skype interviews involve considerable time involvement on behalf of the committee, therefore the candidate pool called for telephone or Skype interviews is generally reduced to three to five individuals and rarely more than ten.

Prior to telephone or Skype interviews, the committee formulates questions for use during all candidate interviews. The process of asking all candidates the same questions allows comparisons to be made among individuals after telephone or Skype interviews are completed. The telephone or Skype interview provides answers to committee-formulated questions that may pertain to candidates' past experiences, work ethics, career goals, and so forth. The questions are typically similar to those asked during an on-campus interview and can be quite specific; these will be discussed in Chapter 5.

It is important to be prepared for a possible telephone or Skype interview for any position to which you have applied. If you are asked to participate in a telephone or Skype interview, you most likely will be notified in advance and provided with times during which the committee is available to conduct the interview. If any of the times presented do not work for your schedule, you can request holding the interview at another time and suggest alternatives. When a common time and date for the interview is determined, confirm all arrangements including the date and time (remember the different times zones), and obtain—if possible—names of the members of the interviewing party. Often the interviewing members comprise a portion of the full committee. Do not agree to participate in a telephone or

Skype interview without preparation. Allow yourself time to organize your materials and thoughts prior to this call. Be physically and mentally prepared.

Physical Preparation

1. Have your CV, the job announcement, and all other application materials you submitted conveniently placed on your desk near your telephone or computer.
2. Have a pen and a tablet available for note taking.
3. Make sure you have a space available in which to isolate yourself—one in which you will not be interrupted by roommates, children, pets, stereo, television, and so forth.
4. If you are having a Skype interview, make sure that your surroundings convey the image you want the committee to see—pleasant background, clean or uncluttered areas, and so forth.
5. Consider using a landline if available to avoid dropped calls or line static. Also turn off such features as call waiting if possible.
6. Have a glass of water available.

Mental Preparation

1. Review the position requirements. You may have applied to several universities; make sure you reacquaint yourself with the specific requirements for that position.
2. Make a list of your accomplishments and skills in relation to the specific position requirements.
3. Practice your responses to various questions (discussed below) that may be asked during the interview. Practice with a colleague, roommate, spouse, or friend. Record these mock telephone interviews. Listen to your responses and presentation, then modify your delivery and responses as you deem appropriate. During your mock interview, practice the following in preparation for the "real" telephone or Skype interview.
   a. Enunciate clearly and speak slowly.
   b. Avoid eating, smoking, chewing gum, and so forth.
   c. Listen carefully to each question and respond succinctly with meaningful and concise answers, which provide complete, inclusive information.
   d. Smile as you talk. Smiling will change the tone of your voice and will most likely project a positive image to the listener.

e. Do not interrupt your interviewer. If you do not hear or understand a question, ask to have it repeated.

f. Take time to prepare your response, if needed, or to collect your thoughts. A moment or two of pause or reflection is acceptable in a telephone or Skype interview. Often after listening to your mock interview you can determine your comfort level in such situations.

g. Avoid "ums," "ahs," "you knows," and other such fillers when responding.

h. Use interviewers' formal titles during your conversation. Titles such as Dr. or Professor are common.

i. Remember to thank the committee member interviewers at the beginning and the end of your interview.

j. Practice taking notes during your interview. Especially notice questions or items that seem of great interest to the committee. When you are asked for an on-site interview, you can use such information to complete additional preparation research into those areas.

k. At the conclusion of your interview and in addition to thanking the committee, ask what the next step in the process will be.

Additional Preparation

1. As mentioned before, try to determine the names of the telephone or Skype interview committee members. Go online and read their biographies. Have that information, along with any photographs of them, accessible on your desk. Learn their names and practice using them in your mock interviews.

2. Research the university, the college, the school, and most importantly the department in which the position is being offered. Learn as much as you can from websites and individuals familiar with the institution and faculty.

3. Become familiar with the research, recordings, and other creative endeavors of the committee members and use this information if or when appropriate.

4. Review the position requirement with an eye toward teaching in that area. For example, if you are applying for a position as a studio instructor you most likely will be asked about:

a. Strategies for recruitment,

b. Your approach to working with students at various levels,

c. Repertoire you might use with students at different levels of ability,

d. Assessment rubrics you would use, and

e. Your philosophy of working with music performance versus education majors, music majors versus music minors, and so forth.

A person applying for an academic position might be asked:

1. If teaching a certain course, what method book might you use and why?
2. What other method books might be considered and available?
3. What types of topics would you cover in a particular course?
4. What type of evaluation system would you use?
5. How might you handle various students and/or problematic situations such as missed exams, excessive missed classes, students not practicing, and so forth?

Prepare as diligently for a telephone or Skype interview as you would an on-campus interview. If this entails writing out responses to various anticipated questions, or preparing note cards with information on them concerning topics, recruitment procedures or ideas, names of method books, your philosophy of teaching, and so forth, then by all means do so. Anticipate as many possible questions as you can, and have prepared questions to ask the committee. Some issues that would be appropriate to address when formulating your questions would pertain to enrollment, types of equipment or facilities available for student use (computers and computer programs, keyboards, practice rooms, instruments, and so forth), student scholarships and/or assistantships, types of events held within the school during the year (concerts, seminars, workshops, symposia, etc.), and goals of the school, department, and faculty.

If possible, form a group of like-minded individuals to conduct mock telephone or Skype interviews. Have them formulate questions from the job description as if they were the interviewing committee and you were the candidate, then reverse roles. Once a mock interview is finished, have your interviewers provide specific and pointed feedback concerning your response and content quality, vocal inflection, and even such things as enthusiasm and excitement level conveyed. Serving as both a "mock" candidate and as an interviewee will provide valuable insight to help you refine your presentations.

PROCEDURES FOLLOWING TELEPHONE OR SKYPE INTERVIEWS AND RECOMMENDATION CALLS

Once all telephone or Skype interviews and recommendation calls have been completed, the committee generally meets to share information. At this point in the search, the basic goal is to decide which candidates to invite for an on-campus interview. If the school can afford to bring in three candidates then the committee will most likely select only three candidates for an on-campus interview. At times however, alternate candidates can be selected in the event that an individual, selected initially for an on-campus interview, is no longer available. While rare, additional candidates may be selected for on-campus interviews after "first round" interviewees have completed their visits.

Candidate names selected for on-campus interviews by the committee are then forwarded to administration. The committee's decision is considered a recommendation and does not bind or commit the administration to act upon that recommendation. The final candidates, once presented to the director, are reviewed. The director assesses the candidates and—sometimes with input from the dean or other administrators—decides to bring one, two, three, or more applicants on-campus for an interview. Depending on the administrative candidate review, either the committee recommendations will be accepted or the committee will be asked to provide additional candidates for consideration. Confirmation of both the number of candidates and often the candidates themselves must be obtained from the dean and reaffirmed by the affirmative action, human services, or equal employment opportunity office. The administrative confirmation process can take from one or two days to one or two weeks. The overall selection of on-campus candidate interviewees can vary widely—sometimes taking as little as a few days to a week or, at times, several weeks.

Either concurrent with the selection of on-campus interviewees or soon thereafter, the committee and/or the committee chair develops an interview schedule. Not only do dates and times for various meetings need to be established, hotels, airline pick-ups, flights, and so forth must all be discussed and coordinated. If the interview process is to cover a two-day period, a daily schedule of events for those two days must be established. The chair and the committee facilitate such events as: meetings with the committee, students, faculty, and administrators, teaching and/or performance venues, meals, concerts, travel from and to airports and the campus, hotel lodging, and so forth for the one- or two-day interview.

It is common that several dates are established on which the interview can be held. The candidates are then called and asked whether they can come for an interview on one of those dates. If there are three candidates, obviously three separate interview time frames must be agreed upon. While the process for selecting and contacting interviewees will vary, the time frame required to do so usually demands a minimum of several days to a couple of weeks to implement.

THE INTERVIEWS

Candidates called for on-campus interviews either have travel plans made for them or most generally are asked to make their own travel arrangements for arrival. (Note: The interview process itself will be discussed in greater detail in Chapters 4 and 5.) Candidates are informed of the activities for which they should prepare during the interview. If a two-day interview process is scheduled for each candidate and three candidates are brought to campus, this process typically will take one and a half to five weeks to complete, dependent on interviewee schedules, university or school schedules (spring breaks, holidays, and so forth), and availability of administrators, committee members, and other such factors.

The search committee is involved in as many aspects of the interview as possible, including viewing research or teaching presentations, attending master classes and recitals, conducting entrance and exit interviews, eating meals with the candidates, and so forth. As committee members gather information on each of the interviewees, notes are often shared formally in brief committee meetings generally before the next interviewee arrives on campus, and certainly after completion of all on-campus interviews.

FINAL MEETING

Once all candidates have interviewed, all information gathered from the interview process is presented, discussed, and evaluated at a final meeting. This meeting is generally called no later than one week after the final interview and frequently is held within days or even hours after the last candidate has left the campus. At this meeting, the committee discusses the candidates' negative and positive attributes. The committee then makes a recommendation to the director. Depending on the administrator, the committee can be charged to recommend none, some, or all of the candidates in either in ranked or unranked order.

The committee, usually the chair, then presents the committee recommendation(s) to their director or dean (their immediate supervisor or administrator). The committee's goal is to provide as much information about each candidate as possible. Often a list of pros and cons on each candidate is constructed and presented in the meeting with the director. Once the search committee has made its recommendations, the director will normally review all candidate materials (CVs, recordings, and so forth). Taking into consideration his or her meeting with each of the candidates and the opinions of the committee, the director selects his or her choices for the position. The director then forwards his or her top choice to the dean for approval. At this point, approval from the appropriate human resources, services, or affirmative action officer is also often needed before an offer can go forward.

The director's recommendation to the dean often includes some general discussion concerning a possible hiring offer package. It is important that both the director and the dean (or the equivalent administrators) be in agreement as to: rank at which a candidate can be brought in, a salary or salary range that can be offered, and other hiring package possibilities that can be extended, such as research funds, computers and equipment, time given toward tenure and promotion, and so forth. Once the dean and the human resources office have concurred with the director's choice, it is then forwarded to the provost (or equivalent administrator) for university hiring approval. Once this approval has been given, the call to make an offer to the chosen candidate can be made and the negotiation process can begin. (Note: The negotiation process will be discussed further in Chapter 6.) The time involved in selecting the top candidate and receiving approval to make an offer of hire can take anywhere from two or three days to two or three weeks.

If you are the candidate chosen to be offered the position, the time elapsed from the submission of your application to an offer of hire may well have taken anywhere from as "little" as one or two months to as long as five or six months. In some "worst-case scenarios" the process can extend beyond six months, to eight months or longer. If you were one of the candidates who had an on-campus interview, it may take as "little" as two to three weeks to discover whether the position was offered and taken by another candidate to four to six weeks, or longer. It is not uncommon for hire offers to be rejected after negotiations. At this point, the position may be offered to the next candidate. Prolonged and/or failed negotiations extend the position status notification time. Eventually however, all candidates are notified of the position status.

Thus, as a candidate, hoping to hear about the status of your application, the wait can be interminable. Hopefully, the information in this chapter has provided you with an idea of the process involved in a university hiring search and the subsequent time lag between application submission and institutional notification concerning your position candidacy status.

While this chapter has briefly outlined the post–telephone or Skype interview procedure, the following chapters provide more information on how to prepare for the on-campus interview, what you can expect at your on-campus interview, and eventually, after you have been offered the position, some guidelines pertaining to the negotiation process. The first step to achieving success at your on-campus interview is preparation, which will be discussed in the next chapter.

4

PREPARING FOR THE CAMPUS INTERVIEW

CONGRATULATIONS! YOU HAVE been asked for an on-campus interview. You are mostly likely experiencing one or more of the following emotions: excitement, nervousness, trepidation, apprehension, panic, expectancy, elation, or a combination of these. Now what? In this chapter, a discussion of the interview process itself will be presented.

Preparing for the Interview

When you are invited for an on-campus interview, you are in essence receiving confirmation that your application materials, contacts made with individuals or referees, and your telephone or Skype (virtual) interview (if you had one) were generally perceived to be positive and strong. Just as you received confirmation that your application and follow-up materials, your "paper trail," were strong (CV, application letter, reference letters, CDs, DVDs, article reprints, transcripts, and so forth), you will additionally know that referees and other individuals when contacted by the committee spoke highly of you, especially if you did not have a virtual interview. If you also had a virtual interview, you not only have reassurance that referees spoke highly of you, but that your virtual interview was strong and positive. You know at this point that at least "on paper," in the eyes of others (your referees and other contacts), and through virtual interview, that you are perceived as a strong potential candidate for the position being offered. Therefore the purpose of the on-campus interview is for the search committee to:

1. Confirm what has been perceived to this point—your strengths in teaching, research or creative activity, and service;

2. Ascertain whether you are a "good fit" with the faculty, school, and university;

3. Assess your potential contributions to the department, school, and university as they relate to their mission and their goals and objectives; and

4. Ascertain your potential for continued success in the field.

Gathering Information

Now that you know your application materials made a good impression, your referees and acquaintances are speaking positively about you, and if you had a telephone or Skype interview, that your style and responses were at least acceptable and perhaps even impressive, it is time to gather additional information about the position.

In the discussion concerning on-campus candidate selection in Chapter 3, you will recall that part of the director, chair, or head's charge to the search committee was to inform them of the number of candidates they could consider being brought on campus for an interview. A relatively common course of action is to bring two or three candidates for on-campus interviews and then, after they have all been interviewed, determine whether any or all of the individuals adequately fulfill the department's needs. Another procedure is to bring one candidate for an interview, meet and decide whether that person should be offered the position, and if not, bring another individual for an interview, until a maximum number of candidates have been interviewed. The committee will, with the information they have gathered, try to determine the most promising, if any, candidate(s) to recommend for the position.

If you are one of two or three candidates being interviewed for a position, you might be wondering if there is an advantage to being the first, second, or third candidate? However, when you are considered for an on-campus interview, you do not generally know if you are the first, second, or third candidate to interview. Hence, this is a moot point for the most part. It is generally thought (Tolan 2009: 1) that, "Interview order doesn't matter—'ordering' has a funny way of being affected by actual interview performance, so again, just do your best and don't overanalyze the small stuff over which you have no control."

Assuming, then, that you are one of the candidates selected for an on-campus interview, you will want to learn as much about the position, the students, the faculty, the school and/or college, and the university, *before* you depart for your interview. Faculty, directors, deans, and other administrators want to know that you are sincerely and seriously interested in the position for which you are interviewing. One way they determine this is by your asking questions about their school, faculty, programs, curriculum, and so forth. Most universities have extensive Internet websites from which you can acquire vast amounts of information about the department, school, and so on. Some universities will send website informaton to their candidates prior to an on-campus interview. Figure 4.1 is an example of such information.

While you may already have a good idea of what you would be teaching, the facilities and equipment you would have available to you, and the level of students with whom you would be working, you will also want to know about additional matters. Some of the information you should gather before your interview is listed below.

1. Committee members: Committee member names are commonly shared with candidates. You should learn about your committee members' backgrounds. Go on the school's website and associate names with photographs. Study each member's area, accomplishments in that area, and research or creative activity interests.
2. Faculty: A listing of faculty by department or area is commonly provided on websites. Learn the names of the individuals in the department offering the position and, as time permits, become familiar with as many other faculty in the school as possible.

University of Miami Bulletin home page:
http://www6.miami.edu/umbulletin/index.html

Frost School of Music Bulletin, main home page:
http://www6.miami.edu/umbulletin/und/mu/index.htm

Music Education/Music Therapy Bulletin for undergraduate programs:
http://www6.miami.edu/umbulletin/und/mu/ed.htm

University of Miami Graduate Programs Bulletin home page:
http://www6.miami.edu/umbulletin/grad/index.htm

Frost School of Music Bulletin for Graduate Programs:
http://www6.miami.edu/umbulletin/grad/mu/index.htm

Frost School of Music homepage:
www.music.miami.edu
On this page, you can click on a "slider" for music education as well as for music therapy. When you click on these sliders, you will be able to watch a video presentation for each program.

Music Education home page:
http://www.miami.edu/index.php/department_of_music_education/

Music Therapy home page:
http://www.miami.edu/index.php/music_therapy/

FIGURE 4.1 Website pages from the University of Miami.

3. Administration: You need to know as much as you can about the administrative personnel: the director, assistant dean, dean, graduate coordinator, and so forth. You may well be interviewing with many of these individuals.

4. Staff: While not as critical during an initial interview, getting to know the staff can be helpful if you have questions during the interview or after you have left the campus. If you know key staff members and can greet them by name, it will help you later if you need to contact them.

5. Programs: Most websites publish their degree program requirements along with other requirements. Become especially aware of those programs in the area of hire and formulate questions you may have pertaining to them. Your knowledge of, and concern for, program development can convey your interest in the position faster than many other means.

6. Tenure and promotion policies: Become familiar with the tenure and promotion guidelines associated with your position. What do you need to receive tenure and promotion? You will be asked directly or indirectly about your knowledge of such procedures, most likely by administrative personnel. Your knowledge of the tenure and promotion process can convey your interest in longevity at the institution as well as your awareness of the factors that lead to long-term employment.

7. Goals and mission statements: Sometimes found in websites, these statements can provide the necessary information to know your "fit" with the existing mission of the school and of the university. Through such statements you can learn where the school's emphasis lies and in what future direction the school sees itself headed. With this information in mind, you can then ask questions about the role each area plays and how it contributes to the mission of the school.

8. Documents: Often schools are willing, upon request, to send you annual, NASM, self-study, NCATE, and other such reviews. These documents hold a wealth of information pertaining to the strengths and weaknesses of the school for which you are applying or interviewing as well as goal and mission statements of the departments and school. Such information can greatly assist you in developing questions that may be asked during your interview.

9. Other: You may also wish to check on the health plans offered by a university. Policies on sabbatical leaves, research support, and so forth should also be investigated. It's never too early to learn about retirement plans. Whether you stay at one university for the remainder of your career or move about frequently, you will want to know the strength of the retirement plan and whether or not you can move retirement funds should you take another position.

The previous items are some of the basic types of information you should gather before your interview. To have a successful interview, you must be prepared to respond intelligently to questions asked of you and to ask intelligent questions. The only way to formulate intelligent responses and questions is to gain information through as many avenues as possible. Thus, be prepared to both answer and ask questions during your interview. Such questions will be presented in Chapter 5.

Travel Plans

Candidates called for on-campus interviews will be informed of prearranged travel plans, or most generally will be asked to make their own travel arrangements. You should be prepared to initially pay for your travel. In most cases you will be reimbursed, but this can take one month or more to occur. If you pay for your travel on a credit card, advance payment may be available by submitting a copy of the "ticket, boarding pass, travel itinerary" and/or the credit card statement to the business manager or similar individual at the interviewing university. However, this may not be common practice. Often, you must meet with a business manager from the school, college, or university when you are on-site and complete forms before the reimbursement process can begin. Once the process begins, payment can take a month or more to "process" and be sent to you.

While not a common practice, some colleges or universities expect you to bear the travel costs of your interview. If you are offered the position, the college or university will then reimburse you, but should you not be offered the position, you may not be reimbursed. By the same token, if you are offered the position and do not accept it, you may not be reimbursed for your travel expenses. Again, this is not a common practice but it does occur. It is best to inquire about travel reimbursement procedures prior to accepting an interview.

The university most often pays expenses incurred while you are on-site. In some instances you may have to initially pay for your accommodation and meals, which are reimbursed at a later date, but generally, rooms, meals, and other accommodations are booked and/or paid for by the school either directly or through committee members, who are then reimbursed by the school. It is important to note that most public institutions do not reimburse some expenses, such as alcohol or extra days spent at the site not associated directly with the interview itself. Again, you should ask before your interview about accommodation and expenses that are reimbursable and those that are not. Often, this type of information will be made available to you, but if not, do not hesitate to ask.

Other expenses incurred during your travel, such as taxi, airport parking, mileage (if you drive to a location), meals while traveling, and so forth, are generally covered by the university, if presented with appropriate documentation. Again, it is better to ask about each university's or school's policy beforehand, so you will be aware of the documentation you will need to secure reimbursement.

Interview Apparel

It is critical that your interview attire, from your first meeting with a university representative to your last, be professionally appropriate. You are making an impression throughout the interview process and your choice of attire is an important component of that impression. During the interview you will definitely be in meetings with students, faculty, and administrative personnel. In addition, you may be asked to participate in concerts, informal gatherings at faculty members' homes, or be involved in a housing tour with a realtor, who is often an associate or friend of a faculty member or administrator. In all of these settings, information is being gathered about you and your deportment and demeanor—all of which is being funneled back to the hiring committee and personnel. From the moment you "get off the plane" to the time you "get back on the plane" you are being evaluated. Your attire will either contribute to or detract from this evaluation or impression. Thus appropriate "interview" attire planning is essential.

What then is appropriate interview apparel? For both males and females, business attire is the most versatile and apposite for an interview. A well-tailored, quality business suit, for both males and females, can be worn exclusively, if desired, to all functions held during the interview. If you prefer not to travel in a business suit or wish to dress less formally for events such as a housing tour, business casual wear is an excellent choice. While quality business suits are sometimes perceived to be somewhat expensive, it is one of the best investments you can make. Well-tailored, quality clothing that is neatly pressed and cleaned, shoes that are polished, and tastefully chosen accessories can help convey the positive image you wish to portray during your interview.

Presentation Preparation

In order for the committee, faculty, students, and administrators to adequately assess your abilities, you will be asked to do one or more of the following: perform; teach in a classroom, studio, or master class setting; present research findings; or other similar tasks. As you plan your presentation(s), it is essential to anticipate your needs. What will you need to successfully present your materials: audio or video equipment, handouts, computer projectors, and so on? What do you, or would you, want the university to provide? For example, if you are a musical performer, will you need an accompanist? If you are giving a lecture, will you need a projector or computer? If presenting research, will you need access the Internet? And so forth. Once you have determined your basic requirements, you must then check with the search committee chair or other appropriate individual to make sure that equipment or personnel to assist you is or will be available.

If handouts need to be made in advance of a presentation, make sure the materials arrive at the interview site well in advance of your visit. Accompanists will also need time to prepare the selections you have chosen to perform: therefore, make sure selections are sent well in advance of your performance. Anticipate as many needs as possible and make any requests well in advance of your interview. Remember, it may not be possible to fulfill all requests, and you may need to modify your presentation(s) based on this finding.

Once you have planned your presentation(s), several practice-runs should be completed to eliminate any errors that may be present in your materials and to establish a comfort level with the delivery of those materials. Your presentations need to be as flawless, engaging, informative, exciting, and in general as professional as possible. Your presentations are a microcosm of your experience, skills, and teaching and learning philosophy. In essence, your interview becomes a snapshot of your approach to teaching and learning as reflected through your professional training and experience. When you have prepared your presentations, ask yourself, "What is the message *I want to leave*? What is the message *I am leaving*?"

In addition to crafting flawless presentations, you also need to be very familiar with them. You must practice transitioning seamlessly from activity to activity without consulting your notes or other references. The interview is a very fluid procedure, and as a candidate you will be expected to move from activity to activity without pause. You may well be expected to perform a recital and immediately proceed to another venue, where you will be expected to talk about the use of dance form in music or present findings concerning the influence of music on societal development. "Warm-ups," if any, are most likely to be brief and time to review notes often does not exist. Hence, it is imperative that successful interviewees be so comfortable and at ease with their presentations that the lack of review, reference to notes, or warm-ups will not adversely affect the outcome. This comfort level needs to be attained in all venues in which you will engage.

At some point prior to your interview you will receive your interview itinerary. Prior to receipt of this itinerary, you will have or should have already been informed of the nature of your presentations, performances, or whatever. But your itinerary will further detail when you will be presenting or performing, when you will be "meeting," and with whom you will be meeting. Your itinerary should further detail when you will be picked up from the airport, when you might be expected to be available for meals, and in general when you might be engaged in activities that are part of, but not necessarily directly related to, the interview itself. Such things as social gatherings, concerts, tours with real estate agents, and so forth should all be detailed in your itinerary. If, after receiving your itinerary, something is not clear to you, do not hesitate to ask for clarification. You want to be, and your host will want you to be, as familiar and comfortable with the interview process as possible prior to your arrival.

One of the groups with which you will be meeting is the interview committee. Most likely you will have at least one if not more meetings with them as a group. You will also interact with individual committee members throughout your various interview venues. If you do not know the members of the interview committee, this is a good time to find out who those individuals will be. As mentioned previously, once you know who is serving on your interview committee, you can go to the institution's or individuals' websites to gain knowledge of their backgrounds and accomplishments. In addition to the committee members, you will be talking with other faculty in the department or school, the director and/or assistant or associate directors, the dean and/or assistant or associate deans, other central administrators, undergraduate and graduate students, faculty from other schools within the college, and perhaps members and supporters from the community.

Depending on the information gathered in preparation for your interview, you will begin to formulate questions about such matters as promotion and tenure criteria, research, travel, performance, or exhibit support, retirement plans, and so forth, mentioned above. Write down these and other questions as they come to you. While some of your questions may eventually be answered due to your own diligence, others may go unanswered or may need clarification. These are questions that most likely are appropriate for inquiry during your interview. Additional information on the types of questions you should be asking *and* the types of questions you will be asked will be discussed in Chapter 5.

Additional Considerations or Interview Preparation Sessions

In lieu of an actual interview, a mock interview can provide valuable information that can help you be more successful. Mock interviews are often conducted in seminars or classes in university settings. Interviewees are often students who are close to or are actively seeking university positions. The interview committee can comprise interested faculty or students or a combination. The setting can be as formal as deemed appropriate to simulate an actual interview situation. Given these parameters, a mock interview may consist of a session in which an interview committee would question the candidate. In addition, a mock interview might include the "candidate" preparing a master class, recital, class teaching, or research session, after which a critique of content and delivery would be discussed. Regardless of the mock-interview format or setting, potential candidates stand to gain a wealth of information pertaining to their readiness for an actual interview. You should complete a mock interview involving as many components of an actual interview as possible. The insight gained from constructive and realistic feedback given by mock committee members will be invaluable to each candidate.

One of the most important points to remember is that "perception becomes reality." The way you are perceived by an individual becomes that person's reality. Mehrabian (1971) believes that people focus on an individual's nonverbal behavior and that nonverbal cues, such as facial expressions, have more bearing in communicating feelings or attitudes to others than the individual's word. Mehrabian believes that positive feelings toward another individual are communicated through nonverbal behaviors such as leaning forward, facing a person directly, touching, standing close or in proximity, using eye contact, and being in a relaxed posture, and that such nonverbal behaviors may be more important than the message being delivered. In addition, Mehrabian believes that some feelings and attributes are conveyed through vocal tone and expression, but not necessary the meaning of the words themselves. Mehrabian developed a formula for the conveyance of feelings and attributes through verbal communication that comprises 7 percent verbal feeling, 38 percent vocal feeling, and 55 percent facial feeling.

Perceptions are formulated based on a variety of criteria, many of which are within your ability to control. Your ability to appear calm and confident, to engage individuals in various settings, and to convey a sense of energy and enthusiasm are in part controllable delivery elements. In their book *The Interview Rehearsal: 7 Steps to Job Winning Interviews Using Acting Skills You Never Knew You Had*, Gottesman and Mauro (1999) discuss ways in which you can hone your delivery skills. Basic delivery rudiments such as posture, proximity, eye contact, gestures, facial expression, and vocal inflection have a great impact how you are perceived. The stronger your delivery basics, the more positively you will be perceived. We shall briefly look at each of these individual elements.

POSTURE AND PROXIMITY

The way we carry ourselves, our posture, can convey the way we feel in a particular situation or reflect our general internal stability. An individual with a downcast head position, slumped shoulders, and collapsed torso conveys someone who is shy, very uncomfortable, nervous, and/or unsure of him- or herself. Conversely, an individual whose body is rigid, whose head is thrust forward, with raised shoulders is perceived as being tense, nervous, and afraid of losing control. Whether this is the reality of the situation or not, our posture conveys a message about our sense of well-being. In an interview, we want to convey a sense of solidity, being in control and being confident. When in a standing position, if our head is upright and balanced, with our body centered and our shoulders relaxed, but neither slouched nor raised, we have the beginnings of what is referred to as an "elevated posture." In an elevated posture our weight is balanced evenly over our legs without locking knees, swaying from side to side, or leaning on one leg. A final elevated posture element is ensuring the arms and hands are not clenched or crossed, not placed in pockets, not fidgeting or wringing, but rather function in a relaxed flowing manner, adding to one's gestures.

An elevated posture should also be maintained when sitting. In an interview there will be several occasions in which you will be seated. The elevated posture in a seated position is maintained when once again our head is balanced and centered, neither thrust forward nor back, and our shoulders are relaxed. When seated in a chair the elevated posture can easily be maintained by sitting toward the front or edge of the chair and leaning slightly forward from the waist. Hands can be placed in the lap or on a surface with a relaxed clasp. For maximum concentration and to again maintain optimum posture, your feet should be shoulder-width apart and be kept flat on the floor.

The elevated posture, in both a standing and seated stance, conveys confidence, poise, and energy. Both the standing and seated elevated posture should be employed whenever you are presenting to a group. It should constantly be practiced and maintained during mock or actual interview situations. The position allows for optimum energy and concentration and portrays a positive image to others. In addition, elevated posture allows individuals to easily employ additional delivery elements essential for optimal results and positive perception.

Proximity can also have a significant impact in your interview. Hall (1990) studied proximity between individuals and suggests there are four categories of personal distance: Intimate (up to 18 inches apart), personal (18–48 inches), social (4–12 feet), and public (12 feet and beyond). Metzler (1977) concludes that a social distance (4–12 feet) will allow for an uninhibited interview. And while the vast majority of your interview contact will be primarily conducted with the social distance guidelines suggested by Hall, you should be prepared to adjust to, feel comfortable in, and prudently use a variety of proximity distances in your meetings and various settings to support your messages.

EYE CONTACT, GESTURES, AND FACIAL EXPRESSION

Other delivery elements that affect perception are eye contact, gestures, facial expression, and vocal inflection. We shall address eye contact next. Maintaining positive eye contact is an important factor in relating to others. Individuals who avoid eye contact, who move their eyes rapidly from side to side or up and down, or maintain a downcast gaze are often perceived as not being as believable, as inviting or welcoming, or as positive and confident as individuals who maintain self-assured eye contact. The components of establishing eye contact are simple. Excellent eye contact consists of periodically taking in all members of a group or class and while doing so establishing individual contact with various members of the group by focusing on one person until they focus on you, at which point you can continue scanning and contacting. As can be seen, establishing positive eye contact is relatively easy to initiate, but many individuals may find it uncomfortable, necessitating further practice.

Gestures help embellish the spoken word. Natural, flowing gestures are those appropriate for the spoken content and support the message being conveyed. If we focus on gestures of the arms and hands, we want movements that are not mechanical or contrived but rather fluid, graceful, meaningful, and supportive. An absence of gestures, or gestures that result from unconscious and/or nervous movements, can seriously impede delivery. Such gestures do not support your message and actually detract from the spoken word. In the same vein, absence of movement, staying in a fixed location, or fixing oneself behind a podium or table tends to inhibit interaction between you and the group, which establishes a physical and a mental barrier between you and your audience. Nervous pacing can produce anxiety or irritation within the group members. Movement that employs change of stance, with varying proximity to the group or individuals, along with upper-body directional change is viewed as inviting and open. It supports the spoken word and encourages positive interchange between you and your audience.

Along with gestures, facial expressions are a major component of nonverbal communication. Even as children, we quickly identified parental facial expressions that conveyed approval, disapproval, sadness, joy or happiness, anger, fear, and so forth. Facial expressions convey a wealth of information to others. Control and awareness of your facial expressions allow you the advantage of knowing what nonverbal message you are communicating. Naturally varying, uncontrived changes of facial muscles, mouth, and eyes are generally perceived as appropriate and positive, while absence of variation or exaggerated and/ or contrived facial movements are questioned for their sincerity. Control and awareness of your facial expressions are invaluable during an interview as you attempt to convey your thoughts, both verbally and nonverbally, in a manner consistent with your intentions.

VOCAL PRODUCTION

So much of what we do in an interview situation is conveyed through the spoken word. While our spoken message is definitely affected by the delivery elements, our vocal inflection can greatly influence our presentation. We've all experienced speakers who are difficult to listen to and we've all heard an exciting speaker, one who is engaging, captivating, and inspiring, keeping us involved and interested throughout a presentation. Plainly stated, an excellent speaker creates interest while a poor speaker causes interest to wane. Using one's voice to enhance a presentation can be compared to a well-composed musical composition. Just as an excellent choral musical work uses dynamic contrast and phrasing, tempo variation, pitch, timbre, and diction and/or articulation to capture an audience, so too can these elements affect spoken vocal delivery.

One of the basic elements that will begin to create excitement and interest in your vocal delivery is the use of dynamics. Obviously, using one dynamic during vocal delivery does not create enthusiasm and may actually generate boredom. As a listener you know how challenging it can become to listen to any type of delivery that is presented at one volume level. Dynamics in music are used to create tension, to set a mood, and to highlight information. Your oral presentations can and should be viewed as the presentation of a musical performance. Think about your message and plan to highlight various sections with appropriate dynamics. And when we speak of dynamics, this also includes diminuendos and crescendos, and their use is equally important in your address. Speak as if you were singing or playing a musical phrase. We are taught early in music training that if a musical idea or phrase goes from a lower to higher pitch we should crescendo and as the pitches go lower, so too should our volume level. Excellent orators keep not only volume in mind, but also dynamics and the aspect of phrasing when presenting. You want to be effortlessly and easily understood without speaking too quietly, being uncomfortably loud, using static unchanging dynamic levels, or by forcing the sound from the throat. A voice well supported by air flow, naturally varying, and with appropriate accents and emphasis is easy to understand and helps engage and captivate the listener. The use of varying dynamics can also add interest to your presentation.

When you combine dynamic contrast and phrasing with tempo variation, your presentations become that much more interesting and you will find that your audience will be more attentive to your message. "Tempo and phrasing" refer to the pace at which information is presented. Speaking too quickly for comprehension or too slowly will cause listeners' interest to wane. A vocal presentation tempo that uses a comprehensible pace and contains moderate variations and appropriate pauses for emphasis will result in higher listener interest and engagement. Therefore, it is of great importance that you vary your vocal presentation tempi throughout your presentations. You may choose to speed your delivery rate to generate excitement or slow it to create emphasis. Occasional use of pauses can be extremely effective in creating tension and also highlighting or placing emphasis on important points. As with a musical phrase, the speaker should treat each idea as a musical phrase adding appropriate dynamics, accents and emphases, and suitable pauses and tempo variations as indicated by the information. If delivered in such a manner, your information will become more interesting and lucid.

Another consideration in your delivery should be pitch. Few things are less exciting than static, monotonous presentations. The pitch of the voice needs to vary naturally for emphasis and to provide for ease of teacher delivery as well as optimum student listening comfort. Additional "color" is added to a presentation when the orator uses pitch variation, but one should be aware that pitch variation must be used with care and judiciousness. Overuse of pitch variation can quickly sound contrived and artificial.

Finally, one of the more important elements in speaking is diction. Clearly enunciating and articulating all consonants and vowels make it easier for the listener to understand you and help you be more easily heard. The use of excellent diction combined with appropriate articulations will enhance the vocal presentation immensely. Using a series of short, accented words in a sentence conveys a different message than saying the same series of words using an elongated and smooth articulation. Avoid "swallowing words, placing them in the back of the throat" and speaking with a lack of resonance and clarity. Focus on clearly articulating each vowel and consonant of every word and delivering each word with a projected and resonating tone.

What you have to say is important. Taking care to make sure you are engaging your audience is eminently important in an interview situation. Using appropriate and varying dynamics, comprehensible tempo and phrasing, along with sufficient pauses and accents for emphasis, will help insure your audience is attentive.

Making sure you are clearly delivering your message is equally important. Suitable pitch along with excellent diction will insure you are conveying, and your audience is correctly receiving, the message you intend. Using various vocal delivery techniques to enhance your presentations is an excellent way to capture your audiences' attention and help them focus on your message. Again, as you prepare for your interview, vocal delivery elements, along with forethought about the way you will be perceived through your posture, eye contact, gestures, and facial expressions, are important considerations in planning interview presentations.

ELEMENTS OF YOUR PRESENTATION

Presentation preparation must include not only delivery techniques but also the materials themselves. When planning every presentation, it is extremely important that you use the basic but effective techniques, which I'll call the "hook," the "overview," the "summary," and the "resummary." The hook is an opening story, activity, question, action, presentation, quote, or even a joke that captures an audience's attention. It's called a hook as it will capture the interest of your listeners. For example, let's say you were going to give a lecture on a famous individual. For your hook you bring in a small, worn, work-shoe. You begin your presentation by showing the group the shoe and proceed to tell them a story about a man who wore this shoe as a child. You talk about a childhood event of this individual, let's say cutting down a cherry tree and the subsequent consequences of this action. The hook introduces your individual in a way that captures your audience's interest.

The hook is brief, as is your overview. The overview basically presents your audience with an outline of your presentation and forecasts the major headings. In our example, you may want to say that you are going to talk about this individual's childhood, his early professional development, his rise to power in the military, and his eventual leadership positions later in life. After your overview, you then begin to talk about each of these headings. Repetition is encouraged to help keep your audience attuned to your outline, so in this example you might wish to say, "I am first going to talk about George's childhood." After you've completed each section, it is important to summarize what you just said and announce the next topic heading. So after summarizing George's childhood you might wish to say, "Now that I've talked about George's childhood, I would like to discuss George's early professional development." You proceed to talk about this area of his life, summarize this section, then say, "Now that I've talked about George's childhood and early professional development, it's time to discuss his rise to power in the military." After each heading, summarize and reannounce your outline topical headings until you've finished your final topic, at which time you briefly summarize each topic discussed. You may wish to reintroduce the shoe again and produce another shoe that represents the aged George and his final accomplishments.

In addition to the flow and sequence of the presentation, you should plan to use various approaches to convey your message. Individuals acquire information through visual, aural, or kinesthetic approaches. For example, some individuals are stronger visual learners than aural or kinesthetic learners, while others may acquire information more quickly through a kinesthetic approach. When you think about the way you will present your information, consider the various ways in which people acquire information, and plan to accommodate the visual, aural, and kinesthetic learners in your audience. Plan activities or incorporate audiovisual systems (CDs, DVDs, PowerPoint presentations, and so forth) to help support your presentation. And of course, practice using all materials thoroughly before your interview.

ENERGY NEEDS

Plan to take some high-energy, nutritional food with you to your interview. As we all have experienced at one time or another while traveling, eating nutritional, well-balanced meals is not always feasible or even a possibility! Flying, or for that matter, any kind of travel, is not conducive to healthy eating. If you are flying to an interview, the chance of you being able to eat much during the trip is slim. Often, especially if you arrive earlier in the day, you may be whisked directly from the airport to the interview site for meetings or presentations. It is a good idea to have some easy-to-consume nutritional foods such as nuts or nutritional bars in your carry-on to eat on your flight. Also, because of the rigors of the interview process and because individuals want to find out as much about you when they have opportunities to converse, eating enough at meals can be challenging. Often during meals, individuals will be asking you many questions. Of course you want to respond to all questions, which can result in not being able to finish your meal or even to feel that you had enough to sustain you. Here again, some high-energy foods packed in your luggage will help you "refuel" when you return to your lodging after a long, tiring but rewarding day of interviewing. Another important interview consideration concerns hydration. Through the process of interviewing (talking, moving, walking, and so forth) you will not only be expending energy but also fluids. It is very important to remain hydrated during your interview. And while you should take care to avoid flopping a water bottle out of a briefcase every few minutes, judiciously consuming water at opportune times is essential. Plan to take bottled water on your flight and if possible to your interview.

Another type of energy need is that obtained through mental prepared-ness. The mock interview process can be invaluable to mentally prepare for an interview. Also, reexamining possible interview questions and going over your responses to them, reviewing the information you've gathered about the uni-versity and the school faculty at which you are interviewing, reading the job description, and so forth are all excellent mental exercises to perform in prepa-ration for your interview.

The use of mental visualization can be helpful in preparing for your interview. Mentally visualize your presentations: see yourself poised and confident in front of your group during your presentation. Visualize yourself in various groups and one-on-one meetings with the search committee, the school director or chair, or the college dean. Visualize yourself as confident, self-assured, calm, and in control.

The night before the interview, spend some time with a friend or family mem-ber, telling them why you would be the best candidate for the position. The pur-pose of such a dialogue is to put you in the right frame of mind for the interview, so *you believe* you are the best possible person for the job. You must believe in your-self if you expect others to believe in you. Of course appropriate rest and sleep are important to be in peak mental and physical condition. Such things as exercising, performing yoga, getting a massage, and other practices can help you be at your utmost mental and physical peak for an interview.

References

Gottesman, Deb, and Buzz Mauro. 1999. *The interview rehearsal: 7 steps to job winning interviews using acting skills you never knew you had.* New York, NY: Berkley.

Hall, Edward T. 1990. *The hidden dimension.* New York: Anchor.

Mehrabian, Albert. 1971. *Silent messages.* Belmont, CA: Wadsworth.

Metzler, Ken. 1977. *Creative interviewing: The writer's guide to gathering information by asking questions.* Englewood Cliffs, NJ: Prentice-Hall.

Tolan, Tim. 2009. The batting (interview) order—Does it really matter? http://www.healthcare-informatics.com/blogs/tim/batting-interview-order-does-it-really-matter, accessed February 23, 2010.

What is a model interview?...It's an interview that
defines a specific purpose—a specific set of data to be
obtained—and then proceeds through conversation to
fulfill the purpose. (Metzler 1977: 9)

5

THE INTERVIEW

THE DAY HAS arrived, your presentation materials are complete and your questions organized. You have captured the interest of the search committee members and administrative team and are now on your way to the interview site. Your immediate task is to convince the search committee team that their interest in you was well founded. Trust that they will be scrutinizing and evaluating what you do and say, how you do and say things, and how you react to things that are said and done. You are in fact auditioning for a job and this is your stage—your audition. Your best is the only acceptable level at which you can perform if you want to secure the position. Not only will you want to review the questions that will be presented in this chapter, there are other things you should and must consider, such as awareness of your deportment from the moment you arrive to the time you leave.

What do you need to know, now that you have accepted your interview? Hopefully, you've planned well for the interview by preparing your presentations, whether they be performances, teaching episodes, research presentations, or so forth. Also, you've hopefully read about and researched the school and the faculty and have contacted individuals who have provided you with additional information. In this chapter we are going to review some of the possible questions that could be asked by the interview committee, students, or other faculty or community members that you will encounter. Possible questions posed by administrators will also be presented, as well as their expectations of you. First, a discussion of the interview itself, focusing on what should and can be expected in an interview, what types of things are being observed and noted, and how you should present yourself in the various settings.

THE INTERVIEW

You will most likely have an itinerary of your interview schedule and will know when you will be meeting with the search committee. The meeting with the search committee is often one of the first—if not the first—meeting you will encounter during your interview. It is not uncommon for the search committee to schedule a meeting with you prior to any other sessions and then an exit meeting after most or all sessions have been completed. Such pre and post meetings allow the committee to ask questions prior to and then after observing your presentations, to receive feedback from you, and to provide you the opportunity to meet the search committee members, ask any questions you may have before and/or after your interview events, and help clarify any issues that may exist. The following, see figure 5.1, is an example of an interview itinerary.

Dr. Harry Hill
Tuesday, February 22—Wednesday February 23

Time	Description	Location
Tuesday, February 22		
7:30pm	Dinner	Allegro Ponce 2530 Allegro Blvd Clinton, PA 288.663.8668
Wednesday, February 23		
7:30-8:30am	Breakfast with Committee Chair	Sir George Golf Course Pick up at hotel 7:30am Meet in lobby
9:00-10:00am	Meet with Dean Kelly Smith	Dean's Office Tillin Hall
10:00-10:30	Tour of Jiller School	Perm Bldg., Tillin Hall
11:30am-1:00pm	Lunch with Executive Council	Faculty Club
1:00-2:00pm	Research Presentation	Lilly Conference Room
2:00-3:00pm	Meet with Students	Lilly Conference Room
3:00-4:00pm	Meet with Faculty and Search Committee	Lilly Conference Room
4:00-5:00pm	Open	
5:00-6:00pm	Class Presentation	Room 254
6:00	Return to Hotel	
7:00	Dinner with Search Committee	Waltz Steak & Seafood 3333Allegro Blvd Clinton, PA 288.663.9898

Accommodations: Courtyard Marriott, Clinton, PA 288.663.2301. Confirmation Number: 8769444376
Hotel Shuttle: Available at curb outside of baggage claim.
Contact Info: George Fritz—777.222.9999(C), 288.663.0745 (O), fritz.g@gmail.com

FIGURE 5.1 Interview itinerary

Perhaps one of the first questions your search committee will ask is, "Why are you are interested in this job?" In other words, what aspects of the position interest you and why? What is it about the department, the faculty in the department, the school, the faculty in the school, the university, and/or the locale that you finding appealing, attractive, exciting, or fascinating? They will want to determine the incentive for your position application. Often your response will be a strong determining factor toward position consideration.

In addition to *your* interest in the position, the committee members will want to determine what you would and/or could bring to the community, university, school, department, faculty, and students in terms of expertise, public relations skills, potential recruitment ability, and ability to enhance the department while working collegially with all faculty. In this task, one of the primary factors the committee will be considering is "fit." They will be determining how well you could perform the job, interact with the existing faculty, work with students, and network with the community. They will want to know how easy it would be to work with you and to determine how flexible your instructional delivery and working relationships would be.

Of interest will be your recruitment ability, your potential to draw and attract the finest students to your area and to the school. What have you done and/or what will you be doing that will appeal to students? What kinds of activities would you most likely be engaged in at an international, national, regional, or state and local level that potential students would find noteworthy? How would you balance these activities with teaching and service responsibilities and expectations? In other words, how would you accomplish your agenda while maintaining an appropriate teaching load and performing your share of committee work? How will you, in essence, be a *star* and a *team player* for the school—be able to promote yourself and still be modest and not overbearing—be interested in national and international venues while significantly contributing to state and local events?

In addition to your search committee meeting(s), the interview will involve meetings with the director (head) of the school, the dean of the college or his/her representative, a business manager, and perhaps community members, as well as separate meetings with students (perhaps individual meetings with undergraduate and graduate students) and faculty within the school. Your ability to work with students will be assessed in some manner, whether it be through a class teaching presentation, master class coaching setting, conducting an ensemble, or providing a private studio lesson. Especially if you are interviewing at a research-intensive university in which research and creative activities play an important role in obtaining promotion and tenure, you will be expected to highlight, in some fashion, that expertise. Whether through a performance, a research presentation or other venue, your research or creative activities will be considered.

The interview typically spans a period of at least one day and often two days, depending on the institution and the intensity and rigor of the interview itself. You should expect, from a thorough interviewer, to spend at least a "full" day or two days on the campus. You will be involved in sessions in which you will have been asked to teach and/or display your research or creative expertise. In addition to meals, informal gatherings such as "meet and greet" faculty get-togethers, concerts, exhibits, or theater productions, your days may be further filled with campus tours and cursory excursions into the community with a real estate agent to view housing. Whether you are at a meal, waiting to enter a theater production, washing your hands in a rest room, walking down the hallway, talking with a secretary, or riding in a car to or from an airport, your conversations will be noted. Your interview will be full and rich, simultaneously exhausting and stimulating, and certainly revealing and illuminating.

This is in essence the interview. The aspects of the interview that need additional attention at this point pertain to the types of questions you will likely be asked as well as the expectations of the hiring team, specifically the administrative personnel.

While it may be impossible to anticipate every question asked in an interview, reviewing and answering questions—such as the ones that follow—can help you prepare for a myriad of inquiries you will encounter. The way you respond to questions and what you incorporate in your responses often includes more information than what is actually asked in the original question. In other words, a well-crafted question not only elicits specific information about a candidate, it also helps reveal the philosophy of that individual, his/her thinking about broader issues, and so forth. Often the answer to the question asked may not be of as much interest as *how* the question is answered. For example, if asked to describe what you liked or disliked in your teaching experience to date and you begin with, "I didn't like this," or "I wish students were better trained," or "I lacked appropriate facilities to provide proper instruction," the committee will note that you tended to focus on what you didn't like rather than what you did like.

Perhaps one of the best ways to prepare yourself for interview questions is to first be secure and confident about your philosophy of education. As discussed earlier, your philosophy of education encompasses your teaching approach (instructional preparation and delivery system), your belief in the way individuals learn (learning theory), the manner in which you interact with others (faculty, students, administration), your approach to evaluation of your teaching effectiveness and the learning effectiveness of those you teach (reflection), the way you organize and conceptualize materials, the way you view things, personal qualities, and so forth.

POTENTIAL INTERVIEW QUESTIONS AND FOCUS AREAS

The following is a list of questions that, while not probably worded identically, are frequently asked during interviews. For ease of review, questions have been organized according to the topics that follow. While some of the questions overlap and could logically be put under other headings, the point of the grouping is to provide some systematic ordering. The order of the question groupings has no bearing on their importance nor on the order they may be asked during an interview. The questions included are not intended to be exhaustive but are provided to help stimulate thinking about your responses to potential questions. Vick and Furlong (2008) and Kuther (2010) contain general questions that may be asked at an interview. Additionally, there are several internet sites that provide potential university interview questions. The following is just a small sample of available site listings:

http://www.hr.arizona.edu/successful_searches/interview_questions,
http:// www.lewisu.edu/resources/careerservices/interview.htm,
http://students.msbcollege. edu/CareerServices/jobsearchtools/Interview.aspx,
   and
http://gradschool.about.com/cs/academicsearch/a/facint.htm.

The headings under which questions in this chapter are categorized are as follows:

1. The teaching-learning process,
2. Ideals and philosophy,
3. Yourself and the position, and
4. Research and creative activity.

The Teaching and Learning Process

- Remembering one of the most successful lessons you have given, would you explain why that lesson was successful and in so doing can you highlight that success in relation to your use of technology, learning theory, delivery or approach, and organizational techniques?
- Can you describe some of the evaluation systems you have used in your teaching to date in relation to student evaluation? Can you explain the strengths and weaknesses of those approaches?

- Describe the type of class goals and objectives, content, and student experiences you would include in a _____ course. What textbooks might or would you use in this course and why?
- Discuss your teaching experience to date and describe what you liked and what you disliked about that experience? What was rewarding about your teaching experience and what was not rewarding? What changes would have made your experiences more rewarding?
- This position involves teaching _____. Tell us what topics you might or would include in this subject or these subjects. Are there other topics that might be important but that you would not include due to time limitations?
- Can you tell us about one of your most challenging teaching episodes while working with a student or students and how you handled and resolved that situation?
- Tell us how you incorporate multicultural education, technology, and diversity ideas and concepts into your studio, classroom, or rehearsal.
- Can you describe one of your typical classroom presentations or studio or rehearsal teaching episodes?
- How do you evaluate your students' work? Describe the approach or approaches you use to evaluate students, and explain why you use that approach or those approaches.
- If a student is failing in your classroom or studio what are some of the causes that might have contributed to that failure?
- You have enough time to work with only one student but two students need your assistance. One student is failing and needs your help to possibly avoid being dropped from the program and the other student needs your help to develop a great book or performance technique that could significantly contribute to the profession. Which student would you assist and why? Choose only *one* student and present your rationale for assisting that student.
- Do you feel you are responsible for your students' success? Explain.
- How much do you feel you contribute to your students' success?
- What teaching techniques and strategies have you used that were effective in helping students master content and skills in your classroom or studio? How did you determine those techniques and strategies were successful?
- Describe one of the most creative lessons you presented and explain why you felt that lesson was creative.
- Are you an effective teacher? How did you come to this conclusion? Explain.

- If a student in your classroom or studio is struggling:
  1. Do you feel you are responsible for the student struggling or do you feel the responsibility is a result of the student's action?
  2. What techniques, creative strategies, and approaches could you use to help that student?
  3. Do you "go out of your way" to assist a student that is struggling in your classroom or studio?
- How do you support students in your classroom or studio who are highly successful? For example: Do you offer extra time and assistance outside of the normal classroom or studio setting? Explain.
- Outside of the university or college grading system, how else do you evaluate student success? Tell us about some identifying factors that would indicate student success.
- How do you know that a student or students understand something you are presenting without testing them or using some other type of external evaluation?
- How do you keep students actively involved in your classroom or studio? Describe some of the techniques, approaches, or activities you use to do so.
- How do you address different learning styles of your students? Describe approaches you use to accommodate these various learning styles.
- How do you begin and end a typical presentation or lesson?
- How do you insure your students' goals and objectives are being met simultaneously with your goals and objectives for the students?
- What is the one "thing" you can feel confident all students will take away from your classroom, studio, or rehearsal at the end of the semester, term, year, or degree?
- How do you structure your classroom presentations, studio lessons, or rehearsals?
- Do you feel you are responsible for student motivation? Explain.
- If I were to walk into your classroom, rehearsal, or studio, what kinds of activities, instructional strategies, techniques, and so forth might I see?
- Can you tell us about a recent instructional technique or technical aid you have used that you believe improved student understanding?
- Given a student who is having difficulty, what would or could you do to help this individual?
- Out of the multitude of materials that could be taught, how do you determine what topics are essential for student learning?
- Have you have changed your lesson plan preparation and lesson delivery as you have gained teaching experience? Explain.

- If students say you are a teacher who is fair, what do you think they mean?
- Please describe your assessment plan in individual (studio settings) and group settings.
- Can you describe one of your most exciting and inspirational lessons and explain what made it so?
- If you have ever deviated from one of your lesson plans, can you explain why you did so?

Ideals and Philosophy

- Why is music, art, theater [your particular discipline] important?
- Why do you think we should study theory, history, or [your area within the discipline]?
- What is your philosophy of teaching, performance, research, or service?
- What is an outstanding teacher, performer, or artist? How would you describe them? What qualities or attributes would they possess?
- Based on your experiences to date, how would you describe the type of person you *most* enjoyed working with and then describe the type of individual you *least* enjoyed working with?
- What is success? How do you define success? What is the determinate that indicates you have been successful?
- How do you think people would respond when asked what they *most* enjoyed and what they *least* enjoyed when working with you?
- How would students who have studied with you describe you as a teacher?
- How would you like your students to view you as a teacher? What qualities would you most like them to have of you as a teacher?
- What aspects of this position would best fit your idea of ideal employment?
- Would you describe your ideal teaching position?
- Part of this position involves community outreach and involvement. Describe how you will effectively communicate with the community and describe some activities you would or could engage in to accomplish this goal.
- What qualities do you value most in your students?
- If I were a student why would I want to be in your studio, classroom, or ensemble?
- Do you have a preference for teaching undergraduate or graduate students? Why?
- What do you feel is important to know about your students? Why?

- Describe your most challenging experience working with a group or an individual?
- Can you describe a current educational trend you consider important and explain how you could implement or have implemented it in your teaching?
- Can you describe an instance when you used information gleaned from research studies in your teaching? Describe the information that you used and how and why you incorporated it.
- How would you deal with a student who has a lot of potential but doesn't seem to be showing sufficient achievement or development?

Yourself and the Position

- How do you see yourself fitting into this faculty?
- Why should we consider making you an offer for this position?
- What attributes do you bring to this position that distinguish you from other candidates?
- Collaboration and interdisciplinary activities are very important at this university. Can you describe a recent project or activity in which you collaborated with colleagues in other disciplines, or could you describe a project that would involve such activity, one that you could implement?
- What would your reference providers, students, colleagues, or teachers say about you?
- What one word would you use to describe yourself and explain why you chose that word?
- If you had five words to describe yourself what would they be?
- If you tailor-made a position for yourself, what would it be?
- What is one of your areas of weakness and what are you doing to eliminate or remove it?
- Why did you want to be a teacher, a performer, a conductor, composer, etc.?
- What gives you satisfaction in your teaching?
- What gives you satisfaction in your research or creative activity?
- Does service activity help fulfill one of your professional goals? If so, please explain.
- How would you describe yourself, more as a team player or an individual achiever?
- What is the greatest strength you will bring to this position?
- What is one of the areas you foresee you would need to strengthen if offered this position?

- How would you like to grow in this position?
- What has attracted you to this university or this position?
- Please describe your system for student retention. What techniques or approaches have you used?
- Can you describe the various successful recruitment techniques you have used and those that haven't been successful?
- Can you describe some innovative recruitment activities you would like to implement?
- Assuming you were hired for this position what changes might we see in the program and in the students after one year, five years, and ten years?
- Do you have any questions for the group?
- Do you feel qualified to teach _____ [something outside your area of direct expertise]?
- Based on your observations to this point, are there any changes in our program that you would like to see or that you would like to incorporate?
- What is your response if a student doesn't like a musical selection that is scheduled for presentation or performance?
- How do you view outreach activities in the community?
- How would you describe your relationship with faculty and students?
- Where do you see yourself in five years? In ten years?
- How do you view the relationship between studio, classroom, and ensemble instructors?

Research and Creative Activity

- What is your current research, performance, or creative agenda?
- What is some of the current research being done in your area?
- Who are some of the leaders in your area of expertise? Why are they considered leaders? Why do you consider them leaders? Do these individuals have different qualities than you?
- Can you describe what your performance, research, or creative venue would be like in five years? In ten years? How might it differ from your current performance or research venue?
- What are some current trends in your (particular discipline)?
- How is your research, performance, or creative endeavor unique within the profession and what makes your creative work distinctive within your field?
- How do your creative endeavors contribute to the field?

- What is your plan to distinguish yourself among your colleagues through your research or creative activities?

Your interview committee members, as well as other members of the faculty, community, and students, will be asking questions of you in formal and informal sessions. You can expect to respond to questions such as those presented previously, as well as many others. Again, it is important that you are secure with your philosophy and your approach to teaching and learning as it will serve you well in your formulating your responses.

In addition to individual meetings and presentations involving faculty, students, and possibly community members, you will undoubtedly be involved in meetings with administrative personnel. The two most likely meetings you will have with administrative personnel will be one with the head of the school (a director or chair) and one with the head (usually a dean) of a larger division (usually a college) in which the school resides. In some instances, the school itself is a college and is one of several colleges within the campus. Regardless of the administrative formation, you mostly likely will have interviews with these two heads. For discussion purposes I shall refer to the unit in which you are interviewing as the "school" and the head of that unit the "director." Further, I shall refer to the larger division in which the school resides as the "college" and the head of that unit, the "dean."

Now that we have this understanding, it is important that you know what these administrative heads may be looking for and the types of questions they will likely ask. Additionally, you should know what you should—and may even be expected to—ask them. The interview committee, students, and faculty are often are interested in different aspects of your qualifications than administrators. In this next section we will discuss the director's and dean's perspectives of your interview.

Directors and Deans

WHAT ARE THEY LOOKING FOR? ABILITY, POTENTIAL, CHARISMA?

What are directors and deans looking for in potential faculty hires? The dean and director are trying to ascertain whether the candidate will work well with his/her colleagues, students, and administration. This is often referred to as "fit." Basically, fit is the ability or perceived ability of a candidate to be comfortable and thrive within various settings, whether social or professional. Administrators want to determine whether others will want to spend time with an individual and whether the candidate displays respect for his/her colleagues, students, and administration. They not only want to know about a candidate's fit with students, staff, faculty, and other administration, the director and dean must also determine whether an individual will be compatible with the school's and university's mission. If the university has a strong research mission, is the individual in harmony with that mission? Does s/he have the potential to prosper given the mission of the school or university? The same concern is sometimes considered when viewing the community. If the university setting is within a rural area and the individual being interviewed is from a large urban area will that individual prosper in such a setting? Will the candidate flourish within the community setting in which the university sits? In general, administrators try to ascertain whether the candidate's personality, general interests, and teaching and research interests will be compatible with those of the school or university and the community. While the director and dean will each make individual assessments concerning these factors, a director will almost certainly consider the search committee's view and the dean will consider the director's view to determine the candidate's "potential appropriateness" for the position, situation, or setting.

An important element administrators seek is the candidate's ability to assist with the growth of a department, school, or college. The following question may be asked, "What will this individual bring to the unit, the school, the college?" Both the dean and director want to know how an individual can: (1) Aid and facilitate departmental growth and development, and (2) Be a supportive and productive member within the unit, school, or college. So in essence there are several factors being considered:

1. The candidate's ability to support and enhance the existing unit, school, or college,
2. The candidate's potential to be productive within that unit, school, or college, and
3. The candidate's charisma or ability to convey excitement in his/her field to students, colleagues, and others.

Let's look at the first issue, a candidate's potential or ability to support and enhance the existing unit.

One question that administrators seek to answer is whether the candidate will be able to assist and support the current faculty or unit.

- How will s/he expand or challenge the program? Does this person match the institutional needs and mission?

- Do they fulfill the needs of the position? What else can they do? Could they perform other duties if departmental needs change?
- Will they be able to take an appropriate share of the departmental load—courses, service on committees, advising, and so forth?

Deans and directors are assessing a candidate's potential to be productive within that unit, school, or college and often are seeking an entrepreneur—an individual or "engine," if you will—who could stimulate and excite an area or school. This may be especially true when a senior-level position is being filled. The director is looking for an individual who has compatibility within the school and one who is able to inspire students and faculty alike; one who can lead by example; one who has the insight to take what exists and create something new and exciting. We've all heard about Nobel Prize winners, individuals who not only create for world good but also simultaneously inspire and enthuse their colleagues in the process. They stimulate and excite others and are a catalyst for positive growth and change. And while an entrepreneur may even be a drain on the time, energy, or attention of the director—with many needs and requests—and even though it may be understood that such an individual will likely seek employment elsewhere after a period of time, it is often this type of individual a director most often seeks.

Barring the necessity for an entrepreneur, administrators most certainly are considering the candidate's potential to obtain tenure and promotion. During an interview, administrators will pose questions that will seek answers to questions that may have already been asked by faculty or students. However, the administrators' perspective may well be different than that of faculty or students.

- Can this individual gain tenure and promotion at our institution as an incoming faculty member?
- If the individual is not able to secure tenure and promotion upon initial hire, does s/he seem to have the potential and capability to do so when the decision will be made?
- If s/he has not taught before, what potential is there for growth in the areas of teaching?
- What research or creative expertise and track record of publications or performances does this individual bring to the position? Based on past performance, will s/he seemingly continue to produce in this area?
- What qualities does this individual display that would support a decision to hire?

- What has this candidate done that would lead one to believe s/he will be successful at this institution?
- What will this individual seemingly be doing in five or ten years? What type of plan does s/he have for continued success in his/her field?

Directors are seeking individuals who can work well within units and departments, support the faculty, and prosper within this framework. But of equal importance is the candidate's pedagogical teaching style. In other words administrators are assessing the candidate's charisma or ability to convey excitement in her field and to inspire students, colleagues, and others. They are seeking to evaluate the pedagogical style of the individual, as well as the interaction between her and students. They want to determine how she will perform, teach, and interact in a classroom or studio setting. To determine this quality a director will generally attend the beginning of any teaching presentation. The first five minutes of any presentation, in which there is a teaching presentation, evaluation, or interaction, will inform the director of that individual's pedagogical style. This occurs through body language, speech, proximity, gestures, and other delivery and interaction techniques used by the candidate.

A quality that administrators assess is the candidate's ability to convey excitement about his field to students, colleagues, and others. In other words, does this individual have a magnetism that attracts others to that personality based on their knowledge of the field? Will he be able to draw recruits to this university when talking about their discipline? Do they make their discipline sound exciting, interesting, and understandable? Can this individual convey knowledge, enthusiasm, and passion for the discipline and hold the attention of the director or dean in conversations about his discipline? Administrators look at the *way* in which candidates show enthusiasm for the field and whether they can pass that enthusiasm on to others, and how they can recruit for the school.

It is important that you know something about the unit, school, college, and university to which you have applied. Administrators may assess your interest in a position based on the knowledge you have not only of the position, but of the school, college, and university. Another way administrators assess your interest is noting how many times you talk about the university position and the goals of the school. In other words how you can or could contribute to the position rather than talking about how the position could benefit you. Thus, you may be asked what you know about the institution, its mission, its standing, and so forth, and about the type of contribution you could make to that mission. The amount of information you've assimilated regarding the faculty, school, college, and university will proportionally convey your interest in the position itself. You are, in the eyes of most administrators, joining a team and they are interested in what you know about that team and whether or not you've thought about your potential role in this team.

In one way or another both the director and the dean will determine whether you are a team player, a prima donna, a "star," a loner, or any combination thereof. While an entrepreneur may at times be sought, rarely do administrators want to alienate the current faculty by hiring an individual who is uncooperative, unsupportive, not willing to work as a member of a group, or one whose actions convey a sense of superiority to her colleagues. And yet, administrators try to get the "best person for the money," especially for positions such as endowed professorships, knowing that if they do hire a "star," she may not stay at the institution for a long time—they are not necessarily "hiring for life." However, if a star is too needy, they soon become a negative influence. Also, at times administrators believe that some faculty members may not want a star because stars may raise the bar or standards to a level higher than some faculty wish it to be. Thus, regardless of the position being filled, it is up to the administrators to determine what strengths someone brings, the energy level that she puts forth, the impact she will have on and with the faculty, and whether or not the candidate has the potential to "put them on the map" and still carry a customary load and become "part of the team." They will be asking questions that help them determine the following:

1. What you would add to the existing mix,
2. How you could enhance the department,
3. What your attitude would be if asked to carry a normal load, and
4. Whether or not you would be perceived as needy, drawing off funds and monies from others for your own wants or needs, making others carry more load because of release time demands for your own agendas, and
5. Whether you would be a good addition to the team.

After all is said and done, administrators must determine whether or not your contribution to the faculty would be viewed positively or negatively. The "well-being" of the unit and school depends on a healthy working relationship among all faculty members, a relationship that reinforces collaboration and respect and avoids dissent, mistrust, and discord. When responding to questions, you should be sensitive to the manner in which you discuss your accomplishments. When discussing your accomplishments and experiences, in addition to emphasizing your individual or solo accomplishments, be sure to highlight the collaborative efforts in which you have been engaged, whether it was through research, teaching, or service—through performances, presentations, or other venues. Your enthusiasm for both individual and teamwork will enhance your value as a faculty member, demonstrating you can function both as a leader and as a team member.

Somewhere during your discussions with faculty or administration you will be asked in some manner or another the question, "Why have you applied for this position?" Your response to this one question can often impact whether you will be seriously considered for the position. Again, responses to this question that are considered to be exclusively personally oriented are frequently viewed negatively. While candidate consideration for a position may include climate, a mate, proximity to family, and a host of other personal *raisons d'être*, these factors should not be the sole, or even the main purpose for your position consideration. Hopefully, the attractiveness of a position surpasses monetary considerations and personal factors, allowing you to focus on your interests in working with a dedicated faculty, within a strong department, with motivated students, in a setting with excellent administrators, or in a university with a mission that is conducive to your professional goals.

If you currently hold a position at another institution you will need to address the reason you are considering a move from that establishment. Focus on the positive when addressing this matter. If you are in a negative situation, do not discuss those issues. Complaining about your current situation does not enhance your credibility as a candidate; instead it may label you as a complainer and as someone who can't be content in any situation. Rather, point out the positives of the position for which you are interviewing. While your interest in moving may be for any number of reasons, wanting to move to a university with a stronger research mission, a strong undergraduate curriculum, or moving to a school that has an extensive graduate program, for example, will be viewed as a stronger motive than moving because you are not happy in your current job.

What Qualities Are Valued by Administrators in Faculty Hires?

Qualities such as your capability to be a leader and yet willingly be part of a team, your potential to obtain tenure, or your ability to enhance the reputation of a division, department, or school while developing an important national or international research or performance agenda, are esteemed by administrators. Other qualities, such as life experiences, flexibility, personality, and communication and deportment, are also valued. Many administrators will seek individuals with life experiences that are connected to their professional endeavors. Administrators may ask themselves: What life in the arts has this person had?

What "real" experiences versus "book learning" have they had to validate their knowledge? Do they have contracts, have they recorded or performed, written and published, what is their connection to real-life experiences? Can they help students get jobs? Do they have connections to the industry? What is their scholarship background: where is the candidate coming from—the school, the faculty? Was it a reputable school with a good environment and can they help students get into such institutions as graduate students or faculty? Can they help students get a Fulbright and can they help students publish, record, or perform? What can they offer to help students reach that next level of prominence within the field? Have these individuals received excellent mentoring that can be passed on to their students? Can they and will they share their knowledge with others?

Flexibility is another quality sought by administrators. The ability of potential faculty to be able to change and adapt to new situations is one that is valued by administrators. Most universities are dynamic, fluid, and changing bodies. Often in such environments faculty are asked to assume new responsibilities, whether it is heading a grant-writing team, teaching a new course, developing new curriculum, or taking on administrative responsibilities. Administrators often view the individual who can demonstrate the ability to be flexible and amenable as one who is valued and a positive asset to a faculty.

Personality is perhaps one of the most valued commodities of any potential faculty hire. Personality forecasts an individual's ability to relate *to* and work *with* others, whether they are students, colleagues, individuals from the community, or others in the field. While you can't change your personality during an interview, you can consciously "put your most positive foot forward" during this process. The interview itself can be an exhausting and strenuous event that requires individual peak performances throughout the course of the experience. Know that your personality will be scrutinized and answers will be sought to such questions as: Does this candidate have a sense of humor? Is this person too business-like, too into himself or herself? How will others perceive this person?

Equally important is your ability to communicate with others and your deportment. It may seem obvious that administrators are looking for an articulate individual, someone who is equally adept at communication in both written and oral forms, and has the ability to convey positive images to students, colleagues, university leaders, and community leaders. The way we present ourselves—the way we appear to others—sends one of the strongest messages even before we have spoken a single word. Your appearance, the way you dress, carry yourself, and engage in nonverbal communication all convey your demeanor or what some individuals call your aura or charisma. The way we communicate through the written form, such as through grant writing, cover letters, CVs, or article publications, or verbally, such as through presentations at community or professional events, all have an impact on our publics. Administrators seek those individuals who potentially will have the most positive public image possible while still attaining and fulfilling the goals and mission for which they will be hired.

What Questions Should a Candidate Be Prepared to Answer?

Some of the questions an administrator will likely ask were suggested in the previous discussion. These will be revisited. Of primary importance to upper administration is whether or not candidates have the potential to gain tenure and be promoted if hired. Therefore you will be asked questions about your research or creative agenda, especially if you are applying at a research-intensive university. Questions that ascertain candidates' abilities to gain tenure and promotion are often directed at their research/creative venues. You will, most likely, be asked questions such as the following:

- What publications, performances, compositions, or presentations have you undertaken and completed in the past three to five years?
- What publications, performances, compositions, or presentations are you currently working on or planning?
- I note that your dissertation was in the area of _____. What did you learn from investigating this area? As a result of completing your dissertation, what other projects, studies, or ideas have been generated as a product of this endeavor?
- Where do you see yourself in the next five years, ten years, in terms of research/creative activities? What types of endeavors, venues would you most likely be undertaking in five years? ten years?
- What long-term projects will you be working on and hope to complete in the next five years? In the next ten years?
- Have you established national or international prominence in your field? If not, how do you plan to establish national or international prominence in your field? What plan(s) do you have to reach or enhance your prominence in your field?
- Can you tell me about ten to twenty possible projects (publications, books, CDs, concerts, plays, directing, and so forth) you would like to undertake and complete in the next ten years?
- What aspects of the research or creative process do you enjoy and how to you plan to continue exploiting those avenues in the future?

- Do you enjoy performing, writing, and so forth?
- Based on your research or creative endeavors to date and after having read our school or university mission, why do you believe you would be successful at our institution?

Another component of the tenure and promotion process, in addition to the research or creativity venue, is that of teaching. If the candidate has not taught previously in a university setting or has limited teaching experience the director or dean will want to determine the candidate's potential for growth. As teaching is an important component in the tenure and promotion process, questions that ascertain candidates' abilities to gain tenure and promotion directed at their teaching ability could include the following.

- How would you rank yourself as a teacher? Explain.
- What are some of your strongest teaching traits, characteristics, skills, or abilities?
- If I were on a promotion and tenure committee and you were asked by the committee to detail those aspects of your teaching that would convince us you were an outstanding teacher, what would you say?
- How would you describe your teaching approach?
- If a member of the community had walked into your classroom/studio/ rehearsal and observed you teaching or conducting what would they tell me about that experience?
- Do you like to teach? If so, why?
- Rank your interest in teaching, research or creative endeavors, and service? Explain your ranking rationale.
- How do you convey knowledge, enthusiasm, and passion for discipline through teaching, conducting, or rehearsing?
- How do you capture and hold the attention of individuals with whom you are working?

In general, administrators are attempting to ask questions and gather information that will help them assess the various qualities you display, ones that could support a decision to hire. First and foremost, administrators want to know whether your interest in the university and the position is sincere. Administrators determine this interest in several ways. One way to address candidate interest is through the candidate's questions about the university, college, school, and department. The questions *you ask* during an interview can be as important as those you answer. Through your questioning and statements it will become apparent whether you have "bothered" to learn about the school prior to your interview. Often, especially when time permits, administrators will send you various types of information such as promotion and tenure criteria, annual reports, and internal reviews. You should become familiar with these materials as your knowledge of their content is another way of assessing your interest in the position. For example, if you had been sent promotion and tenure (P&T) documents prior to the interview, it will be expected, if you were interested in the position, that you have reviewed those materials thoroughly. You most likely would be asked a question such as, "Having read our P&T document and in light of your CV, what do you feel your strengths are in obtaining promotion and tenure here?" A list of specifics should be provided—it doesn't necessarily matter what the list contains—but the director and dean want to determine if you were interested enough in the position to have read and considered the P&T documents and then to imagine or visualize yourself in that process at their institution. Can you articulate the events that must be undertaken to attain P&T?

Finally, "fit" is being determined. If you are applying for a position at a research-intensive institute you should be prepared to talk about your research or creative activity agenda along with your teaching abilities. "How committed are you to the culture of the school?" You should also be prepared to:

- Discuss the kind of school or department in which you want to work.
- Describe the types of activities you would ideally want to be involved with on a daily basis.
- Describe the qualities of your ideal school.
- Discuss your work ethic in relation to the culture of the institution.

Hopefully, you would be describing the school, or at least some of the qualities of the school, at which you are interviewing. This will show the director and dean that you are aware of their school's goals and objectives or mission that will assist them determining whether you are a good fit. Thus administrators are looking for the following:

1. Match: Do you match the institutional needs and mission? Do you fulfill the needs of the position? Are you seriously and sincerely attracted to and interested in the position?
2. Flexibility: What else can you do? Could you teach different subjects if the departmental needs changed? Would you be willing to be flexible?
3. Magnetism: How effectively will you draw recruits? Can and do you make teaching exciting, understandable, and interesting? Do you have a magnetism that will attract talent?

4. Attractiveness and Charisma: What is your proficiency for sharing your enthusiasm of the profession with others as well as your ability to effectively and supportively work with faculty and students? Can you be both a leader and a team player as needed? Will you add to the "attractiveness" of the program or area through your teaching and professional activities?

5. Expansiveness: How will you contribute to, expand, and challenge the program? What strengths could and would you bring to the program?

Sincere interest in the position, potential to gain tenure or obtain promotion, and institutional fit are all factors considered by administrators in determining the appropriateness of any faculty hire. Your ability to fulfill the various departmental needs is essentially being determined through your presentations and through the manner, thoroughness, knowledge, and appropriateness of your responses to questions asked of you as well as the questions you ask.

Questions You Can or Should Ask

Thus far our discussion has focused on questions you should be able to address and on those items with which you should be eminently familiar. What then are the questions that administrators are either expecting you to ask or those you should ask? And are there questions that should be avoided during the initial interview? Perhaps it is appropriate at this point to note that you need to prepare questions for your interview. The absence of questions is viewed as a serious negative, as it is perceived as a lack of interest or seriousness in the position and sends the message that you are only going through the interview process for an ulterior motive. That said, there are questions that should be avoided during the initial interview. Primarily, specific questions that pertain to a job offer or the negotiation process should be avoided during an initial interview. Wanting to negotiate too soon sends the message that you are interested primarily in the financial aspects of the position rather than the position itself. This does not mean you shouldn't ask about salary range and such items, but the specifics of a position are generally delayed if, until, or when an offer is actually made. The negotiation process will be discussed in the next chapter.

Questions that should be asked during an interview preferably follow a progression of those that show your interest in the university, then the stability of the setting, the students, and finally the benefits. Questions that you can ask that indicate your interest in the university could include any of the following.

Interest Questions

- How is the university governed? How are decisions made at the university, college, and school levels? How are faculty involved in those decisions?
- How are benefits, salaries, and so forth negotiated? Is there a union that represents the faculty in these decisions?
- How is the university and the school of _____ viewed in the state as well as regionally, nationally, or internationally?
- How is the school of _____ viewed by the upper university administration, by the dean of the college, by other deans, the provost, and the president?
- How would you characterize the mission of your university, the college, the school, the department?
- What are the strengths of your school and/or the department?
- Describe the typical activities of an assistant, associate, or a full professor in your school in terms of teaching load, research or creative activities, and service.
- How often are school or departmental meetings held? What is the nature of those meetings? Are decisions that affect the school or departments made in those meetings? If decisions are voted upon, who is eligible to vote?
- When was your last national review, such as NASM, and what was the outcome of that review? Can you summarize the findings of your last annual report, both the strengths and weaknesses and the actions you are planning in light of that review?

Questions Pertaining to the Student Population

- What kinds of student support (GTAs, GAs, scholarships, awards, and so forth) are available to students?
- What is the enrollment? Have you reached an ideal enrollment level or are you hoping to increase or decrease enrollment?
- How would you characterize the quality of your entering undergraduate students? Is there a waiting list to enter the school or department? What percentage of students applying for admission is accepted? The same questions should be asked of the graduate students if there is a graduate program.
- What is the graduation rate for undergraduates? For graduates?
- What is the ratio of undergraduate to graduate students? Is this the ideal ratio you are seeking?

- What percentage of undergraduate and/or graduate students, in the various disciplines, is placed after graduation? Describe a typical undergraduate or graduate student placement with a degree in performance, education, etc.
- What is the student composition of your school? Are students from families who have not previously pursued college degrees encouraged? Do they receive any kind of special assistance? Do you attract students from a particular ethnic class or makeup, or a particular social economic class? Do they receive any type of enhanced assistance?
- What kinds of technology are available to students at the university level? What kinds of technology are available in the classroom or studio?
- How well does the library meet departmental needs? Are the reserves adequate? Are appropriate research sources available and free of charge?
- What is the ratio of faculty to students? Do students have the opportunity to work primarily with professors or are classes taught predominately by teaching assistants or adjuncts?

Questions Relating to the Stability of the Setting
- How long has the director of this school or the dean of this college been in place? Is s/he respected by other directors or deans? Is s/he easy to work with? What do you see as his/her vision for the school or college?
- Funding: How is the school, college, or university funded? What portion of funding comes from the state (if any), from endowments, from ticket sales and similar venues, from other sources?
- On average, what is the faculty turnover rate per year? What are some of the reasons faculty have left?
- How difficult is it to gain tenure and promotion? What percentage of those seeking tenure and promotion receives tenure and what percentage of the faculty are currently tenured? If tenure or promotion was denied, what were the problem issues? (Note: for the previous question, you as the candidate should be listening for items such as collegiality, poor student evaluations, not carrying load, narrow focus, lack of appropriate publications, performances, recordings, presentations, etc.) Who is allowed to vote on tenure and promotion issues at the school level? What's the relative importance of teaching, research, and service for promotion and tenure and what is the normal time spent in the various ranks before tenure and/or promotion can or must be sought? What does the tenure and promotion review process involve?

- Is your enrollment growing, declining, or remaining the same? Is that the desired direction of your school or department?
- What do you consider to be the strongest departments and schools within the school or college respectively? How are you supporting those departments and schools?
- Is the position for which I am interviewing a newly created position or is it a position that has been vacated by a faculty member? If this is a vacated position, can you tell me why the faculty member left? Are there any plans for creating new faculty lines in this department? If so, what would they be?

Questions Pertaining to Faculty Benefits

Before listing potential questions pertaining to faculty benefits it should be noted that such questions should be reserved for the *latter part* of your interview with the director or dean. You will first want to establish your interest in the university or school, position, faculty, students, and perhaps even the community before pursuing potential faculty benefits. And while some questions concerning restaurants, churches, night spots and entertainment venues, housing or real estate, schools, and so forth are relevant, they should be kept to a minimum. Questions pertaining directly to specifics of a hiring package should not be asked but general questions, such as those pertaining to health benefit packages, retirement system possibilities, general faculty teaching and research support, and possible salary ranges, can be addressed. Again, reserve your faculty benefits questions for the end of interview.

The following are some potential questions that can be asked in your interview with the director and dean.

- What kinds of faculty support, other than salary, are available for incoming faculty (start-up or hiring package, reduced load for the first year, research assistance, grant availability, grant-writing assistance, research tools such as a lab or equipment, office computers and printers, travel funds, and so forth)?
- What type of retirement plans or programs can one participate in at this university? Do you offer VALIC, TIA-CREF, and/or a state or independent sponsored program? Does the university participate in the social security and Medicare programs or is this an option if other retirement plans are in place? How much salary goes to retirement and what is the university's contribution?

- What type of health plans are available (medical, dental, vision, and so forth)? What are the costs of these programs, and what is the university's contribution?
- What is the salary range of faculty in similar ranks in this type of position?
- What is a normal teaching load for faculty in similar positions and do you typically offer reduced teaching loads for the first year of residency?
- For what courses would you anticipate the person hired for this position would be responsible and what would be the breakdown of undergraduate to graduate offerings?
- What types of research or creative activities facilities and support are available through the school or college and university?
- Are sabbaticals granted?
- What is your policy on spousal hires?
- Are graduate assistants normally awarded to faculty in positions such as the one being offered?
- What are some of the stronger schools or school systems in (city or area)_____?
- What is the cost of living and housing in _____ specifically in relation to the salary the university would be able to offer?

As was mentioned at the beginning of this section, you need to prepare the questions you wish to ask. Through such preparation you will gain insight into the university and its structure, the dynamics of the college or school, the student body, the curriculum, and so forth. As your information base increases you most likely will have additional questions that go beyond the scope of the initial questions outlined here.

Summary of Your Interview with the Director and Dean

Remember that the dean and director are trying to ascertain, in addition to your training, experience, and expertise in the field, how well you will work with them and other administrators, with other faculty, and of course with students. Will others want to spend time with you? Do you display respect for colleagues, students, and administration? Do you have a sense of humor or are you too "business-like," are you too into yourself? In general, do you have the right fit for the position?

Remember too, that in one sense you are not the only one interviewing. Both the director and dean know that you too are assessing the school, faculty, students, administration, and facilities during your on-campus interview. To this end, the job of the director and dean is not only to assess you but to *recruit you* as well. They know that excellent candidates will often be interviewing at several schools. If they feel you are a viable candidate, they will want to know how you can be recruited—and therefore will tend to talk about the benefits of the school—about the strengths of the position.

INTERVIEW ATTIRE AND PUNCTUALITY

In Chapter 4 a discussion was presented on gathering additional information about the committee, school, and so forth, as well as making your travel plans, arranging your interview apparel, preparing your presentations, and becoming aware of how you present yourself to others and how these interactions are perceived. Indeed even some of your energy needs were discussed with suggestions on food you might consider packing to sustain you through the rigors of the interview. Now as you arrive at your destination you need to be aware that your first contact with any individuals from the interviewing site will be noted. Later on, the committee may discuss any information gleaned from this initial encounter. Because this initial meeting will make some type of impression, it is important that your "travel attire" be professional. This doesn't necessarily dictate the need to wear a "coat and tie," unless of course you are proceeding immediately from an airport or other location to the actual interview itself, but it also doesn't mean you should be wearing cut-offs and a t-shirt when meeting your hosts or host representatives. So whenever you arrive at the interview site, be prepared to "meet and greet" your hosts. You are making that all-so-important first impression, which will be a lasting one. Even though you may be tired, hungry, and, dare I say, a bit flustered or even cranky, due to the rigors of the travel itself, dispel those feelings and substitute in their place your joy for having been invited to the interview and for the opportunity to meet colleagues in your profession. Whether you receive and/or take a job offer, you will learn much from each interview you experience. Appreciate the opportunity to interview, and convey that appreciation in your initial greeting.

Once you have been greeted by your host, usually a member of the search committee or a representative (this may be a graduate student or graduate assistant from the department in which the hire is being conducted), you will most likely either be taken to your hotel or to the place that you will be staying to get settled or you may begin the interview process immediately. Generally, if you arrive in the late afternoon, early evening, or late evening you will likely proceed to your accommodation. Often, however, morning or even early afternoon arrivals allow ample time to schedule interview events. You may, for example, be picked up at an airport and whisked off to a meeting upon your arrival. Of course your interview itinerary will detail all of these events and you should secure a copy of the itinerary prior to travel.

If you go to your hotel you will have a chance to "freshen up" after checking in. Sometimes candidates' accommodations are in the home of a faculty member. While some find this a bit less relaxing and more stressful, it can offer a candidate an opportunity to learn more about the school and faculty in a bit more relaxed atmosphere. Remember, however, you are still interviewing even when in your accommodation for the evening. Once you have had the opportunity to check in, freshen up, and/or find a "home" for your luggage, you may be asked if you would like a meal, especially if you arrive around a "meal" time, or you might proceed to the interview site for a meeting to be held later. Sometimes you will be invited to attend a concert, a formal or informal gathering at a faculty home, or other such event. You may be left at the accommodation site and informed of the particular time you will be picked up the next morning for either a breakfast meeting or to proceed to the campus—it is critical that you be punctual for all meetings. At some point, however, you will be with your hosts, partaking of food and drink. Remembering that everything you do is being observed and evaluated, here are some guidelines you might like to remember when dining with members of the search committee.

INTERVIEWING AND DINING

While it may seem strange to talk about meal etiquette, menu selection, or portion consumption when interviewing, candidates have lost job offers due to meal-related activity. Perhaps a short, true story is in order here. I once participated in a search in which my fellow committee member and colleague was to attend a breakfast with a candidate. It was the first meal the candidate had with a committee member after arriving late the previous night. So, first impressions had only been briefly made with another member of the committee on route from the airport to the hotel. My colleague attended breakfast with the candidate and came into my office quite upset. Since there was an hour before the next activity with the candidate, I asked my colleague what was bothering her. She said, "You would not believe what this candidate did! Why, there is absolutely no way I can support this individual." I was rather surprised and a bit shocked to say the least. I could only think that my colleague had found out that our first candidate was perhaps a serial killer or worse. So, I probed for additional information. "What," I asked, "did this individual do?" I didn't really want to know at this point but, on the other hand, I didn't *not* want to know either. My colleague replied, "Well, he simply doesn't seem to know about appropriate professional behavior. You wouldn't believe what he did at breakfast this morning!" My mind was now spinning, I had no idea what was about to be said next. "We were finishing our breakfast when it happened," she proceeded, "it was in such poor taste I couldn't believe my eyes." "What? What happened?" I asked. "You're not going to believe this, but he had a sunny-side-up fried egg and there was some yoke left. He then took some toast, put it in his hand and began to swirl it around the plate! I was appalled," she continued, "how could we ever support anyone like this—he has no professional behavior whatsoever? This candidate has lost my vote," she ended.

As you can see from this story, even the simplest of behaviors can trigger a strong, adverse reaction from a committee member. The moral of this story is: be aware of your actions and make sure you send the message you wish to convey. Meals are especially difficult times for a candidate. When people gather for meals it is often a time for relaxation, enjoyment, and conversation. For the candidate, however, this is the time to be acutely aware of what you say, how you respond, and how gracious you are during the dining process.

When you interview, the committee wants to impress you as well as seek additional information. The act of dining often presents an opportunity for the committee to "wine and dine" you at locales that are respected and generally highly regarded. They want you to relax, and often after a morning of intense meetings or a day of interviewing, relaxing is exactly what you want, *and need,* as well. You are tired and hungry, but this is exactly the time when you need to dip into your energy reserve. While others are relaxing and enjoying themselves they will undoubtedly be asking you various questions. You need to listen carefully to what is being asked and then artfully craft your response. You will be expending as much energy, if not more, during your dining experiences as you would in a one-on-one or committee meeting. Eating is *not* your main objective, rather responding to inquiries must take precedence. To this end, you may well leave the restaurant feeling hungry. If indeed you do, know that you dutifully and thoroughly responded to questions and that the committee was interested enough in your candidacy to seek additional information. Often it is good to leave a meal hungry, especially at an early morning or noon dining venue. If you consume large food portions it will take away from the energies needed for later interview events. To this end, the food you choose at various meals should require the least amount of effort to eat and, if possible, be the easiest to digest.

Here are some food choice suggestions for your dining pleasure. One dining axiom is to avoid foods that have sauces or may cause difficulty eating because of their texture. Obviously pastas with sauce and other similar dishes pose a hazard to your ties, blouses, and so on, as they can become quickly stained. Items that should be or are traditionally dipped in sauces (French dips) or in butter (lobster) pose further "splatter risks" and should be avoided. Items such as French onion soup or similar items prepared with melted cheese that tend to produce long dangling "cheese strings" when eaten should be shunned, as should eggs that are served with a soft yoke.

Some food items require significant chewing during consumption. Salads may be especially problematic as they can be messy at the most inopportune time, they require a lot of chewing prior to swallowing thus making it awkward to respond to questions, and lettuce has the habit of becoming lodged in the most annoying places in your mouth or teeth—avoid salads! Many meats require significant mastication before swallowing, which again leads to difficulty of addressing questions posed by committee members during this process. Obviously, you do not want to talk with food in your mouth and even small bits of meat require considerable chewing. Foods that are or can be eaten without utensils, such as barbequed ribs should be avoided, especially if others are not partaking in such fare.

So you ask what is "safe" to eat. For breakfast, scrambled eggs are easy to eat and can be swallowed quickly with little or no chewing. Oatmeal is also easily consumed, easy to digest, and is a rather tidy, nourishing breakfast food. Lunches can be a bit more problematic but some soups, such as creamed soups, are generally easily eaten with a modicum of potential for untidiness. Certain types of open-face sandwiches, especially those prepared with fish, can be easily and safely eaten with utensils. For dinners, the suggested entrée would be fish accompanied by rice and a vegetable such as green beans. Neither fish nor rice requires much chewing and they are again easily and "safely" eaten, while allowing for an effortless transition to conversation. Green beans do not fall off a fork and are relatively easy to eat, especially if eaten in small amounts. These meal suggestions are by no means exclusive but are presented as examples of items you may wish to consider during your interview.

One question that is often pondered by a candidate during interview meals is price range. Common practice is that your meals will be paid by the interviewing institution, either immediately or later through a reimbursement procedure. In either case, interviewees often wonder about an acceptable price range for a meal especially at dinner where prices for an entrée at a fine dining establishment can be rather expensive. If your hosts order before you, you should take your price range cue from them. You can comfortably order entrées that are equal to or less than that of your hosts. Often however, your hosts will ask you to order first. In this case I would suggest that you order an entrée in the middle or lower middle of the menu price range. Often this type of entrée will be a fish dish, such as baked salmon. Another question that arises is whether or not to order an appetizer. If you do feel the need to replenish your energy quickly before your entrée is served, you should feel comfortable ordering an appetizer. I would suggest that you defer to your hosts, however, as you don't necessarily want to be the only individual ordering an appetizer. If you do order an appetizer ask your hosts to help you with the order choice under the guise that you would not be able to eat all of the appetizer and that you would like to order something that all members at the table might enjoy—even though you may actually be ravenous at the time and would be able to eat *several* appetizers. When ordering a "group" appetizer, be sure to ask the waiter or waitress to bring extra plates, and so on, as you want this to be shared among all members at the table. This same advice can be considered when determining whether or not to order desserts.

Finally, a question often asked is whether or not the interviewee should consume alcoholic beverages during a meal. If you don't consume such beverages normally, this obviously will not be an issue. But many individuals enjoy, for example, a martini before a meal, a glass of wine with a meal, or perhaps even a liqueur as an after-meal beverage. Because you have expended a lot of energy during the course of the day's interview activities and may not have eaten great quantities of food during the process, any kind of alcoholic beverage is likely to affect you more dramatically. For this one reason it may be wise to forego a drink. Also, you want to be at your peak throughout the meal and alcohol tends to dull the senses, something you definitely want to avoid during your interview. But if you decide to imbibe, you should do so only if all or some of your hosts are partaking and only if it is apparent that such behavior would not be viewed as less than desirable. You should also be aware that the cost of alcoholic beverages is often not a covered expense within a search budget and this is especially true, for example, at state or public universities or colleges. Thus, if you do drink, definitely offer to pay for the drink as likely your host will have to pick up the alcoholic beverage tab if you do not.

The intent of the prior discussion was not to discourage you from enjoying your dining experiences during your interview but rather to prepare you for the possibilities of interested, curious hosts wanting to learn about you and the skills and ideas you could bring to their position. They forget that in addition to responding to their questions you too need to eat. For you, then, the enjoyment of eating a leisurely, carefree, and nourishing meal in a relaxed atmosphere should not be a dining excursion objective. Your objective is to convey as much information as is sought by your hosts. And even if you leave the restaurant somewhat less than satisfied, remember, you've packed some energy food in your suitcase, which will fortify you for the remainder of your interview.

POST-INTERVIEW QUESTIONS AND INQUIRIES

Once you leave your interview site you may receive further inquiries or correspondence, most often from a dean, director, or search committee chair. A follow-up email or note thanking you for interviewing or for the opportunity to meet you may be sent. *Do respond* to such correspondence. Your response signals your continued interest in the position, while a failure to respond indicates just the opposite. You may also wish to initiate a similar correspondence to the chair, director, or dean, thanking them for the opportunity to meet and learn about their school.

Similarly, post-screening issues may arise where questions are raised that need clarification. In senior hires, for example, sometimes reference calls are delayed and you may be asked for permission to contact those referees. Again, your prompt reply signals continued interest in the position. Finally, you may have, during the course of the interview, indicated that you were interviewing or had already interviewed at other universities. If you have been offered a position as a result of one of those interviews, you should contact the other universities, usually the director of the school at which you interviewed, as a courtesy. Often if one of those schools is also interested in you, your call may prompt yet another offer.

Sometimes, after all initial candidates have had their on-campus interviews, no candidate is found suitable for the position. At this point additional candidates may be reviewed and brought for on-campus interviews; the search may be extended, allowing for late as well as new applications to be considered; the position may be readvertised; the position may be reevaluated and perhaps reconfigured and advertised at a later date; or the position may be eliminated. In any of these cases, once you have been informed of the outcome, and if you have not already done so, you should correspond with the director, dean, and committee chair, thanking them for the opportunity to have interviewed at their school.

SUMMARY: THE INTERVIEW

The interview process is one that requires significant prior preparation and forethought in anticipation of the on-campus visit, as well as sufficient energy and stamina during the interview. It is a time when you learn about the faculty, students, and administration and they become familiar with you. In the process, everyone will most likely learn more about himself or herself as well. The process is intense, physically and emotionally draining, and yet satisfying. It is a time when you stop to focus on your skills, talents, and abilities and determine how to present and showcase them in the best possible light. Whether or not you are offered the position, you *will* learn from the process.

Once you leave the interview site you will undoubtedly question some of your responses or perhaps some of your questions. You may wonder if your prepared materials were the most appropriate for the situation or if your manner of presentation was strong enough. This is a normal reaction. However, if you systematically prepared for your interview in the manner suggested and performed at the highest level possible when on-campus, you should feel satisfied and indeed proud of your accomplishment. Remember, you were chosen from a group of tens or maybe hundreds of people to interview for a position. This in itself is an honor, and while it may be even more satisfying to be offered a position, a strong interview, regardless of the outcome, will provide future benefits. The professional world is a small place. A stellar interview will always be remembered, regardless of the outcome. Word-of-mouth recommendations among faculty at conferences and conventions, professional meetings, and similar events are not uncommon. Thus, a successful interview will eventually pay dividends, and hopefully one of those dividends will be a job offer, which will be the topic of discussion in the next chapter.

References

Metzler, Ken. 1977. *Creative interviewing: The writer's guide to gathering information by asking questions.* Englewood Cliffs, NJ: Prentice-Hall.

Kuther, Tara. 2010. What to ask during an academic job interview. http://gradschool.about.com/cs/academicsearch/a/facint.htm, accessed November 14, 2010.

Vick, Julia Miller and Jennifer S. Furlong. 2008. *The academic job search handbook.* 4th ed. Philadelphia: University of Pennsylvania Press.

6

THE OFFER AND THE NEGOTIATION

YOU'VE RETURNED FROM your interview and you may have received some type of correspondence acknowledging your on-campus meetings. On the other hand, you may have heard nothing and are now asking, "What is going on?" Provided you were the last candidate to interview for the position, there most likely are lengthy discussions occurring concerning which one of you, if any of you, would provide the most appropriate fit for the position. Of course, if you did not know whether other candidates were interviewing after you, and depending on the number of candidates yet to be interviewed as well as the availability of the candidates, committee members, and administrators to complete those interviews, the process could continue for several weeks.

If, however, the search committee has reached a decision as to the possible candidate or candidates, there will be dialogue between the committee chair and the director. The search committee, in most cases, is a recommending body to the director. It is the director, usually in consultation with the dean, who selects the individual for the initial offer. The search committee chair will share information gleaned from committee members with the director. While it is common for the director to ask the chair *not* to rank the candidates in order of the committee's preference, the director usually asks if there are any candidates the committee deems unacceptable. In any case, a seasoned search committee chair is generally able to indicate committee preference without actually ranking the candidates and thus provides the director with appropriate information concerning the applicants. In other words, if you were the "favorite" candidate of the committee, that information will be communicated.

After the search committee chair meets with the director, the director, who likely has his/her own candidate of preference, will consult with the dean. The dean generally must approve the candidate before the name is forwarded to the university provost or president for final approval. The dean will also weigh in on his/her candidate choice. During this consultation, information summarized from individual meetings with the dean and director will be shared. A frank discussion concerning information from the search committee, whether a candidate is or was interested in the position, whether the school has significant funds, facilities, or other needs sought by an individual to bring him or her to the university, and other such information is shared. Once agreement has been reached regarding the top candidate, a discussion begins regarding the nature of the offer letter. While there is generally a time for negotiation before a final letter of hire, the dean and director, based on their discussions with the candidate during the on-campus visit, will have a fairly good idea of what a candidate might need in order to accept the position. Discussions concerning the overall details of securing sources for items such as equipment, release time, travel monies, research start-up funds, and the like will be occurring. Upon the conclusion of such discussions, an initial offer letter can often be composed.

The director, now armed with this information, will contact the human resources, affirmative action office, or personnel department to seek approval of the offer. It is important once again that the human resources, affirmative action office, or personnel department be consulted and that initial approval be obtained, as this office often grants final contract approval. In Chapter 2, in which the application process was discussed, it was mentioned that you likely would be asked to complete and return an information card to the human resources, affirmative action office, or personnel department. Now is the time this information comes into play. If the university is an equal opportunity employer (EOE), a discussion will be held as to the status of the individuals being considered and those not being considered. Individuals from protected classes and so forth, who would have been encouraged to apply, are given consideration at this point in the process. The director generally must explain his or her choice for candidate in relation to EOE guidelines. Once receiving clearance from this office, the director may then proceed.

If it has already been determined that research or creative activities support items will be part of the offer, the director—sometimes in conjunction with the dean—will contact the vice-president for research, the provost, or other appropriate offices to seek potential support for items such as computers, printers, particular software, perhaps funding for a graduate assistant for the new hire, and other such requisites. It is important that all likely costs can be covered and that a determination of who will cover what costs has been or will be made.

Candidate approval generally must also be endorsed by the provost's and/or president's office. Secure in the fact that permission has been granted, approval for a particular candidate has been confirmed, and funding for the position still exists, the position can be offered to you! Congratulations! You will then be contacted and informed of the offer. Even though a verbal offer is made, the initial offer letter will not be completed until after your discussions with the director. This dialogue will help frame the contents of the offer letter. Often a draft offer letter is sent to insure that essential elements of the verbal agreement have been included and detailed. If there is agreement by all parties on the draft offer letter, it is signed and returned. If changes need to be made to the offer letter, those are noted, and another offer letter is sent with those changes. Once the final letter of hire contents have been agreed upon, another final letter of hire or offer of appointment is generated. When there is complete agreement on the "draft" letter, it may serve as the final contract, provided it contains all essential elements, signatures, and so forth. Eventually a formal contract will need to be signed. Because of required documentation needed to prove citizenship (social security card, birth certificate, etc.) the signing of the contract is often delayed until your on-campus arrival.

What happens if, during the interview or decision-making process, you are offered another position? Is this common? If you have been actively interviewing, you obviously have been a candidate who has attracted interest from other institutions. Depending on the speed at which a search is conducted and when you interviewed, it would not be uncommon for you to be offered a position before, after, or even during another interview. If you are fortunate enough to be in this position, you need to know what course of action to follow. First, unless the offered position is the "dream position" you have been seeking, inform the institution that you are pleased and would like a couple of days to consider the offer. Usually three to five working days are acceptable as a consideration period in most disciplines; however, some disciplines allow a two-week or longer consideration period. During this time frame you may choose to negotiate with the institution (more on this later) or simply accept the offer. However, if you have interviewed at another institution for a position you find more attractive, call the director and search committee chair of that institution, and inform them that you have been offered a position at another institution but are still interested in their position. The director or chair can and will, most likely, apprise you of the current search status. Often, if their search process is near closure and you have been identified as the top candidate, the offer process can be accelerated. In such cases, the director "pushes" the approval process based on your status, being that you have been offered a position at another institution, and can get back to you within a three- to five-day period (or sooner) with his or her offer. If offered another position, you now would have the enviable position of having multiple job offers. Professional courtesy dictates that you decide which position to pursue and convey that decision as quickly as possible to all institutions involved. This will enable each institution to continue their hiring process in a timely fashion.

What happens if you've received an offer, and you determine the university from which you hope to receive another offer is not yet ready to make any immediate decision? What are your options? Once you receive an offer from any institution, a clock or time line begins, and at some point you need to either accept or decline the offer. You can't delay this decision because you are hoping another, more desirable university position may be offered. You must decide to accept or decline any offer in a timely fashion and be prepared to live with that decision. Your biggest risk in declining a "less desirable" offer in hopes of attaining a "more desirable" one is that it may result in not having any job.

Assuming that you have at least one job offer to consider (HOORAY!), in addition to the initial verbal offer, there are at least three steps to yet consider:

1. Questions to be asked at this point,
2. The negotiation process, and finally
3. The final hire letter.

All of these items are closely related and basically contingent upon each other. While your initial offer letter/agreement, your negotiations, and of course your final hire letter are perhaps more stimulating in content, you need to be asking some basic questions at this point to establish a basis for your negotiations.

Questions You Should Ask upon Receiving an Offer

The questions you ask after having received a job offer forecast your requirements for acceptance of the position and help frame the negotiation process. Most of your questions at this point will normally be targeted to the director; however, some questions may be more appropriately directed to the search committee chair. Responses to your questions, directly related to the negotiation process or not, will ultimately provide additional information pertaining to the position, the school, and the university. All of this information will supplement your knowledge of the setting and assist you in the decision-making process.

Some questions asked may be inquiries revisited from your initial interview; however, more direct responses should be expected at this time. For example, questions pertaining to salary should now yield more specific information, and instead of being quoted a salary range, you should now be provided a specific salary or at the very least a very narrow suggested salary range.

Because of Internet postings and access laws you can often get a good ballpark figure of existing faculty salaries received at many public-funded and private institutions. Depending on the culture of the institution, a range of $2,000 to $10,000 or more over a stated salary amount or range can "become available" through the negotiation process. Some universities have hire package funds from outside sources—others have funds that can be obtained for counteroffers. Depending on the response of the hiring institution, you may decide that salary should become one of your negotiation items. Note, however, that some universities have little if any flexibility in salary offerings, but may be able to provide substantial nonsalary items such as labs, computers, and similar items.

Thus, there are questions that should be revisited as they may become items for further discussion during the negotiation process. In addition to salary questions, other inquiries that should be made include the following areas or items:

1. Teaching load assignment and specific course responsibilities;
2. Possibility of reduction in teaching load during the first year;
3. Specific technology equipment (for use in classrooms or for individual research or office), materials (library holding purchases, access to online journals, dissertations, and search sources), teaching and computer lab availability, and online and course development or delivery support;
4. Start-up packages: pools of money available from other offices or sources on campus that may include research or creative activities package monies, equipment, or travel support monies;
5. Availability of internal research grants through the school, college, or university, author support, Fulbright and similar support;
6. Support for article or book publication or CD or DVD production;
7. Summer employment possibilities;
8. Office availability (size, windows, office equipment such as desks, chairs, tables, filing cabinets, bookshelves, etc.) and office equipment (telephone access—long-distance availability—computer and printer options, online access to search sources, email, etc.);
9. Parking;
10. Moving expenses;
11. Relocation services through the university that can assist with rental, leasing, or purchase issues;
12. Other issues you deem appropriate.

Additionally, there are questions that should be asked that may or may not become negotiation issues. Generally, if a senior position offer is involved, some items hold stronger potential for negotiation consideration than for an entry-level position. However, regardless of the status of your position, entry or senior level, you may be interested in responses to the following areas or items:

1. Tenure or promotion timeline;
2. Research, creative activity, and personal budgets separate from departmental budgets and specific to individual research, creative activity, or personal item expenses;
3. Graduate teaching assistantships;
4. Housing, car, travel allowances;
5. Reduction in teaching load for professional services (editor of journals, president of national organizations, and so forth);
6. Annual salary increases that cover cost-of-living expenses, for example (while rare, some private institutions are able to provide such assurances);
7. Endowed chair consideration;
8. Royalties, off-campus consulting, grant or external funding or dual-position consideration, publication or other creative enterprise rights;
9. Spousal hire;
10. Implementation of innovative curriculum, development of specific institutes or programs, founding of new journals or similar venues.

There are questions that should be asked but likely won't become negotiation issues, regardless of the responses, as they are generally not negotiable. Such questions pertain to the following:

1. Health benefits (medical, dental, optical, life insurances, extended leave insurances);
2. Retirement system benefits and available options;
3. Policies on sabbatical leaves;
4. Policies on family leaves;
5. How the position being offered became available: Was it a newly created position or an existing position that became available through retirement, illness, or death, or a faculty moving to another university, not gaining tenure, or moving into an administrative or similar position within the university?
6. Contractual period of hire.

It is common for universities to contribute to, or in some cases completely pay for, health benefit insurance costs. While this normally is not negotiable, you should find out the amount of premium paid by the university toward these costs. Additionally, some universities provide life insurance coverage at low or no cost to the employee. In a similar vein, universities commonly contribute to retirement funds. Again, it is in your interest to determine the university's contribution to your retirement fund. Other information such as the availability of sabbatical leaves, family leaves (such as maternity leave), and other such programs should be investigated and understood as part of your hiring process.

If you did not find out during your interview how the position being offered became available or were not given details, now is the time to discover this information. You may also wish to determine the "normal" turnaround rate of the school's faculty in general. A 5 percent churn or faculty turnaround or retirement is normal. Thus for a faculty of sixty, an average of three new faculty hires can be expected yearly. While an increase of more than 5 percent can happen, it should not occur on a consistent basis. If there is a flux of more than 5 percent on a consistent basis, or if the "churn" frequently exceeds 10 percent, this could indicate problems within the school. The candidate should investigate such activity.

Finally, an additional item not generally open to negotiation is the term of your contract. While there may be exceptions, it is common university practice to offer faculty contracts based on an academic year, commonly a nine- or ten-month period. Faculty members, regardless of rank or tenure status, are reviewed each year using various performance criteria. Faculty members meeting those criteria are subsequently issued another yearly (academic) contact. Because members of faculty work for a fixed (agreed) period, after which time they are considered for rehire and are either issued a new contract or not, some may consider this to be a fixed-term contract (USLegal 2012). Regardless, the point here is that some items are not negotiable and your contractual period of hire, along with other items mentioned previously, list among those items.

Teaching Load Assignment or Reduction in Teaching Load

Universities, colleges, and schools all have different concepts of what a "full teaching load" should be. Research-intensive universities generally have "lighter" teaching loads offset by "heavier" research, publication, or creative activity expectations, while teaching-intensive colleges may expect little, if any, research, publication, or creative activity, but may have significantly heavier teaching loads. Teaching loads are often described in terms of credit hours, with a full academic load varying

Assignment of Normal Work Load Credit Expected of Faculty Members

**24 = Full Faculty Load Per
    Semester**   **Load Credit**

1. 3-credit-hour lecture course (maximum 3 preparations/semester) 6

2. 2-contact-hour performance class 3 or methods/laboratory course 3

3. Performance lesson. 1.33

4. Performance repertory class. 1.33

5. Small chamber or jazz ensemble coaching. 1.33

6. Directed ensembles (load calculated at 2 x contact hours). 3-8

7. Student teaching supervision (minimum 5 visitations per student
    per semester) 2

8. Faculty ensembles: Piano Trio, Woodwind Quintet, Brass Quintet . . . . .3 (4 for leader)

9. Division chair (not Area Chair) 6

10. Area coordinator (coordinator within Divisions). 1.33

11. M.M. thesis or D.M.A. document advising (per 3 hours of advising). 1.33

12. Ph.D. dissertation advising (per 3 hours of advising) 1.33

Class size adjustment to normal load credits for 3-credit-hour lecture courses.
   Undergraduate Level:
     below 10 students - multiply normal load credit by .8
     10-25 students - normal load credit
     above 25 students - multiply normal load credit by 1.2
   Graduate Level:
     below 5 students - multiply normal load credit by .8
     5-10 students - normal load
     above 10 students - multiply normal load credit by 1.2

FIGURE 6.1 Illustration of school of music teaching load calculation.

between twelve and twenty-four credit or load credits per week, depending on the individual university formula. The example that follows, a twenty-four-load credit formula, is a sophisticated example designed in an attempt to ensure work-load equality across the multiple and diverse responsibilities faculty members carry.

Another formula, in contrast to the formula above, would be one in which four three-hour classes taught during a semester or quarter comprise a full work load. It is often assumed that in addition to teaching the courses or lessons, faculty members will be available for office hours, master classes, advising, extra assistance outside of office hours, committee service, and recruitment efforts, along with responsibilities for professional or outside service and/or research, publication, or creative activity. For example, if you were in a semester system and were assigned a 3/3 academic area load, you would teach three three-credit courses or the equivalent each semester in addition to other assigned or assumed duties and expectations. Any combination of teaching load may be assigned: 3/2, 2/2, 4/5, or like combinations, depending on the institutional, college, or school criteria. The assigned teaching loads generally remain constant for a significant period. As an entering assistant professor with little or no college teaching experience, you should ask what a normal load is for your area. Generally, unless there is some type of outstanding circumstance, you will be assigned that normal load. However, if you are entering as a senior professor, you may wish to negotiate for a reduced teaching load. Possibilities for teaching load reductions may be granted because you are:

- assuming a position that includes responsibilities as an administrator within the department, school or college;
- the head of an institute or hold a major office in a professional organization, such as the editor of a major journal or president of a large, professional national organization within your discipline;
- a nationally or internationally touring soloist, member of a major performing ensemble, recording artist;
- a frequent nationally or internationally known presenter for a commercial or professional organization;
- responsible for oversight of major research grants or funds and subsequent responsibilities associated with those grants.

Often with senior-level positions there is an assumption that the individual being sought should have a national or international stature and would therefore be involved in activities that would bring acclaim and prestige to the institute. Such individuals should—and would most likely be expected to—negotiate reduced teaching loads to continue such national or international activities. Load adjustments may be granted on a permanent basis or perhaps negotiated annually.

As either an entering or senior-level incoming professor, you may be able to negotiate a reduced teaching load for your first year of employment. Such temporary load reduction is often granted to allow you to establish your research agenda, develop courses, begin establishing yourself professionally in the community, state, and nation, and to "learn the ropes." A load reduction might include being "protected" from serving on any or too many committees or a reduction in course load. Course load reductions may be for the academic year or perhaps for just one quarter or semester but normally do not continue past the first year.

In addition to your teaching load, the specific courses you will be teaching should be discussed and even detailed. While this may have been outlined during your interview, now is the time to discuss the details of your assignment. Will you be teaching mostly undergraduate, graduate, or a combination of undergraduate and graduate courses during each semester or quarter? What specific undergraduate or graduate courses will you be teaching? Are these courses in your major area of interest and training? Are they the types of courses you would like to teach or does a large portion of your teaching responsibility comprise "service" courses? Are there specific courses you want to teach and would be available to teach? Generally, the specific courses you most likely would be teaching have been determined, but there is often flexibility in course assignments at this point.

Start-Up Package and Research, Creative Activity, or Teaching Support

Many universities offer both entry- and senior-level professors "start-up" packages. A start-up package can be worth hundreds to thousands of dollars. Start-up packages are generally temporary (one to two years in duration) funds or materials designed to assist an incoming professor in the development or continuation of endeavors, such as a particular field of research, technological development such as online curriculum or course development, and/or equipment and software to support similar endeavors. Support can be given in the form of travel monies to undertake research or to attend conferences or symposia, or monies for research-related equipment and software or instructional assistance. In the sciences as in the fine arts, researchers often need specific equipment to continue or undertake a particular line of research. Instruments to measure lung capacity, software to run specific computer programs, and similar items can all become part of a start-up package. Computers, printers, labs, and other technological support are commonly provided in such packages. Thus, depending on your needs and your ability to convince the hiring administrators of your needs, your start-up package can be worth thousands of dollars.

Along with a start-up package, it is common to ask for moving expenses. Many universities are able to cover some or all of your moving expenses. Some universities can assist with faculty rental units or other such relocation services. Certain institutions have temporary (one to five years) faculty housing units that offer excellent accommodation at minimal expense.

Another commonly negotiated item is an office. An initially assigned office can often become *permanent*, so the size of your office, its furnishings, whether it has a window and such things as accessibility to parking, all become important negotiation items. You will likely spend considerably more time in your office if it is comfortable and conducive to your pursuits. It is to both the director's and your advantage to secure a comfortable, inviting workspace.

The ability to park your vehicle is as important as an office. Therefore, one of your first considerations may be parking availability. Some university campuses have extremely limited faculty parking. Part of your negotiation process may include the "privilege" of being able to "purchase" an on-campus parking permit, especially if such permits are limited. Often, in such situations, faculty are placed on waiting lists to purchase parking permits. If this is the case at your prospective university, negotiate for the opportunity to purchase a parking permit immediately.

You may have other parking considerations due to the nature of your position. The proximity of parking to your office may be an issue if you normally carry large amounts of equipment, instruments, or other materials to and from your office. Whether the parking area is covered may be an issue in colder climates. If your teaching load included night classes, security issues should be considered. Special parking privileges (being able to park in a multitude of areas, including normally restricted zones due to the nature of your position) may be among your requirements. And while it may not be a negotiable item, it is important to be aware of parking costs.

As you think about your research or creative activity and teaching needs and the possibility of securing an appropriate start-up package to support those endeavors, remember it is often easier for administrators to secure equipment (computers, printers, or specific technology), software (programs for musical notation, statistics, architectural design, or drafting), and other similar materials from other campus sources. Monies, as opposed to equipment, are generally more difficult to secure, and while some funds for research, travel support for conferences, and such may be obtained from graduate schools, general university research funds, or perhaps from dean, provost, or president's funds, most funds come from the school itself, which may have limited resources. Thus, if your start-up package requests lean more toward equipment needs rather than actual monies, the university may better be able to support your requisites.

While start-up packages are provided for both entry- and senior-level professors, entering senior-level professors can often ask for and secure additional support. It is not uncommon for senior-level professors to request, in addition to normal start-up items already mentioned, additional materials, which may include:

- an ongoing or annually refundable research or personal budget, separate from departmental budgets, that is specific to individual research or personal university expenses;
- a permanent graduate teaching assistant assigned directly to the senior professor;
- special facilities such as a computer or electronic lab; or
- support to start a research center, recording studio or label, or similar ventures.

If a senior professor with an established lecturing, touring, or performance schedule is hired, a request may be made for paid, long-term leaves or teaching assignments that may include infrequent and limited student contact. "Educational property" may include such things as royalties from books, copyrights, patents, and so forth. Individuals often negotiate agreements with the hiring institution to retain royalties, copyrights, patents, and funds secured from off-campus activities, such as performance recompense, publication royalties, commissions from original works, and/or other creative enterprise rights or reimbursements.

In some cases, especially within private university settings, guaranteed minimum annual salary increases, more frequent sabbatical leave consideration, endowed chair consideration, and other such items can be negotiated. Also, it is very common for a senior-level professor to negotiate for early tenure and/or promotion consideration. Many universities will not transfer tenure to individuals entering as associate professors. Thus, this individual can negotiate for early tenure consideration. In the same vein, an individual who wants to be considered for promotion from associate to full professor may negotiate for early consideration. And finally, while it is perhaps more common to upper-level administrative hires, spousal hires can be considered as part of a senior-level professor hire. Some universities will insure your spouse would be provided with an appropriate position in the university should you accept the position. Other universities have policies against spousal hires in the same department but may allow a spousal hire in another school or college, while some universities disallow spousal hires throughout the institution. Often such policies can be waived through negotiation.

It is wise to keep in mind that making requests during negotiations does not necessarily insure their availability. Keep in mind that what you ask for should be in proportion to your professional standing, output or potential, experience, and other considerations. Asking for things beyond the scope of your qualifications may well be considered an indication of poor judgment on your part. However, do consider your needs when accepting a new position. **This is an opportunity that may never again be available to you**.

The Offer and the Negotiation

There are several definitions of the term "negotiation." Simply stated, negotiation is a process that involves entering into discussion to reach an agreement. The negotiation process can, at times, become an intense and involved procedure, one that is conducted through telephone calls, emails, and depending on proximity, personal visits. Regardless of the means of communication, negotiations often involve multiple back-and-forth exchanges and considerable time involvement. Apart from the initial stress or time commitment allotted to the process, it is one of the most important procedures you will undertake as a university professor. For those who accept their first position and never move, the negotiation process will frame your entire professional higher education career.

There are several fine books on the art of negotiation, such as Diamond (2010), Lewicki, Saunders, and Barry (2008), and Shell (2006). While you may find these materials useful, it is important to consider that many negotiation strategies found in sources are based on an adversarial approach, the assumption being a disagreement that needs resolution, a solution reached, and so forth. The negotiation process you enter into with a university administrator differs from many business negotiations. Basically, the major difference is that there is no conflict or disagreement to be resolved. By entering into the negotiation process, the university is at least initially stating that you are the person who provides the "best fit" for the position, and you are acknowledging the position is one that you find attractive. Essentially, you are entering a negotiation as associates and colleagues who respect and trust each other; colleagues working toward a common goal to fill an open position. The goal is to reach a mutual agreement amenable to both you and the university. Ideally, this agreement should be reached while cultivating a positive working relationship, an association that would continue for many years.

NEGOTIATION STEPS

Before beginning your negotiations, rank your priorities, differentiating between needs and likes or wants. By prioritizing your needs, you and your potential employer or director will be able to focus on essential items first and, as time permits, items of lesser importance later. Remember, the director may not have the ability to fund all of your needs and in such cases will seek assistance from the dean, provost or president, graduate college, and others. Knowing your top priorities will help the director prioritize his or her efforts in meeting those needs and identify those needs necessary for a successful negotiation. Ask yourself, "What is my goal?" and "What are my 'must-haves?'" Identify those things upon which you can and can't compromise. If you request a lab for immediate use but the school cannot provide one for two years, would you be willing to wait? Can you compromise on that time line? While your decision may be based on a combination of factors, you must determine the point at which you accept or decline a job offer, identify your bottom line—know "when to walk away" or "when to sign on the dotted line."

It is essential to write down and prioritize your needs.

- Prior to your negotiations you should email, fax, or transmit in some written form your prioritized requests to the director. Prior notice will allow the director to investigate the possibility of securing funding, equipment, software, and so forth from various sources, within and outside the unit.
- If you negotiate face to face, begin the process by providing a list of your prioritized requests. This will assist you in remembering important items, alert the director to your needs, and help you both stay focused during the negotiations.
- Discuss your most critical needs first. If these needs can't be met, there may be no need for further discussions.
- During and after each discussion, *document* your conversation, sending a copy to the director and keeping one yourself. This will enable both of you to begin another discussion knowing what "has" and "hasn't" been addressed.
- When negotiating by telephone, in addition to having made your needs known prior to the conversation, it is very important to take notes during the conversation. After finishing your conversation, take the time to add more detailed comments to your initial notes. As in face-to-face meeting notes, you should send a copy of your telephone notes to the director and retain one for your files. It is important that both you and the director know what you perceived during your deliberations and the conclusions you reached, if any.
- If you negotiate by email, all correspondence should be saved. Remember, emails are legally "open records" at public institutions, so exercise care in what you communicate in your emails. If clarifications are needed, communicate them to the director as soon as possible.
- After all email, telephone, or face-to-face negotiations have been concluded, a summary of the outcome of those discussions should be submitted. Clarity and understanding are paramount in your discussions. Documenting your negotiations will facilitate this understanding.

While some of your negotiation item requests may be based on personal and/ or family item needs, refrain from sharing such information with the director (health, religion, politics, etc.). The negotiation process does not require you to explain "why you are requesting" something, nor does the director necessarily want you to share those reasons. "Don't try to be the director's best friend." S/he is your "prospective" boss, not your "imminent" friend. Many directors will ask you not to share personal information with them unless of course it is concerning an issue of your employment or functioning within your job. In other words, don't nonchalantly or casually share personal information with the director while you are negotiating unless absolutely essential.

In all negotiations, regardless of format, it is imperative that professionalism, honesty, and integrity prevail. You must be prepared, present your requests in a positive manner, and provide rationale for your requests.

At this point in our discussion it is perhaps best to summarize some of the issues addressed thus far before further discussing the negotiation process. The following are issues that have been discussed, and can and should be considered at this point of the hiring process:

- When you are offered a position it is acceptable to ask for some time to consider the offer. Generally three to five business days, unless otherwise stated, is an acceptable period to consider an offer before returning your decision. Obviously, an earlier response is also acceptable.
- Make a list of professional needs and wants for any given position. Then, when an offer is made, modify that list as needed.
- After you are offered and you decide to pursue the position, you will then enter the negotiation phase of the offer. This process involves back-and-forth conversations in the form of personal conversations, emails, or telephone calls. Some directors actually "coach" you as to what you "should be asking for" during these discussions, especially if this is your first university position. If the director doesn't provide coaching, you should carefully review and consider some of the items previously outlined in this chapter under the headings "Questions You Should Ask upon Receiving an Offer," "Teaching Load Assignment or Reduction in Teaching Load," and "Start-Up Package and Research, Creative Activity, or Teaching Support." Additionally, such information can be obtained from faculty at your prospective university or at the institution where you are currently teaching or completing a degree. Ask faculty what you should or could be asking for in a hiring package. For example: "Can I get a CD made?" "Can I get multiple sessions with the recording engineer?" "Are certain research labs open and available to me?" Thus, you will most likely be negotiating for salary, items in a start-up package, research and teaching support.

- As you near completion of your negotiations, an initial offer letter may be drafted. The offer letter generally is composed using a standard or frequently used boilerplate format. I refer to this as the "initial offer letter," as some of the letter details may be modified, due to omissions or additional negotiation. A typical "boilerplate" offer letter, from the University of Arizona, can be seen in Figure 6.2.

In Figure 6.3 an offer that is less formal in format but that conveys the same type of information is illustrated.

Date

Name
Address
Phone
Email

Dear xxx,

The search committee, students, and faculty enjoyed experiencing your teaching, recital, and the other activities that constituted your interview at The University of Arizona. I enjoyed discussing your career and performance goals, your approach to teaching and recruiting, and how your passion for students informs your ideas for institutional and professional service. We are enthusiastic about the multitude of talents you will bring to our institution, and note the passion and energy you have demonstrated during your interview.

It gives me great pleasure to offer you an appointment as an Assistant Professor of Music in the School of Music. This position is effective beginning xxxx for the xxxx-xxxx academic year and provides you with an annualized salary of $xx,xxx. This is a tenure-eligible appointment under the Conditions of Faculty Service (see the *University Handbook for Appointed Personnel* at http://w3.arizona.edu/-uhap) and is subject to the final approval of the President and the satisfactory outcome of any pre-employment screening activities or criminal background checks that may be required under University policy or Arizona Board of Regents policy 6-709.

As a faculty member you will be required to participate fully and with distinction in both undergraduate and graduate education, carry out advising duties, committee assignments, administrative and other duties as assigned. Teaching assignments in the School of Music, under present policy, consist of a maximum of 12 credits of MUS (non-applied) per semester or 18 credits of MUSI (applied) lessons per semester for faculty members who are actively engaged in research/creative activity. Your teaching assignment will normally consist of undergraduate and graduate MUS/MUSI courses in xxxxx, plus various duties as determined by the Director. This may include up to x hours of xxxx,

and/or ensemble conducting/directing. In addition, you will be required to serve on graduate committees. Additional teaching of music courses or workshops during any of the inter-sessions or summer semesters would result in additional income.

All faculty at The University of Arizona are required, on an annual basis to present evidence of sustained excellence in teaching, research and service to establish merit and to set goals and expectations for the following year. The University has established a third year probationary review to assess your progress toward tenure. In your case, your retention review would occur in xxxx-xxxx. Your mandatory tenure review would occur no later than xxxx-xxxx.

FIGURE 6.2 "Boilerplate" offer letter.

You should become familiar with all School, College and University criteria and procedures relating to the tenure and promotion process. Please review both the College of Fine Arts and School of Music criteria as outlined in our current P&T documents, and Section 3.11 of the *University Handbook for Appointed Personnel*. The website for this Handbook is http://w3.arizona.edu/~uhap/ .

We will support you with a new computer (up to $x,xxx), and a one-time resource allotment of up to $x,xxx (costs to be shared 50/50 between the College of Fine Arts and the School of Music) to assist in establishing suitable teaching and learning materials, special equipment, professional travel, or otherfaculty development projects. Monies left unused by February 1, xxxx will revert back to the School of Music. xxxxx will advise you on the procedures to be followed. Ownership of any materials or equipment purchased with these funds must necessarily remain with The University, but will be available for your use throughout your employment at UA.

You will receive a packet of information describing the benefits programs at The University of Arizona. Information describing the benefits program is also available on-line at http://www.hr.arizona.edu. Your benefit coverage is effective the first day of the month after your date of hire or eligibility date, providing you enroll within the first xx days of that date. If you do not enroll within the xx-day enrollment period, you waive your rights to participate until the next annual open enrolment period. Under certain circumstances, you may be eligible to enroll or modify your elections if you experience a qualified life status event change.

Effective with your date of hire or eligibility date, you will be enrolled automatically in the Arizona State Retirement System (ASRS) as the default retirement plan. Appointed Personnel of The University of Arizona have a one-time opportunity to elect participation in the Optional Retirement Plan (ORP). Election must be made on the appropriate forms and returned to Human Resources within xx days of your date of hire or eligibility date. If you take no action within your xx-day election period, your retirement enrollment will permanently remain in the ASRS plan.

This letter constitutes the full terms of our employment offer and supersedes all other commitments, either written or verbal, that may have been made to you.

I am required to call to your attention the fact that Arizona Board of Regents policy provides that misrepresentation of an individual's qualifications or credentials in securing employment at the University may be grounds for dismissal. The Immigration and Control Act requires that you produce certain documents that authorize you to work in the United States. On or before your first date of employment, you must present to this department original documentation to establish (1) true identity and (2) eligibility to be employed in the United States. Please consult with xxxxxx for further information regarding this requirement.

I would appreciate receiving a response to this offer as soon as possible. You may indicate acceptance by returning a signed copy of this letter to me at the above address. Please call or e-mail me at (xxx) xxx-xxxx, xxxxxx@email.arizona.edu, if you have any questions about the School of Music, The University of Arizona, or the terms of this offer. We look forward to you joining our tenure-eligible team!

Sincerely,

Peter A. McAllister, Ph.D.
Director

xxxxxxxxxx (signature/approval) Date

FIGURE 6.2 Continued

March 3, 2011

Job Offer to Deanna Zonda

Salary, benefits, and details, in no particular order:

Salary. We would offer you $48,000. The faculty salary scale is based on discipline and on prior experience in the field.

Typically, there is an annual upward adjustment in salary and additional boosts when one receives tenure and later promotion to professor.

Background Check. Sewell University requires a background check on all new full-time employees, so our signing a contract is contingent on successful completion of that check. Unless there is a major issue that would disqualify one from college employment, the results of the check are kept confidential within Human Resources.

Moving Expenses. We would provide up to $1,500 in moving expenses. You could use part of these funds, if you wished, to travel here to look for housing. We cover mileage for getting your car here, as well. Anything that gets you, your dependents, and your possessions closer to PetiteLanding we would cover. Receipts for all expenses (except mileage) are required. IRS regulations require us to report paid moving expenses as income.

Retirement Contribution. The University contributes an amount equal to 9% of your salary to your retirement account, which can be with TIAA-CREF or AIG-VALIC. You may contribute whatever you wish, up to IRS limits.

Tenure Year and Rank. You would come in at the rank of Assistant Professor. Sewell University requires 6 years to tenure. You would apply for tenure and promotion to associate professor in the fall of 2016, and it would take effect in fall 2017.

Degree. The requirement for this position is that you have a Ph.D. or D.M.A. in music.

Sabbatical and Leave Policy. You would qualify for a paid sabbatical after 6 years. Currently, that is one semester at full pay or a full year at half pay, regardless of the pay received through fellowships, etc. If you get a grant or fellowship or become independently wealthy, you may also take up to a year's leave of absence at any time. If you have a grant that provides release time for research, we can also accommodate that. The University also has a generous paid family leave policy.

Contract Period. Although faculty members are paid and have benefits over 12 months, their obligation to the University is for 9 months, roughly the last week of August through the first 3 weeks of May.

Course Load. The annual teaching load is 5 courses (20 credits). You may also take a partial leave for some number of credits, especially if you have salary coming from a grant. Another way to do it is to have release time built into a grant, where the grant pays for an adjunct to teach one or more courses; of course, we would need to make sure that a competent adjunct were available as a substitute.

Technology/Office. You would have a furnished private office equipped with a computer, your choice of Mac or PC, and software that you might need.

Start-up Funds. To help with starting a program, we will provide start-up funds of $25,000. These may be used to purchase instruments or for other appropriate expenses; up to $5,000 of the $25,000 may be used for your research, travel to conferences, etc. You may carry these funds forward into future years, if you wish.

Conference Travel. In addition to the start-up funds, we would provide up to an additional $1,100/year in travel funds; you may draw on these first, before expending your start-up funds for travel.

FIGURE 6.3 Less formal offer letter.

University Grants. Each year, the College gives out 8 or 9 competitive research grants of $3,000 each to faculty members. When you get one of these, you can't apply again for two years.

External Grants. We have two grant writers who help faculty members with grants; they have their hands in over 100 grant submissions each year. They also help students and faculty members obtain Fulbright Fellowships; we have ranked second in the nation in our category for the last few years for the numbers of Fulbrights received by our graduating seniors. We are also committed to providing necessary matching funds for external grants.

Department Funds. Each faculty member receives $250 annually to spend on journal subscriptions or other professional expenses.

Life Insurance. The University carries a life insurance policy on faculty members equal to 1.5 times annual salary. Sewell University pays the premium.

Health Insurance. Sewell University currently pays the full premium for health insurance for individual employees. If you were to insure dependents, there would be a charge for them. Costs are outlined on the HR website. Annual enrollment begins on April 1 each year, and benefit premiums might change at those times.

Dental Insurance. Sewell University pays the premium on dental insurance for employees. Family coverage extra.

Eye Care. Sewell University has a vision insurance plan. Coverage for employee and family extra.

Tuition Benefits. There are tuition benefits for dependents, both at Sewell University and at tuition-exchange colleges. If you are interested in the details, you should check with Human Resources.

Disability Insurance. Sewell University carries free disability insurance on all employees that pays 100% of salary for 6 months, followed by 60% thereafter.

FIGURE 6.3 Continued

The Hire Letter

If you agree on the initial written or oral agreement made during your negotiations, the next step is to receive the formal letter of hire. The "hire letter" is a formal agreement between you and your employer, and as such is an important document. You should retain a signed copy of your hire letter in a secure location. It is not uncommon for universities, colleges, or schools to experience changes in administrative personnel. When a change in administrative personnel occurs, or when questions arise, the hire letter can be referenced pertaining to assignment, benefits, and other such matters. Additionally, the hire letter is often used during the tenure and promotion process, as it contains several items pertinent to your employment. Therefore, should there be any agreed-upon changes in assignment, benefits, terms of employment, or so forth, from your hire letter, you should request and retain a written and signed copy of those changes and request that the updated copy be placed in your official employee files.

Once you sign and return your hire letter, a "contract" most generally follows. Issued by the university, the contract or contract letter will most likely include your salary, dates of employment (beginning and/or ending dates), and basic information concerning benefits. Often, unless you are able to be on campus, you will need to sign your contract letter upon your arrival. Federal law requires vetting of legal status to be employed in the United States for state-funded, assisted, or aided positions, such as university faculty position, and you will need to show proof of citizenship by presenting usually two or more of the following types of documents: state-issued driver's license, birth certificate, social security card, and passport. It is often important that at least one of your documents includes photo identification. Unlike the hire letter, your contract is generally a document that is renewed annually. Other documents you should be receiving or should have already received are: The school handbook(s) and, if available, the college and university handbooks, booklets on benefits packages and options, booklets on retirement options, and any available faculty orientation materials.

There are several basic elements that should appear in your letter of hire. The basic components of a hire letter should minimally indicate the following:

1. Salary;
2. Appointment period: generally an academic year, which is construed as a nine- or ten-month period, depending on the hiring institution;
3. Indication of load assignment or strength: 3/2, 2/2, 4/4, etc.;
4. Start and end date;
5. Full vetting of legal status to be employed in the United States;
6. Hiring package details: monies for educational materials, research materials, moving expenses, etc.;
7. Reasonable time allotted to accept the offer (usually days not weeks). To be official, the letter must be signed (a signed fax is official as long as the original letter eventually follows);
8. Specific areas of responsibility, if not necessarily specific courses: for example, trombone studio, elementary methods, and so forth;
9. Timeline to go up for tenure and promotion and, in some cases, specific criteria needed to achieve tenure and/or promotion.

Figure 6.4 illustrates a sample of a "letter of hire."

University of Western Wisconsin
School of Music

November 1, 2010

Susan H. Tocsins
1113 E. New Lane
Old Lane, WI 52913

Dear Dr. Tocsins:

Following our recent discussions and after consultation with my faculty, I am pleased to offer you the position of Assistant Professor of Choral Music with the School of Music at the University of Western Wisconsin, beginning Fall, 2011.

You will receive an annual academic base salary rate of $55,000 plus the standard University of Western Wisconsin benefits contribution for the 2011-2012 academic year. The academic calendar runs from August 15 to May 15. There is the possibility of summer teaching with additional compensation.

I am writing with details of the offer of employment and I have enclosed the original letter, plus one copy. Please review and sign one copy indicating your agreement with these points, and return it to me.

1. The initial appointment will be for three years, beginning August 15, 2011 through May 15, 2014. Your appointment will be at the rank of Assistant Professor on a tenure-track. As with all faculty members, you will be reviewed for continuation at the end of your three-year initial appointment. At the end of six years, a tenure decision will be required. All faculty members are reviewed annually through the awarding of indefinite tenure.

2. Your teaching assignments have been determined in consultation with Professor Charles Charge, area coordinator for choral music. They are outlined below for the 2011-2012 academic year:

Following is a general description of the teaching duties required of this position: For each term (we have three, ten-week quarters), I anticipate a total workload of two courses to include teaching a course in choral methods (and related laboratory) or conducting, and directing a choir. Additionally, you would also be responsible for supervising practica.

3. In addition to your regular teaching assignments, you will be expected to assist with student recruitment and advising, supervision of and serving on committees for graduate student research projects. Additionally, all faculty members are expected to serve on committees and perform other appropriate University service.

4. You will be eligible for faculty travel support similar to all full-time faculty members in the School of Music, which is presently averaging $750 per person per year. You will also be eligible for an additional personal funding source or Academic Support Account (ASA) of $1,500 per year under the current guidelines from Academic Affairs for tenured and tenure-track faculty that can be used towards professionally related travel, supplies, equipment, and can be carried forward each year if not completely spent.

5. You will be eligible to apply for a New Junior Faculty Award Program to be awarded shortly after your contract is approved in the amount of $2,000 towards equipment and supplies (such as a computer workstation for your office) and an additional stipend of up to $6,000 in the summer of 2012 to support research and creative work (supplies, equipment, and travel) or it can be taken as additional pay. These funds can also be carried forward to a new fiscal

FIGURE 6.4 Letter of hire.

year if not expended in the first year. We will provide you with details on this program during your first term at the University. In future years, beginning Fall 2012, you will become eligible to apply for Summer Research Awards, which is a campus-wide competitive program that supports research and creative endeavors for faculty.

6. You will be expected to establish and maintain an active and productive program of creative activity in scholarly research and publishing, appropriately related to your area(s) of expertise.

I believe this covers the major points of the verbal agreement we had. Please feel free to add additional points for my review that you believe I may have missed. We will need a reply no later than Monday, November 7, 2010.

I am very pleased that you will be joining our faculty, and look forward to working with you in the future. I wish you the best of luck on your move to the University of Western Wisconsin. Please contact me should you have additional questions.

Sincerely,

Chip Chargeship, Director
School of Music

My signature below indicates I agree to the above conditions of this appointment:

_____

Choral Music Candidate Name   Date

FIGURE 6.4 *(Continued)*

Summary

A higher education job offer, especially your first one, is one of your most exciting professional experiences. You have been selected from a host of individuals and deemed the most appropriate person for the position. This is indeed an honor and perhaps, after weeks of waiting and questioning, a major boost to your self-confidence. The subsequent negotiation process should therefore be viewed as one in which you and the hiring institutional representatives attempt to reach an amenable agreement—one intended to benefit you and the university. If the position is one that you desire, then both you and the hiring institution can work from the basic understanding that *you* want the position and *they* want you in the position. During the negotiation process you will articulate your needs. The university in turn will decide how to best meet those needs. It is important to remember that the university negotiation process is one that is based on sharing a mutual goal and that both parties are willing to expend the effort to produce positive results. Keeping a positive and open mind during your first negotiation will most likely enable this goal to be reached.

References

Diamond, Stuart. 2010. *Getting More: How You Can Negotiate to Succeed in Work and Life*. New York: Three Rivers Press.

Lewicki, Roy, David Saunders, and Bruce Barry. 2009. *Negotiation*. New York: McGraw-Hill/Irwin.

Shell, G. Richard. 2006. *Bargaining for Advantage: Negotiation Strategies for Reasonable People*. 2nd ed. New York: Penguin.

USLegal. 2012. http://definitions.uslegal.com/f/fixed-term-contract/, accessed December 31, 2012.

7

YOUR FIRST DAYS ON CAMPUS AND BEYOND

HOW EXCITING! YOU accepted a university position, your move was successful and you secured a dwelling in your new locale. You've paid deposits for electricity, water, gas, and so forth, established new banking or financial institutions, sent out changes of address, and notified the USPS of your forwarding address. New home email and Internet and other services (cable, telephone, newspaper) have been established, your car, home, rental, and other insurances have been updated, and your vehicles have been inspected, registered, insured, and licensed. It seems like you've been working forever, but you've only just begun. While your home environment may be in order, save unpacking some boxes and frequent inquiries of "where did I put that," your university preparation awaits you.

Your First Days on Campus

You need to allot at least one week, two would be better, *before* classes begin to find and settle into your office, secure parking permits, sign remaining official documents, choose your benefits packages, attend various orientation, faculty, and welcome back meetings, secure university IDs, locate classrooms and classroom equipment, find the copy machine, secure copy machine codes, obtain a faculty mailbox, print out class rosters, prepare syllabi, and so forth. Occasionally universities will secure some of your material needs prior to your arrival, such as office and classroom keys. If you are on a campus that does some of the legwork for you, consider yourself fortunate. Regrettably with reductions in staff and other support becoming more common across higher education campuses, plan to complete most, if not all, of these tasks yourself.

WHAT YOU NEED TO KNOW AND DO BEFORE CLASSES BEGIN

If you have not received a copy of your faculty handbook(s), health and benefit booklets, and other such documents, now is the time get them. Some of these documents may be obtained at new-faculty orientation sessions. Often at these sessions, new faculty learn how to obtain ID cards, select their preferred benefits, note retirement options, and perhaps become familiar with technological software and programs available for classroom and research endeavors. Once you receive your documents, read them carefully. Faculty handbooks should provide guidelines pertaining to annual reviews and promotion and tenure criteria, to travel fund and grant availability. Your benefits booklets outline important information pertaining to your medical, insurance, retirement, and other programs. While it may not be exciting reading, it certainly is critical reading.

DOCUMENTS

Before you begin your on-campus journey, you should locate the following documents: (1) social security card, (2) birth certificate, (3) driver's license, (4) passport, and (5) green card—if appropriate. These are the types of documents that most institutions now require to receive or sign "official" documents. Usually two or three forms of official documentation are required to secure keys, ID cards, parking permits, as well as provide proof of citizenship (enabling you to sign your contract, etc.). Additionally, you may need supplementary documents to secure your parking permit.

PARKING

Unless you are within walking distance of the campus, you'll need to drive your vehicle to the university. Most likely you will not yet have received your parking permit. To secure your permit you may need to show proof of ownership (title), provide license or vehicle registration information, and perhaps even show insurance information or present a university ID. Often a letter from the school's business manager, director, or college dean, certifying that you are permitted to purchase a parking permit (further forms to take with you or secure), may be required. Temporarily however, you may be wondering: Where can I park? The one thing you *don't* want to do is park in university parking without a permit or in any restricted areas that require a university, city, or state permit. You will not be exempt from fines (usually much more than they should be) and parking enforcement is generally *very* vigilant prior to and at the beginning of a school year. Generally, you can find a parking lot that offers an hourly or daily rate to park your vehicle. You may need to walk some distance to your destinations, so plan accordingly.

What is involved in getting a parking permit? In Chapter 6, it was recommended that you negotiate the right to purchase a parking permit. If you did not do this and parking is severely restricted on your campus, you may find that you will not be able to secure on-campus parking immediately. You may be placed on a parking permit waiting list and wait months and perhaps a year or more to secure on-campus parking. Let's assume that you *are* able to purchase your permit. First, you must find out where the parking permits are processed. The parking division is often housed in a separate building that may be some distance from your school. Once you have an idea of the parking division location, you'll need to know the documents required and the cost and form of payment needed to secure your parking permit. Here is where it can get sticky. In order to secure your parking permit you may need to have both a university ID and a letter from the school's business manager, director, or college dean, in addition to your title/registration, license, and insurance. You may find that payment for your permit can only be made through a paycheck deductible item process. Hopefully you will be "in the system" and identified as a faculty member so that this form of payment can be established. However, should you need a university ID or letter of consent and you don't have it, you will need to get those items to proceed. It will behoove you to determine the specific documents and documentation needed to secure your parking permit *before* you walk across campus.

If you can't get a parking permit immediately or if the parking locale is too far from your office, where can you park to get books and supplies into your office? Often loading zones or controlled parking zones for official university vehicles are located near university buildings. Limited in number, loading zone parking spaces can often be used by anyone who follows the posted time limitation (parking no longer than 10–15 minutes for example). At some institutions, a service or loading zone permit is required to park in such areas. Such permits are often held by personnel in the school office and can be checked out for temporary use. Some loading zones allow parking after business hours—for example, you may be able to park in a loading zone near your office after 6 p.m. and before 7 a.m. Monday through Friday and anytime on Saturday or Sunday. Whatever the rules governing such areas, you should be able to get books and supplies to your office with a bit of planning without having to lug them great distances.

UNIVERSITY IDENTIFICATION CARDS

One of the more important "documents" needed on many campuses is a university identification card. Depending on your university campus structure, your university identification (UID) card can allow you to secure keys and parking permits, access library materials, utilize computer labs, and a host of other things. Your UID may be one of the first cards you want to get, after signing your contract. As with a parking permit, you may need a letter from an appropriate authority identifying you as a certified, employed, faculty member, along with a driver's license, passport, or other identification.

UIDs are often issued in a central location on campus. Again, make sure you have all documentation required to get your UID before you begin your journey. One reason to begin your preparation process early is to avoid standing in line, waiting to get your UID. While some campuses provide special access for new faculty and staff members, often such services are not available. A first come, first served policy is generally in force. If you arrive for your UID when the majority of incoming students are also attempting the same task, your wait may be prolonged. Remember too that your UID is generally a photo-ID. Like your driver's license photo, your UID photographs may likely be the first and last one taken at that university, unless of course your UID is lost or stolen. So, like a driver's license, remember this photograph will be for posterity—a condition that may or may not be an issue for you. Generally UIDs are produced immediately on-site or are given to you after a brief processing period.

KEYS, ACCESS TO OFFICE, CLASSROOMS, BUILDINGS

Another one of your more immediate needs will be keys and access to your office, classrooms, and buildings. While there are a variety of modes used to gain access to your office, classrooms, and buildings, such as cards that are slid or run through a scanner (such as those found on most hotel rooms) or door keypad codes, the key remains the prevailing mode of entry on most campuses.

Where can you get keys? Again, like the parking permit and UID, the center that issues keys is often located in a not-so-central, on-campus location. The procedure for obtaining keys varies from institution to institution, but usually some type of permission form or computer-transmitted documentation needs to be secured before you are granted any key. If you need a key to more than one room, it generally requires a separate permission request per key. Thus, if you know you need more than one key, try to get them all at once. This will save you several trips to the "office of the keys." Permission for receipt of a key is generally received from a business manager, building superintendent or manager, or similar staff member. Frequently there is a charge or deposit for each key received, which can be as little as $5.00 per key to more than $50.00 per key.

Think about your keys needs. You will need a key to your office and perhaps a key to access the building in which your office is housed. You may need a key to each classroom you use, especially if no master classroom key system exists. Other key considerations may be for labs, equipment rooms, computer rooms, storage lockers, stereo, playback, or projection cabinets or rooms, meeting rooms, conference rooms, and perhaps concert halls. Remember that each key you check out increases your level of responsibility, so decide which keys you could "live without" and those that are essential to your day-to-day or week-to-week operations. Often, the central office can temporarily check a key out to you for rooms that you might use infrequently.

Key identification cards are regularly issued with keys. A key identification card notifies any security personnel that you have permission to possess that key. Depending on the security issues at the institution, periodic security checks may be implemented. Individuals in buildings and offices that can be accessed only by keys may be challenged to produce evidence they have a key and key identification card. If this is the policy at your institution, you should carry your key identification cards. Additionally, it may be necessary to annually update or renew these cards.

YOUR OFFICE

Hopefully, you've negotiated for an office that meets your standards and needs prior to your on-campus arrival. If you had the foresight to do so, you should have requested that your office receive a fresh coat of paint, floors were cleaned, polished, and repaired, or that the carpet was replaced. Now you need to locate your office and obtain access to it. Most central offices will have a master key that you can briefly borrow that will allow you access to your office until such time as you obtain your office key. The central office staff will also be able to tell you where your office is and most likely provide you with such essentials as paper, pens, pencils, staplers, and so forth. Additionally, the office will be able to tell you where your mail box is located (this is generally in the central office itself), provide you with any outside access code to your mailbox, and provide you, when required, with an access code for the copying machine.

The size of your office and whether or not it has a window is often dependent on your status and rank, due to availability or negotiations, or both. Sometimes too, offices are shared with other faculty members or with graduate teaching assistants. You need to determine your office equipment, some of which may have been determined during your negotiations (computer, printer, scanner, software, grand pianos, and so forth). The amount of office equipment you desire may be dependent on the room itself and whether or not you will be sharing that room. The school generally provides bookshelves, file cabinets, office chairs, and the like. However, if you have special needs, such as an office chair that offers additional lumbar support, you should plan to purchase such items on your own. University office equipment tends to be utilitarian.

While most faculty offices provide local and long-distance telephone as well as Internet access, you may need codes to use them, especially when making long-distance calls. Computer, printer and Internet access setup, and other such technical operations may need to be performed before you can utilize your equipment. Certain software programs may also require special access codes. Most often the central office can direct you to the right personnel to help you with each of your issues.

One nice touch offered by many universities is a faculty or staff art loan program. Many faculty members avail themselves of this service. The faculty member goes to a central location, selects available artwork, and then signs it out for a specified period of time. Much like checking out a library book, artwork loans can be renewed or works exchanged after a given time frame.

CLASSES

You may have the following questions when it comes to your teaching assignment:

- What am I teaching?
- How many private students do I have each day or each week?
- How many classes do I teach each day or each week?
- When do classes begin? What is the procedure for dissemination of class materials?
- Have I taught any of these classes before or will they be "new preparations?"
- Do I have classes that are coordinated with others? In other words, do I teach one section of a course that is also taught by others, in which the expectation is that students, regardless of section, end up learning the same materials? If so:
  - Who supervises these?
  - What are the expectations?
  - Is there a standardized curriculum?
  - If there is no standardized curriculum, what topics must be covered and in what detail?

- Class rosters: Where can I get these?
- Books: Have they been ordered? If books haven't been ordered, how can I order books? How can I secure a desk copy?
- Syllabi: Are there syllabi on file from previous instructors for my course(s)? If so, how should I modify my classes? Should I change the classes?
- What are the expectations for each class?
  - Are labs required?
  - Are clinical experiences required for state certification?
  - Are certain performance criteria to be achieved at various levels and are there juries at the end of the term to assess those criteria?
  - Are there performance or publications requirements or standards?
  - When teaching classes or in my studio, are there requirements of which I should be aware that are associated with departmental standards or expectations, state requirements, school expectations, and so forth?
- Where are my classes, labs, studio master classes, and so forth?
  - What equipment is available to me in these settings (playback, recording, projectors, stands, appropriate chairs, cameras, Internet access)?
  - How and where can I get equipment needed for classes?
- If I need equipment that the school does not have, or there is equipment that needs to be replaced or repaired, is there a budget that can be used for these purposes? What is the procedure?
- Conductors, ensembles, directors:
  - Have concerts for my group(s) already been scheduled? If so, what are the details of those concerts?
  - If I need to schedule concerts, how do I proceed?
  - Are auditions needed? Are they scheduled? What is the procedure?
  - Do I have a budget and, if so, what is it? What procedures are needed to secure funding for various venues?
- Who prepares programs, PR materials for concerts, and so forth, and what is the procedure for doing so?

Most information you seek can be obtained from the following individuals: The director, the area coordinator, the business manager, the central office personnel, or the building supervisor or room scheduler.

The director will be able to inform you of your teaching assignment and if you have a budget. Your area coordinator will be able to provide details concerning your teaching assignment, such as whether any of your classes need to be coordinated with others, and if so, the details of that coordination; whether or not books have been ordered for those classes; expectations for the courses; meeting times, length, and location of your classes; the equipment in those rooms; and how you can obtain student rosters. While the area coordinator may have syllabi of your courses, schools that are accredited by NASM, NCATE, and other such organizations are required to have current syllabi on file in the central office. Also, many central offices can provide you with the procedure for checking out and the location of equipment you need that may not be available in your classroom. The business manager will inform you of the procedures needed to order equipment, place repair orders, and the like. While the director will be able to tell you if you have a budget, the business manager will additionally be able to tell you the amount of funds you have in your budget, how to access those monies, and inform you of any restriction that may be associated with those funds. The building coordinator is generally the individual who schedules rooms and hence will have information pertaining to room and concert hall use. If you have concerts and they have been scheduled, the building coordinator will have that information. If you need to schedule events the building coordinator can assist you in that endeavor. Depending upon the size of the school, an individual may be assigned to produce all programs, public relations releases, posters, and other materials.

ADVISING

If you are fortunate enough to be at a university where undergraduate and graduate student advising is handled by staff, you will not need to be concerned about an advising obligation. However, many schools require faculty to perform this task. If this is the case, both undergraduate and graduate students will be seeking you out for advice on scheduling and graduating. This is a profound responsibility, as inappropriate or incorrect advice could result in a student having to spend additional time and money to complete degree requirements.

One of your first tasks is to talk with your area coordinator to determine who your advisees are and what forms and information you need to properly advise these students. You will need to become aware of normal student course loads, any course sequencing that is required, audition or testing requirements needed to get into certain classes or levels of courses, and of course, knowledge of those courses essential to degree requirements. In addition, such things as information concerning juries, orals and written comprehensives, proposals, testing for certification, and similar data must be at your command and shared as needed. You will need to have access to student files, either electronically or on paper, and you will need to know how to locate and update those files and how to access information pertaining to each student's progress in the degree program. An advising commitment is one that requires considerable knowledge and preparation.

ORIENTATIONS, RETREATS, AND MEETINGS

While you are busily setting up your office and preparing for classes, you must also know that such planning will be interrupted by a host of preclass meetings. Each of these meetings is intended to assist you in your preparations or inform you of events that are deemed important. One such assembly, the university-wide orientation meeting, is designed to assist all new faculty members in a host of ways. Depending on the university, faculty will receive everything from information concerning health, retirement, and insurance plans to learning about computer-assisted programs available for class organizational and delivery purposes (registering grades, recording attendance, receiving homework, scheduling assignments, posting reading materials, and communicating with students). Often specific new faculty orientation programs are additionally held by schools and colleges and are designed to familiarize you with library and computer access or search programs and inform you of promotion and tenure guidelines, availability of grants, and so forth.

Health insurance, retirement plan, and life insurance orientations are designed to inform you of your choices in these areas. Many university health plans provide options from which you can choose: PPO, HMO, EPO, and other health coverage, as well as options to participate in dental, optical, and other such programs. Once you choose a health plan, it is generally enforced for one year and cannot be changed until the following year or sign-up period. Life insurance programs vary, but usually extra-term life insurance is available on a yearly basis. Retirement plans often are not changeable once you select a program. It is in your best interest to investigate all retirement plan options carefully as they become increasingly important as you near retirement. Common retirement options include: state retirement programs, AIG-VALIC, TIAA-CREF, IRAs, and social security or Medicare.

You most likely will have college or school retreats or meetings prior to the beginning of classes. Retreats, often held off-campus or in an on-campus location other than the school itself, are frequently designed as "think tank" sessions and involve all faculty. This is a good time to meet your colleagues. Usually from a morning or an afternoon to one or two days in length, retreats provide forums for administration, faculty, and staff to present and develop ideas pertaining to curricular innovations and to establish new guidelines, goals, or objectives. In lieu of retreats, many schools and colleges hold meetings. These meetings, generally one to three hours in length, are held to inform faculty of such things as:

- Exciting news (grants, donations, and/or endowments received, new programs, increases in state funding formulas),
- Informational items (upcoming accreditation reviews, deadlines for travel funds, research grants, university funding formula changes, class size policy changes, and so forth),
- Introductions ("new" faculty, staff, and administration members, and assignment changes of existing faculty), and
- Accolades (awards received by faculty, staff, administrators, special recognitions for books published, national professional position appointments, receipt of Fulbright awards, and so forth).

The purposes of the college and/or school meetings are to inspire, motivate, and instill pride within the organization. Meetings are generally upbeat in nature and often accompanied by refreshments or even meals. And unlike the retreat—the focus of which is more often directed toward development, planning, or problem solving—meetings, in addition to informational dissemination, are frequently intended to "fire up the troops."

Other meetings that may cut into your preparation time are area or divisional meetings, those meetings within your own department (music education, studio instructors, brass and woodwind instructors, and so forth). Generally area meetings are working meetings, intended to provide guidelines (such as a discussion of the organization of multisectional offerings), to strategize (to plan undergraduate and graduate course offerings for the upcoming year or more), or to discuss pressing issues (changes in guidelines from a national accreditation agency that immediately impacts course content). And while these meetings may be more directly related to your expertise, they still require your time and attention.

OTHER

There are a few other items or questions to which you will definitely want answers, but these don't necessarily need to be addressed prior to the beginning of classes. One such question is: When do I get paid? You may be so busy preparing that you forgot that you are actually getting a salary and as such you will receive payment. As a new faculty member your payment may be delayed until you've taught for a period of time. If this is the case, you obviously must do some financial planning to get through this "dry period." Payments can be weekly, biweekly, or monthly. Also, unless otherwise stipulated by you, the distribution of your salary will be completed during your contract period (nine to ten months). Most universities have options that allow you to disperse your nine- to ten-month salary over a twelve-month period, thus providing for income during the summer months, when you may not be receiving any additional income. The faculty member, however, must generally request this option. Items pertaining to your salary and payment options can be obtained from your business manager.

Grant, travel request, and other funding proposal application deadlines are often due shortly after classes begin. And while additional funding request deadlines may be available, many faculty submit their requests early, during the first round of application considerations, when ample funds are still available. If this is the case at your institution, then you definitely need to be prepared to submit your proposals at that time as well. Deadline for such submissions can generally be found online, from the director, or colleagues.

SUMMARY

The following summarizes the preclass activities discussed in this chapter. You may be engaged in some, all, or more events than listed. Whatever your preclass tasks and responsibilities, know that course preparation time will be limited. Plan accordingly.

Tasks, Responsibilities, To-Do List

- Plan to attend new faculty university-wide orientation meetings.
- Allow time to read/review all handbooks, booklets, and so forth.
- Find and carry with you (at least until you have secured all necessary documents and materials) your (1) social security card, (2) birth certificate, (3) driver's license, (4) passport, (5) green card—if appropriate (6) proof of vehicle ownership (title or vehicle registration) and perhaps vehicle insurance information.
- Take credit cards, checks, and cash to use for incidental expenses.
- Procure documents needed and then secure your
  1. University identification card,
  2. Parking permit,
  3. Keys (access to office, classrooms, and other buildings).
- Locate your office and secure any equipment, supplies, and materials you need.
- Identify courses to be taught and the location and other such details pertaining to those courses.

- Gain ample knowledge about any student advising commitment you have.
- Attend all preclass meetings: university orientation, school or college retreats, and area meetings.

Of course, it perhaps goes without saying that your major task is to prepare for your courses. Your preparation must outline and detail the semester's or quarter's activities. If you have questions about course preparation, course syllabi, and similar issues, there are numerous books that can assist you such as those by Schoenfeld and Magnan (2004), Johnson (1995), and Conway and Hodgman (2009). Your colleagues are also there to assist you in this endeavor. And of course, while we all would like to design the most informative and best-organized course immediately, reality dictates otherwise. Most professors spend years revising and/or completely restructuring courses in attempts to present the most salient information possible in the allotted time frame. Be patient with yourself.

Beyond Your First Days

One of the more important things you can do is find a mentor to help you through the first few years of university teaching. Often, school directors assign you a mentor. If this is an individual with whom you can easily work and talk, do not hesitate to consult him or her as often as needed. Your mentor understands his or her role and should be happy to assist you. However, not all assigned mentors work out, nor do all directors assign mentors. Your task is to find a mentor, an individual with whom you can discuss issues, ask questions, and seek advice. Ideally your mentor will have been at the university long enough to understand the "in and outs" of the system and will also have had positive experiences working with colleagues and difficult issues (i.e., politics). This individual doesn't necessarily need to be in your area or even in your discipline, but they must be someone you trust and can rely upon.

During my years of teaching I found trusted mentors to guide me through the perils of university structure. One of the individuals I worked with as a doctoral student became a valued mentor. Dr. James Sherbon, Professor of Music Education at the University of Texas, Austin, the University of North Carolina, Greensboro, and the University of Oklahoma, was that individual. During his tenure, he taught a doctoral-level course in which he offered erudite advice on succeeding in university settings. As he guided many individuals through their careers, he continued to seek their own sagacious advice. The following contains some of those guiding thoughts compiled from years of teaching.

GUIDING THOUGHTS

There may not be two items more irksome, troublesome to faculty members than workload and salary. The ideas of "fairness" and "pulling one's weight," are frequently used when discussions of workload and salary arise. What is fair and how one pulls one's weight vary from discipline to discipline. For example: if you are an entering assistant professor in a fine arts discipline and expect to get the same salary as an entering assistant professor in business, you are going to be first shocked and then unhappy—shocked because you will learn that the business professor will be getting thousands more than you, and unhappy because that won't change. Workloads also differ by discipline, and a full load in one discipline will be a "light" load in another. Most faculty understand those provisos, and while they may not like them, they understand them. Given those caveats, even though faculty know they "may be fighting over scraps," they want that struggle to be equitable among themselves.

WORKLOAD

When thinking about your workload, even if it was negotiated, factors to consider are: (1) What does your director expect of you? (2) Did you inherit your workload? (3) How does your load compare with your immediately related colleagues? (4) Is there a formula for workloads (*read your faculty handbook*), and how does your load match the stated loads? If you are uneasy about your workload, first talk to your area coordinator. S/he needs to know of your concern and may be able to assist you in your discussion with your director. Additionally, any changes made to your workload may well affect the area offerings. Next, make an appointment with your director, informing him/her of your concern or topic. A good approach when meeting with your director can be, "Can you help me?" or "I need your advice." Prior to this appointment, assemble documentation, such as the numbers of students, number of classes, amount of work you are facing that haven't been articulated. Take this quantitative documentation (in writing) and ask (don't complain) about the distribution of your load. *Do not* make demands! Present your documentation at the beginning of the conference. Such accurately prepared information can be analyzed during and after your conference. If the job situation you inherited is not flexible or to your liking, don't complain, make the best of it. You can work to resolve issues as you gain experience.

Remember also that faculty workload comprises not only classes and lessons. While attendance at concerts, recitals, festivals, symposia, and other such activities is often expected, you do have control over the number of events you attend. Analyze your work environment. Do you have a student "open door" policy or do you maintain fixed or by special appointment "office hours?" An open-door policy can be disruptive to a positive work environment, insuring that you will be taking work home with you. Service on committees is also an item that you may be able to control. If you find yourself overwhelmed, cut back, when possible, on the amount of effort you give to various committees. Often such extra efforts, while welcomed, are not essential to the smooth working of a committee.

One component of workload is recruitment. Faculty are typically are expected to recruit students for their studios and to fill ensembles. As a masterful recruiter, you may find yourself in your second year with thirty students and no teaching assistant (TA). And while your director may not be able to reduce your load or provide a TA, you can implement selective recruitment techniques in the future, ones that balance recruiting or auditioning and your load with the needs of ensemble directors. On the other hand, a double-reed studio likely may not achieve a full studio load.

At times, due to departmental needs, you may need to teach a course out of your specialty area. Go to your new job prepared to teach almost anything, as you may not know your entire assignment until you arrive, enrollment begins to settle, and somebody discovers that an additional section of Theory 101 is needed.

Regardless of your workload, you are expected to meet classes as scheduled. I have known several individuals who have said "I was hired to do research," or "I am a performer, I can't teach while I'm on tour." While this may be true, your first obligation must be to your students. The director should be notified and must approve planned absences (tours, conferences, etc.) in advance. Lessons missed should be rescheduled at times mutually satisfactory to teacher and students. Classes may also be rescheduled, a guest lecturer may be arranged, or an equivalent outside assignment given. Faculty who schedule special rehearsals, make-up lessons, etc. should make every attempt to avoid conflicts with other regularly scheduled activities.

While you don't want to have the "heaviest" faculty workload, you don't want to be perceived as having a "cushy" load either. The collegial perception that you are "pulling your own weight," in the department and school, is important. There is a tenuous balance between the three legs of the stool—the balance between what you do, what you are expected to do, and how that is perceived.

SALARY

One often-repeated mantra in academia is "You will never be satisfied with your salary." Even though you've negotiated the best salary you thought possible, before you realize it, you'll learn that another faculty member negotiated a better salary, or that new assistant professors are being hired at your current salary. When you are promoted to associate professor or full professor, you'll find that your salary begins to stagnate while the new hires come in with seemingly inflated salaries. You might see very small across-the-board annual increments, if any, and you might even experience salary decreases, camouflaged as furlough days.

A phenomenon that comes under the heading of "life isn't fair," the longer you are at an institution, the more you will learn about perceived salary inequities among your colleagues. Individuals with national acclaim and years of excellence in teaching, research or creative activity, and service may often be receiving lower salaries than the latest entering personality. Salary increments and merit pay (if available and if added to your base) can enhance your salary, as can internal awards that carry permanent monetary stipends. However, merit pay awards often seem unfair as the largest merit pay awards frequently seem to be given to undeserving faculty or to faculty in areas other than your own. How then can you increase your salary? Perhaps the two most consistent methods are: (1) take a position at another institution that offers more money, or (2) get an offer from another university and use that as a bargaining chip to increase your current salary. With the latter option, however, you run the risk of receiving a handshake and a congratulatory pat on the back as you exit the director's office on your way to pack your office after informing him/her of your new offer. Another way to enhance your salary, not necessarily through the university system, can be described colloquially as "Doing more gigs!" Developing a business outside of the university structure is somewhat common, especially among professors who hold tenure. This requires a delicate balance between fulfilling your university obligations, your available energy, and your lifestyle. If such salary increase approaches are not available to you and your salary remains static, you may decide to leave or you may decide to stay—knowing that other positive factors of your position outweigh salary issues.

TENURE

In most higher education institutions, the decision to grant tenure is separate from the decision to offer a promotion. And while the two decisions often occur at the same point in a young professor's career, they can be distinct enough to discuss separately.

What becomes most easily attainable to some and most challenging to others is the receipt of tenure. Even though the process may be unnecessarily tedious or laborious for all seeking tenure, why do some individuals struggle and others not? The answer lies in one's area of focus and on the application process.

Every individual has an interest area that is stronger than another. While you may enjoy teaching, you may relish the challenges research or creative activity present, and vice versa. When individuals accept a position, they are in essence indicating their strength of interest in the areas of research and creative activity or teaching. Accepting a position at a university that is research intensive means that you will need to excel in the area of research or creative activity to meet tenure requirements. Accepting a position at a teaching-intensive university implies that teaching and perhaps even service are relatively more important in securing tenure than research or creative activity. If you are struggling with the tenure requirements, you need to ask yourself "Did I accept the wrong position?" If you are in a research-intensive setting and you don't enjoy research or creative endeavors, you may well have chosen the wrong institution and will struggle, if not fail, in your attempt to receive tenure. The knowledge of your setting, combined with your interests, is essential to your success.

Let's assume that you have chosen the appropriate institutional setting for your skill and interest set and you are working toward tenure. The questions that follow may be ones that frequent your mind on your tenure journey.

- How do I know "what counts" or what is most important when developing my tenure dossier?
- How much of "what counts" do I need to be tenured?
- How do I know if I'm "on track" toward tenure?
- Where can I look for tenure guidance?
- What is the process for getting tenure?
- How do I prepare a tenure package? What's included, what should I be doing to assemble such a package?
- What happens if I don't get tenure?
- If I get tenure at one institution and then take a position at another institution, can my tenure transfer?

We shall begin with the first question—What Counts?

What Counts?

Many institutions cite excellence in teaching, research, and service as important criteria for tenure. And while this may be true, reality dictates that one area or perhaps even two areas are weighted more than others. Teaching may be more important at one institution than research, or vice versa.

Where can you find out what areas are most important in the tenure decision? The first place you should check is your own department or school. Especially in schools or colleges of music, criteria for tenure may differ somewhat from university criteria in that music areas equate creative efforts, such as performances, to those in academic endeavors, such as publishing. Read your school's tenure guidelines carefully as they will have been written with an eye toward equating creative activity with academic efforts. Next, read the tenure guidelines provided by your college and then the same guidelines issued by the university. Should you still have questions, and most likely you will, consult with a mentor, colleague, or administrator. Also, many institutions have regular tenure orientation meetings, which you should attend. You should, after consulting these sources, have a good idea of "what counts."

Once you know "what counts," prioritize your daily activities so you are doing those things that develop a strong tenure dossier. In one of my first university positions, I worked with a colleague, "George," who was having some issues with annual reviews. George bemoaned the fact that his annual reviews were not strong. George knew "what counted" and what didn't, but his problem, as he stated it, was that he loved to help others and often *didn't have time* to complete the amount of research the university had prioritized as essential for tenure. He said he enjoyed doing research but just ran out of time. George was afraid that should he increase his focus on research, he wouldn't be able to help students. I countered with the statement, "What help would you be to students should you not get tenure?" We came up with a simple solution. Every time I saw George, I was to ask him what he was doing and ask him "Does it count?" George eventually got tenure and attributed some of that success to his ability to focus and prioritize his daily efforts.

You, too, need to ask yourself the question, "Does it count?" Prioritizing your daily work output to include the production of tenure-important materials is not selfish. Indeed it's just the opposite, as you are helping students by insuring you will get tenure and will continue to be able to offer your expertise and guidance for many years.

How Much of "What Counts" Do I Need to Be Tenured?

I once interviewed at a university where, during the interview, the dean of the college stated, "Of course you know, should you decide to take this position, that we expect our faculty to publish at least two juried research articles a year in the most prestigious journals in your area. While teaching is expected to be good and service appropriate, in order for you to receive tenure, we expect this type of publication effort." After that conversation, I had no doubt what I needed to secure tenure. Obviously teaching was important, service was the least important, and research was heavily weighted in the tenure formula.

So, how much of "what counts" do you need? Talk with your department chair, your director, your mentor, and your colleagues, especially those who are members of the tenure review committee. They will not only be able to tell you what kinds of efforts are most important in tenure decisions, they will be able to tell you how much effort, in their estimation, you should allot to the various areas. Given such information, you then formulate a tenure plan. Remember, too, that quantity (the number of performances, publications, the number of committees you serve on, and so forth) needs to be balanced with the quality of those endeavors.

How Do I Know if I'm "On Track" Toward Tenure?

If you are at an institution that conducts annual performance reviews, your performance review will be one indicator of whether you are on a positive trajectory toward tenure. Sit down with your department chairperson or director and discuss your performance review. Honesty and forthrightness are paramount in such discussions. Remember that everyone has some type of weakness, so do not become argumentative or defensive when such weaknesses are pointed out and examined. Take notes and, if possible, secure a copy of the review for your files. If you do not have annual performance reviews, it would be advisable to request one from your director.

Most institutions conduct pretenure reviews. If, for example, your tenure decision is made during your sixth year of teaching, a pretenure review might be conducted in your third year. Whatever the timeline, the pretenure review personnel will assess the appropriateness of your tenure trajectory. While pretenure reviews aren't necessarily binding, such assessments often have an impact on the ultimate tenure decision. If, for example, weaknesses are articulated but aren't eventually addressed, the ramifications of this neglect would impact a tenure decision negatively. Conversely, a positive review is a strong indictor of a positive tenure trajectory.

Annual performance or pretenure reviews are designed to help you attain tenure. Do not view them as punitive but rather understand that such reviews are your administrations' and colleagues' best assessment of your trajectory to tenure. Your colleagues and administrators are your support team. They want you to succeed just as much as you want to succeed.

Where Can I Look for Tenure Guidance?

In addition to your colleagues and school's administrators, many institutions have tenure guidance meetings in which tenure procedures and guidelines are outlined. These meetings can be held at the college and/or university level and are designed to provide information and address specific questions.

Some schools have mentoring programs in which an individual is assigned as your mentor. Your mentor is often an individual who has extensive experience with the tenure process, has tenure him/herself, and is your guide, ready to respond to your inquiries. Your mentor may be from within your school or may be from another school but regardless of the area, s/he can provide appropriate insights into the tenure process.

Talking with nontenured and tenured colleagues from other areas can offer you valuable insight into the tenure process. Because individuals must ultimately adhere to the same general tenure guidelines, sharing information and experiences among your nontenured and tenured colleagues from other areas can be time well spent.

What Is the Process for Getting Tenure?

While there will be institutional variation, there are common elements within the tenure procedure which include:

- Commonly, annual, two-, or three-year assessments, with a more extensive review being held at a midpoint during the tenure evaluation period.
- The collection of documentation to support a tenure bid. This information will highlight your contributions in the area of teaching, research or creative activity, and service.
- Outside letters of review, frequently requested from individuals in other institutions. Outside reviewers are leaders within your area of expertise and are held in high esteem by the profession. Outside reviewers are frequently asked to comment on the quality of your work, its impact in the field, and your potential to contribute significantly to the discipline, as well as the quantity of your output.

- Multilevel reviews, which include: a department or school tenure review committee assessment, the chair's or director's recommendation to the dean, a college level tenure committee evaluation, the dean's recommendation to the provost, a university-wide tenure committee review, and finally, approval by the provost, president, and/or board of trustees.

Once the final decision has been made by the provost, president, and/or board of trustees on your tenure request, you will be informed of the decision. Eventually your colleagues will be informed of the decision as well.

How Do I Prepare a Tenure Package? What's Included, What Should I Be Doing to Assemble Such a Package?

Assembling or preparing your tenure package is not something you should plan to complete overnight. While the contents of tenure packages will vary with the institution, they are generally quite involved. All candidates must adhere to specific institutional guidelines, including explicit instructions on the inclusion of prescribed materials, limitations on the page length of documents, and so forth. Common elements of tenure packages include the following.

- Your curriculum vitae, often in a format prescribed by the university.
- A narrative statement that identifies themes that have unified your career. To be written in a language and style that are accessible to individuals in all disciplines, your narrative should:
  - describe who you are professionally,
  - show why you are an asset to the school, college, institution, or profession, and
  - highlight accomplishments and achievements in the areas of teaching, research or creative activity, and service.

When writing your narrative, use phrases from documents written by individuals within and outside of your field. Use such statements when discussing and supporting your productiveness, describing your contributions, and highlighting the impact your efforts have made to the profession. By doing so, you will avoid a common problem of sounding ostentatious or self-important. When you answer the following questions, you will have begun the formation of your narrative essence.

- How have your research or creative activities impacted the profession and contributed to the field or to your institution?

- How has your teaching impacted students, their lives and careers?
- How has your service contributed to the university community and the community at large?

For many reviewers, your narrative can provide one of the most powerful affirmations for support of your tenure. Once you have written your narrative, show it to as many colleagues and administrators as are willing to read it and provide constructive feedback. Ask them for their initial impression and the impact of your message. Your narrative must convey your thoughts as gracefully, convincingly, and eloquently as possible.

Supporting data or documentation, including publications, reviews, programs, syllabi, teaching evaluations, conference presentations, list of classes taught, and so forth, may be requested. In my experience, gathering and organizing supporting materials, especially those covering many areas and a long time frame, is very time consuming and can demand hours of collecting and categorizing.

Your tenure package collection begins as you assume your first position. Saving and filing information that may become important for documentation purposes is an ongoing activity. The sooner you can obtain clarity as to which documents are essential and which are less important for tenure, the sooner you can begin your tenure collection journey.

In addition to your collection and documentation efforts, begin to develop and showcase your professional skills at state, regional, national, and international levels. Many institutions require outside letters of review. In order for people to know who you are and to be acquainted with your work, you need to showcase your talents in venues seen by colleagues from other institutions. When the time comes for outside reviews to be solicited from those colleagues, they will be familiar with your work and willing to write on your behalf.

What Happens if I Don't Get Tenure?

If you don't get tenure, you need to ask yourself a couple of questions. First, did you do everything you could do professionally to meet the institution's criteria for tenure? The most common reason for not getting tenure is failing to meet institutional criteria. Ask yourself: Was this academic setting the best fit for me? Not getting tenure doesn't mean an academic career is inappropriate, but it may mean the institution was inappropriate.

In spite of fact that the majority of individuals serving on your tenure review committees are conscientious, there are times that you might be denied tenure for political reasons. If this occurs, there are legal avenues you can pursue. Such legal avenues will be articulated in your institution's tenure documents. These are frequently time consuming and costly. It may be to your advantage to leave the institution and seek employment elsewhere. Negative environments are not beneficial to professional growth. Often it is better to seek a positive, nurturing environment, even though it may be difficult to do so initially. I have known at least one individual who found herself in this type of situation, but I am happy to report that she is now employed at a very highly regarded higher education institution and is held in esteem by her colleagues and administration.

If I Get Tenure at One Institution and then Take a Position at Another Institution Can My Tenure Transfer?

Generally, tenure is not a transferable quantity, but an institution can more easily grant you tenure if you already hold tenure at another institution. Often, if your new institution does not award you tenure when you take a new position, they may grant you years toward tenure. What this means is that should the tenure process normally take six years, an institution can offer you a modified tenure timeline. They can, for example, shorten the tenure decision process from a six-year to a three-year process. If you remember the discussion in Chapter 6 on negotiations, you may also recall that many things are negotiable provided ample justification exists to do so. This is often a negotiable item.

A Summary of the Tenure Process

Applying for the right position is your first important decision in securing tenure. The proper fit between your career goals and objectives and those of the institution must exist. As you arrive on campus, find out what is required for tenure, then organize your activities so that everything you do, or almost everything, has those requirements as an overlay. Ask "Does it Count?" Does what you are doing count significantly toward your tenure and promotion, and if so, how much? The things that count the most should get priority each day. Remember, if you don't get tenure, you can be of no help to your students. Balance is the issue. Work smart: give things that count for tenure priority and then do other things.

Part of the tenure process is documenting what you do. Some universities have an annual review process that will tacitly enforce, at least annually, documentation of your efforts. If you are not at an institution that offers some type of online documentation process, create a "professional box" or file drawer or use your computer to document professional activity whenever you do something of even minor significance. Depending on your organizational approach, you can categorize these activities under appropriate headings or sort out the documentation at a later date. If you wait until the end of the year to document your portfolio, many events or activities will have been forgotten and data scattered.

As you approach your annual, two-, or three-year review, and ultimately your tenure deadline, seek out faculty members who have recently been through the process. Read and study all handbooks pertaining to the process and ask your director or other appropriate administrators for assistance in reviewing and/or preparing your documentation well before the due date. This necessitates ascertaining the due date—normally it is much earlier than you anticipated. Additionally, ask your administrators if there are tenure orientation meetings. Often schools, colleges, or universities provide tenure orientation meetings. Get to know your professional colleagues from other institutions around the nation, as you will eventually need their support in your tenure bid. Finally, once you are awarded tenure, remember how you strove to attain that accolade, and maintain that commitment to excellence. The tenure process normally involves the assessment of three stated components: Research or creative activity, teaching, and service. While success in these areas is essential for tenure, they are also the components upon which higher education careers are built.

PROMOTION

Promotion refers to the process of movement through the ranks, such as movement from assistant professor to associate professor or associate professor to full professor. The granting of tenure does not guarantee the awarding of promotion, or vice versa. Nevertheless, the criteria for the receipt of tenure are often similar to those for promotion. It is common that, for example, an assistant professor who has spent an appropriate amount of time in rank will be considered for tenure, and at the same time be considered for promotion to associate professor. Exceptions exist to the granting of tenure and promotion during the same time continuum, but the awarding of tenure and promotion are frequently discussed together.

RESEARCH OR CREATIVE ACTIVITY

Find your niche—a project or area (research or performance related) that sets you apart from the rest of your department or colleagues. Focusing on a specific area will not only help during the reappointment and tenure process, but it will help you establish national recognition sooner than if you have several interest areas.

Balancing teaching, performing, practicing, and research is challenging. If your university values research or creative activity highly, then build an active and aggressive research agenda. Make time to write, perform, and present—get your name out there. Begin your research or creative agenda as soon as you arrive. The refereed publication procedure can be protracted. The review process itself can take several months to years to complete, and that, combined with the time it takes to have your publication appear in print once it is accepted, can be quite lengthy. In a similar vein, it can take years for musicians to be offered performance opportunities in prominent halls or with esteemed recording companies.

Take opportunities whenever possible to travel, go, and do! If your institution promotes teaching first, but at the same time wants you involved in professional development, wants you to attend conferences, and wants to see a research and publication agenda, then determine that balance as soon as you can during the first year and respond accordingly.

If your university places high value on obtaining grants, you should consider more grant-writing activities. Most higher education institutions encourage individuals to seek grants as the university takes a portion of the grant funding. Additionally, grants enable the hiring of teaching assistants, the procurement of equipment, and often lead to additional, related contractual opportunities.

TEACHING

In addition to developing your research/creative agenda, your first year should focus on teaching. Focus on your students. Be prepared to spend significant time in class and lesson preparation, and to that end, understanding the academic and/ or performance needs of your students. Meet them where they are, and plan to provide the tools and skills necessary to carry them beyond that point.

Create syllabi and course structures as soon as your course load is identified. Your preparation will be critical to student success and respect. The impression you make on students will soon be conveyed to other students and faculty. Enjoy your students, focus on their growth and success. Be a model of professionalism for your students. They will emulate that model.

Throughout the year, note your successes and failures, and develop a plan for your second year. How could you improve the program, department, or school? Eventually you will determine, if you have not already, your "niche" in the department.

Maintaining office hours and meeting with students in one-on-one conferences is an integral part of teaching. If you post office hours, keep them. Nothing is worse than for a student to come to your office at the appointed office hour and for you not to be there. Office hours and student conferences are intended to provide for professionally related discussions. **Never allow students to confide in you about potentially explosive situations without first informing them that whatever they say to you might require you, by law, to repeat what they tell you in front**

of a jury or judge in a court of law. Never speak about colleagues or administrators to students. What you say can and will be used against you.

If you decide to have an "open door" policy, you may find that you must take work home frequently and in greater amounts. Many individuals equate an open door policy with "no home life." The benefit of an open-door policy is student access.

Part of the teaching process is evaluation—student and often peer evaluation. Unfortunately, student evaluations are frequently viewed as having little value. While this may or may not be the case, you will receive both positive and negative feedback, both of which can be valuable. Negative feedback can be initially devastating, but well-constructed negative feedback can provide insight on your teaching as much as, and at times more than, positive responses.

Some schools conduct peer evaluations. In such situations, colleagues are invited into your classroom to take notes and make observations on your teaching content, delivery, and appropriateness as well as your interaction with students. Frequently such evaluations are used as part of the review and/or promotion and tenure process. Peer observation comments and reports are generally available for review. As with student observations, both negative and positive comments may be made. Your task will be to use all information in a manner that is constructive and aids in your professional development.

SERVICE

The concept of service can initially be confusing. Service involves university committee work and contributions to professional organizations outside the university. Service does not generally include pouring punch at the chancellor's faculty reception or singing a solo for a local church service. You will need to become active in some type of "meaningful" service soon after your arrival. Try to get appointed to a committee that doesn't take much work but has high visibility, as some committee work appointments are inherently more demanding than others. Appointments outside your school often are more prestigious. Committee work both inside and outside your school will help you become familiar with your colleagues. As important as committee work can be, limit your involvement. If you have not been appointed to a committee, volunteer for one. You will most likely be welcomed and your colleagues will appreciate your commitment.

POLITICS

Know that higher education is very political. As a nontenured faculty member, you must get the "lay of the land" with regard to "playmakers" in each department or school. When you enter a new position, it must be with the understanding that there are any number of issues and faculty agendas at play. Especially when there is division among individuals, learning the political and personal agendas that exist between faculty members may not be easy, but is paramount to your success.

Do not get involved in a battle between two colleagues! Do not take on "causes" for others. If you are forced to take a stance on an issue, it's best to listen and talk with individuals first before taking that stance, especially when you don't have tenure. Learn how to negotiate the political minefield without angering your colleagues.

As you learn the "dynamics" of your school, whether vindictive and unpleasant or positive and encouraging, you will discover supportive faculty whom you "want to know." There are also "power brokers," individuals who have the ear of other faculty and administrators, whom you "need to know." There may well be nonsupportive and/or temperamental faculty within your area or school. Learn to deal with temperamental faculty members and avoid confrontations. Being successful in the arena of university politics often requires that you "listen more than you speak" and dictates that you "show respect for all faculty."

COLLEGIALITY

So important is collegiality that should you alienate your colleagues, you might want to start packing your bags. Your colleagues, especially those in your immediate area, are your working partners. In order to cultivate the relational and business side of your work, you need to treat faculty and administration with respect, strive to understand their personalities, viewpoints, and "issues." Treat them as you would like to be treated.

As quickly as possible, develop relationships with faculty or colleagues. Open lines of communication not only with your immediate colleagues, but also with all members of the faculty. Make yourself seen—walk the hallways periodically, especially during class changes when students and other professors are likely in the halls. Get out of the office. Introduce yourself to all colleagues in the building. Attend as many recitals, concerts, and other events presented by your colleagues as possible, especially in the first years of your position. Not only will your support be appreciated, you will quickly meet other colleagues.

In many universities, social gatherings are very important to the establishment of collegial relations. An important result of socializing outside school is that your colleagues may afford you more trust and better understand there is more to you than researching, performing, and teaching. While major parties aren't necessary, getting to know some of your colleagues outside school is generally healthy and productive.

COMMUNICATIONS

One type of communication is referred to as "self-promotion." While many feel that self-promotion is not required or is a practice we are not accustomed to pursuing, it is a needed form of communication. But, as in so many things, self-promotion needs to be practiced in moderation. Informing your colleagues, students, and especially administrators of deserved and prestigious accomplishments may be the only way that such information is communicated. Do not hesitate to "blow your own horn," but never loudly, nor too frequently.

More commonly, communication is associated with the daily transmission and acquisition of information. As a new faculty member, you have much to learn. Don't be afraid to ask questions. There may be differences between "how you do it," "how we do it," and "how it's supposed to be done." When you have a question concerning procedure and similar issues, communicate with supervisors and colleagues. While face-to-face conversations are generally a preferable form of exchange, emails now provide a quick and documented form of transmission. You may find that:

1. you must initiate communications, people won't come to you,
2. asking for help is preferable to demanding it, and
3. silence is not always "golden."

Successful communication can save you from a "world of professional blunders." Don't take anything for granted—talk, talk, talk, ask, ask, ask.

WORK ETHIC

Establishing or redeveloping an appropriate work ethic can be challenging to a first year professor. For those just finishing a graduate degree, the balance between doing those things that benefit them directly and assisting others (students, committees, colleagues) is difficult. While it is important for you to work diligently (and sacrificially) to establish yourself as a highly qualified, indispensable educator, you must also be aware of developing your tenure and promotion dossier. Stay focused—do not get seduced into playing in extra ensembles, being on numerous committees, or teaching additional classes beyond your "normal" load, and so forth.

Know what has to be done for your tenure and promotion, prioritize and stick to a plan. Work to develop a reputation as the professor who has abundant energy and new ideas, and who works diligently to attain goals. One of the most important things you can learn for your own benefit is the art of saying "no" at the appropriate times. Of course, the "appropriate time" and to whom you use the word "no" is an important consideration; however, we often "give in" to requests—the consequences of which can affect our own professional advancement.

Be aware of what are sustainable practices during the first year and beyond—be realistic and don't over do it. Meet with your director, mentor, and/or coordinator and make a plan for teaching, research, or scholarship that fits the guidelines of your department—and again, stick to it: avoid extra assignments, stay focused.

Again, decide whether you will have an open-door policy or not. If you have an open-door policy, plan on having less time for other activities when you are away from the office. Open-door policies encourage student visitation and reduce your office preparation time. If you choose to implement an open-door policy, know that you will need to complete your research, planning, practice, and other activities outside of the "regular" workday.

To be successful as a university professor, you must be highly organized. You can be a skilled professor and have a dull or even brash personality, but also be highly organized, and you can be successful for many years. Conversely, you can be a skilled individual with a terrific personality, but be terribly unorganized, and you may frequently be looking for a job.

So while you should be prepared to work hard and consistently through that first year, know also that you are paving your own path. Choose it wisely. Be flexible, but know your strengths and weaknesses and communicate your ultimate professional goals to your administration and department.

BUDGETS

As a new faculty member, there are many pitfalls you must avoid, but nothing may cause you more grief than not adhering to budgetary guidelines and procedures. "Following the rules" isn't always glamorous or the most efficient way to secure equipment or items you want, but where money matters are concerned, it is the *only* way to conduct business. A young colleague I knew tried to circumvent the budgetary guidelines and procedures, either because s/he was not aware of them or chose not to follow them. While there was absolutely nothing underhanded or criminal in the use of the monies, suspicions were raised. It took my colleague several months to "straighten out" that mess. When it comes to budgetary matters, the adage "It's much easier to get forgiveness than permission" *does not apply*.

Learn and follow purchasing and budgetary guidelines and when in doubt about procedures, ask someone for clarification (usually your business manager). And while it may be tedious learning to navigate administrative procedures, forms, and requisitions, in budgetary matters, it is time well spent.

THE PERFECT JOB

Whether your first position ultimately becomes your final position, or your first position becomes a stepping stone to another, "A job is what you make it." Few of us step into the *perfect* job. We create our perfect job starting with our first position. What makes a job perfect is the fulfillment and contentment received from "doing what you are doing," feeling that you are valued and needed, being recognized for your contributions, and having a positive work environment and collegial relationship. In essence, the perfect position allows you to develop your career in the direction you have envisioned.

Generally, hard work, high-quality research, well-prepared concerts, recitals, presentations and lectures, and professionalism (holding offices, being on task, being organized) are eventually noticed and rewarded, although it may take a bit of "horn blowing" on your part. Your activities are not necessarily completed for recognition or reward, but rather to fulfill your chosen career direction. Your activities are indicative of your personal development and your advancement as a leader in the profession. In what area do you wish to focus significant research, creative, teaching, or service efforts? What do you want to be known for in your profession? What is missing from the current program? Is there a long-desired departmental or professional *need* that you can identify and fulfill and be recognized for doing so immediately? This is the quintessence of a fulfilling and successful career in academia. Doing what you want to do through the fulfillment of requirements in your assignment.

Collegiality is, as mentioned previously, a key component to the development of a successful career. We give our colleagues either a reason to support us or a reason not to support us. Respect and support of your colleagues will often be returned. Clearly, giving your colleagues a reason to support you is a goal that can assist you in a host of professional and career-oriented endeavors, including the receipt of tenure and promotion. Collegiality not only refers to your immediate colleagues but to your administrators as well. During your career, you are likely to encounter administrators with a wide variety of leadership styles. Here, too, you must be sensitive to their needs and respect their goals as they relate to your needs and goals and those of the school or college. Your key to career success can be paved through sensitivity, adaptation, and accommodation.

Until you find that situation which allows for the development and fulfillment of your professional duties, you may not be happy. If you are not happy where you are, find a place that will make you happy. As you change and develop your professional career, your needs may also change. What once may have been an ideal situation and a "perfect fit" may be no longer. Not all universities and departments are alike and with due diligence you will find your perfect position.

SUMMARY

When you begin your assignment, it doesn't really matter what your successes have been, the question you need to ask yourself is "What can I do here?" While past successes may have gotten you your assignment, it's your current actions that dictate whether or not you'll keep it. Position retention is based on many factors, but finding the balance between research or creative endeavors, teaching, and service in relation to institutional guidelines is paramount to your success.

An important key to your success is the relationship you create with your colleagues, administrators, and students. Their support is needed to enable your success. Create and foster strong, positive relationships with your colleagues; you will need their support! Create a work environment that is supportive of students and colleagues and ensures a productive workspace. The following concluding thoughts may assist you in your professional journey:

- Don't take things personally. The old saying "it's just business" goes for institutions of higher education too!
- Balance personal and professional life.
- Be open and flexible. Don't let that new degree, honor, award, or accolade go to your head. You still don't know everything and you never will.
- It is not the product that's important but rather the process and journey.
- Listen *to* learn.
- Your ultimate career goal is to "Absolutely be the best at what you do."

Developing Your Career

Your first steps to the development of your career perhaps have already been accomplished. You've completed your degrees and secured a position. Perhaps you are well on your way to securing tenure and promotion but the tangible elements of developing your career are not all that is required to complete the fulfillment of your calling. Developing your career is as much about "knowing and discovering yourself" as it is about accomplishing tasks.

While struggling with the anxiety of surviving in the job, dealing with the pressure from obligations that compete for your time and energy, overcoming the sense of isolation, coping with stress from professional matters that overflow into nonwork areas causing family and other personal relationship tensions, or experiencing dissonance about the rewards you receive for your work, higher education music faculty's greatest struggle may be that of developing a career. Why? Because developing a career is not just about investing time in projects or performances or doing what "counts" for tenure or the next promotion, developing a career is about you—it's about knowing what makes you do the things you do—it's about knowing what makes you content.

So much of what we are told concerning the acquisition of a position—getting tenure, being promoted, or succeeding in your position—may seem like political gamesmanship or merely a formulaic approach to job procurement and retention. Developing one's career depends on your responsibility to demonstrate incontrovertible hallmarks of leadership and character. According to Schoenfeld and Magnan (2004: 151–2) the hallmarks of leadership are one's ability to:

- Know yourself as well as your colleagues and students,
- Seek self-improvement,
- Set the example which others emulate,
- Take responsibility and make timely and professionally informed decisions,
- Be professionally proficient and instill that quality in your students through example.

Hallmarks of character include your:

- Integrity, maturity, and confidence;
- Compassion, humility, tact, and flexibility;
- Self-discipline, decisiveness, initiative, and endurance;
- Coolness under stress, sense of humor, and creativity.

Our growth as responsible members of the higher education music community moves from a self-centered or self-acquisitioning mode to one that is intently focused on assisting others in reaching their potential. During this pursuit we learn about self and others, transforming that which is meaningful only to self to that which is of importance to the larger audience. Through self-growth we become increasingly aware of our responsibility to positively affect others. Your career development is dependent upon your well-being and vitality. Understanding how you fit into and modify the environment in which you work is a key to success.

According to Menges and Associates (1999), faculty well-being and vitality are associated with career development and success. Individuals capable of recognizing the environment in which they best thrive, of understanding and recognizing their inner needs, are then capable of seeking or creating such an environment, thus allowing for career development and enhancement. Being able to identify yourself among the various faculty types may enable you to better understand the motivational incentives upon which you thrive and assist you in creating an environment that allows those incentives to exist. Below are eight faculty types (Menges and Associates 1999: 218–23) thought to identify motives that promote faculty well-being and vitality. As you read each of these faculty types you may identify with various statements or motives that can aid in the identification your motivational requirements. The faculty types are characterized by activity, skill, or interest, as follows.

- Competence in scholarly teaching
  Through reading, research, publication, and active participation at
  professional conferences, these faculty members keep abreast of new
  developments in their fields and constantly infuse old courses with fresh
  information. What they teach is constantly changing and developing, the
  way they teach is thorough and sustains their scholarship. Their range of
  knowledge is likely to encompass related and even unrelated disciplines.
- Competence in pedagogical knowledge and skills
  These individuals acquire a variety of techniques and strategies for
  communicating the intricacies of topics in their disciplines. Teaching
  is scholarship driven, not technique driven and no class is exactly like
  another. They know what works with students because of all the formal
  and informal classroom research they do.
- Competence in classroom leadership and management
  Effective leaders in the classroom, these faculty members are not simply
  good managers of students but, in greater measure, leaders of students.
  They earn the respect of students and become emergent leaders. Students
  in such classes with such faculty acquire a sense of community, work
  diligently outside of class, and eagerly participate within the classroom.
- Goal management in teaching and learning
  Faculty members under this heading are characterized as setting
  challenging and important goals for self and students. Goals are selected

to be compatible with each other and in harmony with their colleagues and students. Quality is preferred over quantity and goals give purpose and meaning to their work, while inspiring those who work with them.

- Autonomy in academia
  These individuals balance their need to be self-determined with their need to be collaborative—learning to play alone and together. They seek sufficient autonomy, not independence, and desire only enough professional freedom to grow, express their talents, and achieve their goals. They feel in control, not restricted by the choices of others, or by shortcomings of their environments. They guard the freedoms they need to do their work and invest themselves in those environments that provide sufficient autonomy.

- Social support and collegiality
  Weaving their lives into the institution where they work, these individuals prefer working with others and are likely to have done most of their research and other professional work with colleagues or students. They probably had, and also served as, mentors and some of their closest friends are colleagues. They are trustworthy, warm people in whom others confide.

- Rewards and recognition
  External incentives are important to this group of faculty because of what the external incentives represent. External incentives do not by themselves motivate this individual but rather help define the recognition this individual believes s/he has earned.

- Feedback for generative production
  Under this heading faculty are identified as receiving delight in sharing the value and meaning of their knowledge with students. They see themselves as purveyors of hope and stewards of human potential. It's why they do what they do, to have an immediate effect on others.

Faculty vitality and wellness can also be determined through the types of activities in which they are engaged. If you observe higher education music faculty, you may notice they spend a lot of time in teaching-related, research and creative activities, and service directly related to institutional goals, yet most of them are engaged in numerous other activities. While their careers may be partially defined as those activities directly associated with assigned university duties, careers are more than this—music faculty are more than their positions—music careers are more than administrative assignments. If you look at higher education music faculty, you will find them engaged in a host of activities—activities that may loosely or tightly be aligned with institutional expectations but certainly not assigned by administrative fiat. Faculty are assigned to teach classes and serve on committees, but other roles help define their careers. As a member of a higher education music faculty, you may be engaged in any one several musical activities, none of which are assigned by the institution, some of which may include:

Chair of summer music festival programs
Conductor of community orchestras, bands, choirs
Conductor, director, or administrator of musical youth groups or organizations
Performer in community orchestras, bands, choirs
Composer
Featured clinician for music companies or self-employed clinician
Book author
Member of a chamber music group (touring or nontouring)
Speaker or clinician at conferences
Member of semiprofessional or professional orchestra, opera company
Participants in theater productions,
Editor of a journal
President, vice-president, treasurer, secretary, and so forth of a professional Organization
Touring soloist
Adjudicator at festivals (international, national, state)
Director of church groups,
Director of community musical organizations
Private music teacher
Method book composer
Fund raiser for local groups: boy's or girl's choirs, and so on
Entertainer: member of a jazz, dixie, easy listening group, and so on
Teacher or conductor of summer institutes or festivals.

While many or all of these activities may seem to be related to a higher education faculty member, they are not assigned duties. These are roles in which music faculty choose to involve themselves that in turn define and enhance their careers. As you define your career and activities, they will simultaneously define you. Hence, your higher education career is guided by your instructional responsibilities as well as by your chosen professional activities outside institutional obligations.

The field of music in higher education has, like so many other fields, undergone change due to funding cutbacks, scrutiny and interference from politicians, criticism of such practices as the granting of tenure, reorganization of academic and business structures, pressures to adhere to burgeoning external regulatory guidelines and policies, and mushrooming technological changes. As a musician, you about to enter a profession that is increasingly market driven, and yet will offer you the freedom to structure your own career development path through creative endeavors. The ability to be decidedly self-directed, motivated, organized, and task-oriented plays an integral role toward your success as a university music professor.

Academia and You

Whether you are a skilled conductor, an accomplished performer, a budding theorist, a consummate musicologist, an up-and-coming composer, a published researcher, or a brilliant music educator, your reasons for applying for and ultimately accepting a music position in higher education may be multifaceted. Some individuals love the process of interacting with students; others enjoy teaching but also appreciate the challenges presented through research. Still others thrive with a plethora of performance venues or in-service-oriented settings. Higher education allows for exploration in all of these areas in varying degrees. As a musician in a research-intensive setting, you will be expected to produce copious amounts of research-oriented materials (compositions, grants, CDs, DVDs, juried research articles, books, national or international performances, etc.), while still being a stellar instructor and offering appropriate support to the service area. In teaching-intensive institutions, your focus should be directed toward your students, with special attention to assisting students in and outside of the classroom. Service at a teaching-intensive university may be as important as, or even more important than, research. Ultimately, your career success as a higher education music professor is contingent on choosing a school at which you can accommodate its mission while also being able to engage in the types of activities that are rewarding and gratifying to you.

As you prepare for the higher education music job market, you will shift your emphasis from that of being evaluated to being the evaluator, from being taught to teaching, from being directed to conduct research to directing research. When you were screened and selected for your potential to succeed as a music graduate student, your emphasis was on navigating the academic waters as a student. Now, as a higher education music professor, you become the leader, the individual guiding others in their quest for development and enhancement. In this role, you become independent, reliant on internal drive and motivation. Guidance you once sought from your professors will now be sought from you. A career as a higher education music professor requires a modicum of conformity while simultaneously demanding creativity and independence. You must be prepared to "play well in the proverbial sandbox," to follow directions and guidelines while demonstrating your facility as a visionary and innovator, expanding the boundaries of originality, acceptability, and creativity—to conform, yet be a nonconformist.

Welcome to the world of higher education!

References

Conway, Colleen M., and Thomas, M. Hodgman. 2009. *Teaching music in higher education.* New York: Oxford University Press.

Johnson, Glenn Ross. 1995. *First steps to excellence in college teaching.* Madison, WI: Atwood.

Menges, Robert J., and Associates. 1999. *Faculty in new jobs: A guide to settling in, becoming established, and building institutional support.* San Francisco: Jossey-Bass.

Schoenfeld, A. Clay, and Robert Magnan. 2004. *Mentor in a manual: Climbing the academic ladder to tenure.* 3rd ed. Madison, WI: Atwood.

Index

CPSIA information can be obtained
at www.ICGtesting.com
Printed in the USA
LVHW030343151221
706184LV00011B/1263